# Acting on Impulse

## Reclaiming the Stanislavski Approach

### A practical workbook for actors

John Gillett

*methuen* | drama

First published 2007

Methuen Drama
A & C Black Publishers Limited
38 Soho Square
London W1D 3HB
www.acblack.com



ISBN 978-0-7136-7758-4

A CIP catalogue record for this book is available from the British Library.



This book is produced using paper that is made from wood grown in managed, sustainable forests. It is natural, renewable and recyclable. The logging and manufacturing processes conform to the environmental regulations of the country of origin.

Cover design by Andrew Evans

Illustrations by Jannis Labelle

Typeset in 10/14pt Glasgow XL

Printed and bound at Caligraving Ltd, Thetford, Norfolk

# Contents

# Acknowledgements

The gestation period for this book comprises all the years I have studied and worked as an actor, director and acting teacher. I am indebted to all those who gave me encouragement over the years, particularly the late Nancy Diuguid; to all the actors and other practitioners with whom I have done workshops, classes, and productions and who have tried out my approach; and to those who kindly agreed to read my first draft, or parts of it, and made helpful suggestions: Simon Dunmore, Charlotte Kasner, Andy de la Tour, Edda Sharpe, Jan Haydn-Rowles, Bryan Oliver, Dr. Helen Castle, and Steven Helliwell. My thanks to Mikhail Mokeiev and Hamish Glen for allowing me to interview them. I also want to acknowledge the value I've gained from those who have gone before and written on the Stanislavski approach and who have helped me to clarify my own ideas; these are recorded in the bibliography. Particular recognition goes to Robert O'Neill and his Actors Workshop, where I first studied Stanislavski and Michael Chekhov and heard their authentic voice, which set me on my way, and without which I would not have written this book. My deepest thanks go to Christina Gutekunst, a truly inspired and insightful voice teacher, who has given unstinting and loyal love and support through good and bad fortunes, who has spent many hours working with me on productions and projects and discussing the book, acting theory and practice, and theatre ideals – probably at risk to her own sanity!

# Foreword

All actors want to be truthful. The sense of truth we feel in ourselves is our greatest gift (as actors, and as humans). How do we find it onstage? All actors want to transform. Playing yourself gets boring (indeed, being bored of playing yourself might be why you started in the first place). How do we change?

> *It's possible that some British drama schools can cover varied acting and theatre styles without necessarily delivering enough on basic acting process in a way that makes students feel confident, easy and equipped to deal with full and truthful character creation in any period and form.*
>
> from Chapter 16

No kidding. As an actor, and lately as a director and artistic director, I see that drama schools are not producing graduates with a workable theory of acting. I didn't go to drama school, and though I've gone to class since I started work and tried to keep up with my studies, my lack of a consistent approach has always troubled me. I want to work hard. I know that when things fly, it's because you've put in the spadework. I want to be inspired. I need to find what John Gillett calls 'the conscious process to enable actors to reach inspiration more often'. Well, this book really helps. It's a comprehensive and detailed guide to the Stanislavski approach. There are at least four techniques of character-building in here that I've never seen before (and can't wait to try out in the rehearsal room), and the description of Stanislavski's principles of objectives and obstacles is clear, complete and thorough. It will enable you to analyse any scene. The cry of the actor at sea 'I don't know what I'm doing!' should, with the application of the principles outlined in this book, become a thing of the past.

*Acting on Impulse* is really two books – it's a manual, full of enabling, easing exercises, always championing what works. And it's also a scholarly biography of the Stanislavski approach, which has at its heart a deep respect for the artform and its practitioners. The Stanislavski approach is one of the subjects most bluffed about in the theatre (I've been guilty of it myself). We think we know what Stanislavski was on about. We know less well what he actually said – or more importantly, how what he said evolved and was taken up by students and disciples later. An important part of this book is its coverage of the canon of acting teaching – back through Lev Dodin, Uta Hagen and Stella Adler to Michael Chekhov and Stanislavski himself. There is enough biographical information here to give you a sense of continuity – but there is also a teasing challenge to look further and investigate these other teachers in their own right. And that is as it should be – one of the joys of this book is its inclusivity – if it's useful, it's in. We never know when some new inspiration or insight may help, or revitalise our tired acting muscles. And just as we hope never to stop working, so we should also try never to stop learning.

Being an actor shouldn't stop when you leave the rehearsal room. Very few British books on acting think to comment on an actor's social conscience - John makes a persuasive case that a healthy social conscience is an indispensable part of the complete actor. As long-time members of the same Equity branch, I know that his belief in the collective informs everything he does, and his passionate call for a common artistic language is both thrilling and persuasive. Acting is not magic, it's common sense (by which I mean, based on those senses which are common to us all). The more shared the sense, the greater the magic. This is not a beacon that's easy to keep alight. It can be rubbish being an actor in Britain. Staying positive is hard; the industry model is not our friend. But the strength of Stanislavski's approach is that it is democratic. It is collaborative. It works best within an ensemble and it stands in contrast to the star system that believes in order to look good, all around you must look terrible.

Olivier's famous retort to Dustin Hoffman's exertions on *Marathon Man*, 'Dear boy, why don't you try acting?' has always seemed to me unfair. Hoffman gives a wonderful performance in *Marathon Man* (in a different way so does Olivier, come to that). I've always thought that in standing up for the organic against the representational, Hoffman was on the right track. If an actor would rather try to live than pretend, and finds his method fruitful, and it doesn't make him impossible to act with, he should be allowed to work in any way he likes. But it's hard. The actor who chooses not to 'try acting', but instead searches for beauty and simplicity in their work, needs support and inspiration. This book provides it.

**Samuel West**

# Introduction
## – acting in context

> *There can be no true art without living*
>
> Stanislavski

## Why do we act?

I start with this question because it is so fundamental and important for any actor and it also raises other questions that concern the content of this book. For example, why did people act *originally*? Why do we act *now*? Why *should* we act? and *How* should we act?

The origin of theatre was in religious ceremonies conducted in early communities. The first theatre developed in Greece when one actor replaced the priest, assumed the character of a god or hero and entered into dramatic dialogue with a chorus of fifty to convey a particular story and theme. Play festivals were held which the whole community was required to attend. People acted in ancient Greece primarily for social reasons as part of the community. Plays had clear messages about recurrent violence, the nature of justice, betrayal, passion and revenge, and so on. Much later, Shakespeare wrote political and philosophical plays exploring the contradictions within the human psyche of the time and a society in transition from feudalism to capitalism. In more recent times, Shaw, Ibsen, and Chekhov made moral and political critiques of society in their plays. The tradition continues up to modern writers from Bertolt Brecht and Arthur Miller to contemporary dramatised public enquiries, satires and revivals of Schiller. I take it for granted that if plays are to survive and be valued from generation to generation they have to be entertaining on some level as well as instructive and enlightening; by contrast, relatively few plays have survived which are solely light entertainment.

This leads to the next question: Why do we act *now*, in the twenty-first century, in a situation where we have not only theatre, but television, radio, and film, and proliferating cable, satellite and digital TV channels, videos and DVDs, internet movies, podcasts and mobile phone downloads? We live surrounded by new technology that quickly becomes outdated and presses us to catch up. We also live in a culture where live performing arts have not been valued by successive governments to the extent that they are in France and Germany, for example, and theatre is engaged in a constant struggle to survive. The idea of public service broadcasting by the BBC is as much under threat as the rest of our public services, now affected by private sector involvement, internal markets, and sale of important resources. 'Reality' shows, fly-on-the-wall 'documentaries', 'idol' competitions and a myriad makeover programmes compete in the titillation market and replace drama. Profit-led, market-oriented policies dominate government thinking across the board. A pervasive cultural view now seems to be that anyone can be famous, you are what you wear/drive/consume, grab wealth quick and look out for number one. Of course, there is an alternative and opposite consensus: that live theatre – and quality TV and a sustainable film industry – are important and public subsidy here should be raised to European levels and recent cutbacks reversed; and, in the wider perspective, that we need to resist the domination of the world, its peoples, culture and environment, by a few rich nations with their neo-liberal policies and super corporations.

In this context, responses to *Why do we act now?* will be predictably varied. Some may want fame and fortune – to get into films or soaps and become a star. Some may tend to exhibitionism. Some say it's what they're good at and it's all they can do. There is another response, and one that appears to me more logical and credible given what actors have to go through. The training of one to three years requires commitment and discipline, as well as ability. Then, in fees, living expenses and student loans, training can leave you £30,000–£40,000 or more in debt. You then face a business where there is up to 90% unemployment for actors at any one time, and where average weeks worked amount to around eleven per year. The actor's minimum weekly wage in a subsidised regional theatre is £350 (from April, 2008). Much work on offer pays nothing. Getting an agent to help you find work can be difficult, as can launching yourself as a small business, finding *any* job, let alone continuous work, and building a lasting career. The drop-out rate is high, and fifteen hundred or more actors come onto the market from drama courses every single year. To find the determination, positivity, and stamina to deal with all this, most actors have a much deeper desire and need to act than just being pricked by the spur of fame or exhibitionism alone.

Some have a strong desire simply to be good entertainers who can give people pleasure. Good though that aim may be, I think many actors go beyond this and see acting as an interpretive and creative skill/craft/art that communicates to an audience the *reality of human experience*, through which they can be stimulated, enlightened, moved and provoked, as well as entertained. It might prompt them to question their relationships with other people and the world around them, and, maybe, even to try to improve life. This is arguably the role of all art in society: to help people more fully understand and get their bearings in the world through means not possible by simply reading newspapers, factual books, or from formal education; by means that are not just cerebral, but relate to our subconscious, senses, emotions, intuition, sexuality, imagination, and experience – to our whole humanity. This is particularly the case in that most directly and fully human of all art forms, drama, and gives the answer to the third question, Why *should* we act? Most actors in my experience are very conscious of themselves as being part of a wider humanity, and want to communicate themselves and the experience of others to others.

It's to these actors that this book is aimed primarily. Drama, in whatever medium, also offers the opportunity to live a variety of lives; not to be confined to one life, job, country and epoch, but to experience more of the invariably unrealised potential of a human life. Since the Renaissance, the infinite possibilities for human development have been clear. Equally clear has been the ability of societies to frustrate and destroy that potential. We've travelled from the multi-dimensional richness of Shakespeare's characters to the trapped and disembodied souls of Beckett. It's the job of actors to portray both, and all types in between, truthfully; to serve the author and communicate interpreted content fully to an audience in a way that *affects* them. Otherwise, we're left with *deadly theatre*, an emptiness we just consume mechanically.

The last question, *How* should we act?, relates directly to this and is at the heart of this book.

## Pretending and experiencing

What sort of acting approach, process and style best serves the role of the actor as expressed above? I'm referring here to any form of performance in which recognisable human beings are presented in some way – not just so-called 'naturalistic theatre' (a concept I'll come back to later), and including Shakespeare, Restoration, Shaw, or even the Absurd and Brecht.

As in the fields of politics, philosophy, art or science, acting has produced its own opposing theories and practices and correspondingly different results. The highest quality of British acting is usually defined by what we see in the West End and from leading companies like the RSC and National Theatre. The acting style I believe to be most rooted here for historical, cultural and economic reasons comes from a specific view of, and approach to, acting. It also exists in other countries throughout the world, including America, home of the 'Method'. This style is best and most often described as Representational acting. Uta Hagen, the renowned German-American actor and teacher also calls it Formalism (*A Challenge for the Actor*, Scribner, 1991). This has not been given much analytical definition in Britain because it's taken for granted. The style in opposition to this, most associated with the approach of Konstantin Stanislavski, the Russian actor, director, teacher and founder of the Moscow Art Theatre (MAT), is what I shall call Organic acting, but referred to by Hagen as Presentational acting (*Respect for Acting*, Macmillan Publishing Company, 1973) and Realism (*A Challenge for the Actor*), and also called 'inside-out' acting, and less helpfully, 'Method' and 'the system'. I'll stick to Representational and Organic because I think these terms are more inclusive, clearly understandable, and describe the approach and process which produce two different types of performance.

I'll venture a differentiation of what is involved in each style:

- Representational acting is essentially *pretending*. Organic acting is *experiencing*, believing in and living through the circumstances and actions of a theatrical reality; living truthfully in imaginary circumstances.

- With Representational work the character is outside you, the actor. It is visualised with the conscious brain and then *imitated*, like holding up a drawing of a real person. The character is described and shown, represented at a distance. Organic acting involves *recreating human experience*, using the actor's own makeup – mind, body, senses, emotions, imagination, will, intellect, experience – as the raw material through which they will be transformed into the character. The real experiences and processes we go through in everyday life are reproduced through observation, imagination, and recreation in rehearsal and performance, following natural, justified, truthful steps.

- Representational acting presents an *externalised manner* or emotional state, and consciously determined actions. Organic acting is essentially *doing*, creating physical and psychological actions leading from inner impulses generated by the circumstances in which you exist.
- Representational acting focuses on the *outside form* of character and creating *effect*. Organic acting works usually from the *inside out* to create what Stanislavski called *'the life of the human spirit of the role'*. Conscious preparation is aimed at reaching the actor's subconscious, to develop the inner and outer action of the character, with external physicalisation following.
- Representational acting, as a result, follows *fashion* (e.g. patterns of phrasing and intonation associated with certain performers; a trend for 'naturalistic' and monotonous delivery; or particular facial expressions from TV sitcoms). Organic acting is *universal*, drawing on a depth of human experience that transcends fashion.
- Representational acting is more *cerebral*, relying on conscious decisions and 'choices' to define the character, although the appearance may be that the actor is working from 'instinct'. Organic acting uses the *imagination* more, sometimes working consciously but only to free the intuition.
- Representational performance is *premeditated*, consciously worked out and pre-programmed. The actor is outside the action, *consciously observing and controlling*. Organic performance is *spontaneous* and free within an agreed structure, so the actor can be *involved* and *in the moment*: that is, live through the part in every moment and every line while maintaining artistic control.
- The Representational approach primarily considers *how* to do something. The Organic approach considers *what* and *why* something is happening, and allows how it happens to develop naturally from that.
- Representational acting demands that the actor plays and *fakes emotion*, because the actor is only acting, it's not real. Organic acting involves allowing *experienced emotion* to flow from the action as a natural human response.
- The Representational process often involves *dependence* on the director, to find out how to play the character. The Organic one demands *independence*,

because you need to harness an awareness of self to an understanding of the character, and create it from you.

- The Representational acting company is more likely to be *individualistic*, and involve a fragmented mix of interpretations and styles, and possible competitiveness. The Organic company will aim to work as a team with a cohesive style and understanding, as an *ensemble*.

In simplified table form the differences look like this:

| Representational acting | Organic acting |
|---|---|
| pretending | experiencing |
| imitation | recreation |
| manners and states | impulses and actions |
| external form | inside to outside |
| effect | 'life of the human spirit' |
| fashion | universal |
| cerebral | imaginative |
| premeditated control | spontaneous involvement |
| how? | what and why? |
| faked emotion | experienced emotion |
| dependence | independence |
| individualism | ensemble |

What I haven't done here is to talk about the Representational and Organic *actor* because actors often cross over into using a combination of approaches because of their mixed training, varied influences in the industry, and different directors' work processes. An actor may not be wedded to one of these ways of working, and a British actor is as capable of a fully organic approach as any other: 'What I write does not refer to one epoch and its people, but to the organic nature of artists of all nationalities and of all epochs,' said Stanislavski. Equally, the nature of the actual performance may be as varied as the approaches used, as Stanislavski observes in *An Actor Prepares* (Penguin, 1967): 'Side by side we see moments of living a part, representing the part, mechanical acting and exploitation.'

There have been, and are, clear representatives of both schools, of course; Organic acting didn't begin with Stanislavski. His 'system', evolved through his work at the Moscow Art Theatre and its Studios, was only recorded on paper from 1935, resulting in what we know in English as *An Actor Prepares* (1936), *Building a Character* (1949), and *Creating a Role* (1961) – the first two books were originally conceived as one volume, *An Actor's Work on Himself,* covering both inner and outer technique, but editorial pressure forced its publication in two parts. He developed his process to solve the problems he and other actors faced in keeping performance alive, fresh and truthful, stopping it becoming stale, mechanical and empty, and in finding and recapturing the inspiration and immediacy that so affected audiences. What he came up with was not some abstract theory, but a process based on his observation of actors like the Italian, Tommaso Salvini, Mikhail Shchepkin, the Russian 'father of realism', and his follower, Glikeria Fedotova, whom he considered great because of their natural reproduction of human experience. He wrote down and taught what actors actually did to recreate human life onstage. On the other hand, there were alongside these actors declamatory, external, unbelievable actors, who applied a crude Representational approach.

One of the clearest, and most often quoted, demonstrations of the conflicting styles was in the performances of two renowned European actors, Sarah Bernhardt and Eleonora Duse, at the end of the nineteenth century. Bernhardt was all show, mannerism, and flamboyance. Duse was truthful, spontaneous and lent her own being to a character. In 1895, in London, they played the same part, Magda in Hermann Sudermann's *Heimat,* in separate theatres and were both observed and reviewed by Bernard Shaw for *The Saturday Review.* (Published as *Duse and Bernhardt* in *Plays and Players, Essays on the Theatre* – Oxford University Press, 1952.) He picked out Bernhardt's 'childishly egotistical' acting, her 'stock of attitudes and facial effects', her 'inhuman and incredible' beauty, her artful, clever 'nonsense' and ability to make you admire and champion her so that the audience wildly applauded her at the end. He summarises: 'She does not enter into the leading character: she substitutes herself for it.' With Duse, he notes her natural appearance, 'the illusion of being infinite in variety of beautiful pose and motion', her range 'which immeasurably dwarfs' that of Bernhardt, and that behind every stroke of her acting is 'a distinctively human idea'. The most famous observation, though, was of Magda's unexpected meeting with the father of her child, whom she has not seen for twenty-five years, and who comes to the family home with flowers: after the formalities are over, Duse came to examine his face after all those years and was so open and involved in the moment that a real *blush* spread across her face, what Shaw perceptively describes as 'a perfectly genuine effect of the dramatic imagination'.

In Shakespeare's day even, there must have been a similar distinction in style, otherwise why would Hamlet make these comments about the Player's depiction of the slaughter of Hecuba's husband, Priam, by Pyrrhus?

Is it not monstrous that this player here,
But in a fiction, in a dream of passion,
Could force his soul so to his own conceit
That from her working all his visage wanned,
Tears in his eyes, distraction in his aspect,
A broken voice, and his whole function suiting
With forms to his conceit? And all for nothing!
For Hecuba!
What's Hecuba to him, or he to Hecuba,
That he should weep for her?

So involved is the Player in the action of the speech, so engaged is he with the plight of Hecuba that his whole being adapts to his imagined reality, and real tears fill his eyes. Further, there are physical changes: his face pales, his voice breaks, and his whole bodily expression matches to the imaginative impulse. Belief in the imagined reality brings emotion through the action and physical embodiment of the whole experience. A classic example of Organic acting.

Difference between the experienced and demonstrated styles of acting existed between Molière's company and his rivals in the seventeenth century, and between leading French actors in the eighteenth century such as Mlle Dumesnil and le Clairon.

Of course, in recent times, the greatest British exponent of Representational acting has been Laurence Olivier, and brilliant as he may have been in external description of a character and physical effect he resisted any sort of organic involvement. If it happened by accident in a performance, he was known to disavow it because he felt he was not in total control. Even on film, Olivier clearly fakes emotion, acting it out and not feeling it. It's part of a theory advocated by the nineteenth-century French actor, Benoît Constant Coquelin (1841–1909), author of *The Art of the Actor,* and other Representational actors today, that you should feel anything *only* in rehearsal, after which you should imitate the emotion, because if *you* feel the audience won't. I still hear this even from young actors. Coquelin says: 'The actor does not live, he plays. He remains cold toward the object of his acting but his art must be perfection'. Stanislavski adds: 'And to be sure, the art of representation demands perfection if it is to remain art' (*An Actor Prepares*). The imitation and illustration of life has to be totally convincing. If you see someone faking emotion it can be embarrassing, doubly so on film. On the other hand, if you see an actor experiencing genuine feeling – that is, without indulging, wringing it out, and forcing it – which fits the demands of the production and the author, then if you have any compassion you will most likely be moved. I think this is even more the case now we are acclimatised to some excellent film acting from around the world. Olivier set a style for British acting to which many British actors, at least onstage, and sometimes on film too, appear to be glued.

Just as Coquelin's style was opposed by that of Henry Irving in the nineteenth century, representatives of a more organic acting approach have been prominent here in the twentieth century – many would say pre-eminent – for example, Peggy Ashcroft; John Gielgud, who praised Stanislavski's 'practical wisdom' in his preface to Sonia Moore's *The Stanislavski System* (Viking Press, 1965); and Michael Redgrave, who called himself 'a disciple of Stanislavsky' in his autobiography (*In My Mind's Eye,* Weidenfeld & Nicolson, 1983). However, our industry and training do not generally encourage the development of organic actors in the mode of Innokenti Smoktunovsky, the Hamlet of Kosintsev's film, and the Vanya from the Moscow Art Theatre production of *Uncle Vanya* seen in London some years ago; or actors such as we saw in the Maly Drama Theatre of St Petersburg productions at the Barbican of *The Possessed, Uncle Vanya,* and *Platonov.* It's true we have a number of drama schools of quality, a wide range of theatre companies offering a depth of good, professional performance, and a strong and lasting tradition of acting strength. However, is it justified to show that particular breed of British national and class arrogance and say continually, 'We have the best theatre and actors in the world,' when you consider the two hundred plus *subsidised* theatres in Paris, the national theatres in every major German city, the acting quality demonstrated by the Russians, and the depth of the great American film actors? I'm sure we're justifiably envied by some people somewhere, but this sort of generalisation is not constructive towards other countries' actors or ourselves. It papers over the cracks in our culture.

## Coherence and confusion

It will be clear from what I've said so far that I believe the Organic acting approach to be the most appropriate for communicating human experience. For this to flourish fully, actors need sustained periods of employment and development combined with a coherent, unified approach to work and training. Unfortunately, in reality our arts and entertainment industry is not very conducive towards that.

### Work

Economic and cultural factors combine to undermine our development and quality of the work, and the possibility of a more organic form of performance. The old repertory system no longer operates as a training ground. Actors rarely work for a season of four or more months on a number of different plays, learning their craft, becoming more versatile, getting to know a particular audience. Usually jobs last less than two months, then it's on to the next scratch company, or a wait, the job centre, or the 'fill-in' job. Consistency of employment and sustained development are not usual. For reasons of tradition and economics, rehearsal periods are, and have always been, tight – usually around four weeks; less in 'fringe', where most likely you won't be paid either. Cast sizes are invariably smaller and productions fewer than they once were. In 2001, this situation was temporarily improved by an injection of an extra £25 million into subsidised theatre by the government, creating what Derby Playhouse described as 'a mini-renaissance'. Some companies were able to expand rehearsal lengths, and improve the range and quality of their productions. However, to the fury of the theatre world, the government then announced three years of standstill funding for 2005–08, which means a cut of at least £30 million in real terms. More and worse cuts are now looming and threaten to make the situation even worse.

There are exceptions to the norm. A few companies like Stoke Victoria, Northern Stage and Dundee Rep have run companies with an ensemble of actors on long contracts, with a common approach and philosophy as well as closer contact with the community. The RSC is now aiming to return to the ethos of its early years and a company engaged for possibly two years; whether it will have a coherent way of working with common goals and reject the star system, or whether it will simply be a company on long contracts with through-casting, remains to be seen.

Whenever Russian or other ensembles come to the UK to play there is usually enormous critical praise: *The Financial Times* on the Maly Drama Theatre of St Petersburg: 'The greatest acting in the world? ... these Petersburgers are a lesson to us all.' Only recently, though, has there been a more concerted push for this sort of company to be established in Britain, and that came from the trades unions, Equity and the Directors' Guild of Great Britain, who organised an Ensemble Theatre Conference at the ICA in London in November 2004, with invited representatives from the Maly and the Stary Teatr, Poland. The conference recommended that ensembles should be created in each major population centre, and that the virtues of ensemble theatre be seen as important for the future health of British theatre. How sympathetic government ministers will be to this given their plans for funding cuts remains to be seen. Ensemble theatre is often seen as a 'foreign' collective sort of thing and distrusted.

Many young actors now get their first jobs in TV, commercials or film, but these don't usually last long and may be rare. Sometimes a talented newcomer might not work much at all in ten years. Sometimes actors work regularly for twenty-five years and then it just stops. Some people never stop working. It's an unpredictable life, which reinforces the point that actors have to be clear about the importance of their work and totally committed if they are to survive all the pitfalls, rejections and disappointments of the business.

## Attitudes

- In some areas of the business, in theatre and television, there is still hostility to any mention of Stanislavski, whose name is invariably equated with 'Method' and sets off a series of knee-jerk responses to actors allegedly wasting time preparing and mumbling in corners. The old instructions of 'say the lines and avoid the furniture' and 'just get on and do it' are still very much part of industry thought. With short rehearsals as well, directors' approaches are often on the pragmatic side and impatient of 'process'. Directors of whatever age and background have been known to panic quietly and push for the final results at the start of rehearsals. A Stanislavski-trained actor will often have to fight their corner and prove by results.

- There is a myth that the Stanislavski approach has seeped through to the very core of British theatre, and some anti-'naturalists' would say it has sapped its very lifeblood with its anti-theatre poison. In over thirty years I have only worked with two directors who applied – and then only sometimes – a rigorous organic process. A number have paid confused lip-service to Stanislavski but ended up enforcing the Representational norm. Some of his ideas and tools are co-opted (for example, units, objectives, actions) not to produce more experienced, truthful work, with the actor at its centre, but yet more Representational productions, albeit ones that may be clearer, more intelligent, and with a stronger director's stamp on them. Stanislavski becomes Anglicised and stripped of his radicalism, a bit like Che Guevara on a T-shirt. How many genuinely inspiring books on acting are written by British actors, as opposed to jokey anecdotal memoirs and autobiographies? Compare this state to the countless books on acting process by Americans and Russians such as Uta Hagen, Stella Adler, Sanford Meisner, Robert Lewis, Harold Clurman, and Michael Chekhov, among others. Where is the sense of social conscience and idealism in *our* acting literature? These qualities are out there, actors have them, but we don't talk a lot about it because maybe it doesn't seem very 'British'. Unless you work in educational theatre, actors in the UK don't talk much about theoretical influences on them – is it fear of censure from a common home-grown hostility towards theory, ideology, methodology or anything else with 'y' on the end? Maybe it seems too French, German, American or Russian?

- Another myth presented as a conventional wisdom is that the approach of Stanislavski and his successors *only* applies to 'Naturalism', by which people seem to mean anything that appears natural as in everyday life and upon which there is no apparent comment. The terms 'Naturalism' and 'Realism' were given definition as schools of writing in nineteenth century France. Gustave Flaubert, through *Madame Bovary*, became the most notable exponent of Realism, characterised by methodical and objective observation and research, and the writer's attempt to live imaginatively the characters' world and experiences. Each book had to have a message evident to the reader. Naturalism, most associated with Emile Zola and Guy de Maupassant, applied scientific method to the study of human realities, and focused on the influence of physiology, environment and circumstances on psychology. It was full of descriptive detail and working class experience. Maupassant, however, broke with Naturalism and 'enumerating the multitude of insignificant incidents which fill our existence' (Preface to *Pierre et Jean*, 1888). He said 'the realist, if he is an artist, will search not to show the banal photography of life, but to give us the more complete vision, more striking, more authentic than reality itself'. He chose the most characteristic aspects of reality to create 'the selected and expressive truth'. Surely this is the key characteristic of Realism: selection of different aspects of reality to convey a particular world view.

People now frequently define Naturalism as 'a slice of life' and include Chekhov, televison and film drama, and modern gritty plays – 'kitchen-sink drama' as it was called in the fifties and sixties – but the content of all this work is highly selected and structured, in other words, Realism. Even documentaries and docu-dramas are carefully edited and are not just a purely objective record.

In Stanislavski's productions of Chekhov the acting aimed to be natural to life and they were full of *naturalistic detail* designed in careful production scores: *The Seagull's*, for example, called on characters to wipe away dribble, blow their noses, and clean their teeth with matchsticks, but that doesn't make Chekhov 'Naturalism', in its original or revised definition. Stanislavski himself later criticised his production for reliance on external detail at the expense of inner truth (*The Moscow Art Theatre*, Nick Worrall, Routledge, 1996). Nevertheless, the play and Stanislavski's production plan contained elements of comedy, tragedy, symbolism and detailed construction of atmosphere.

Further, Stanislavski's Moscow Art Theatre (MAT) seasons didn't just include Chekhov plays, as we might be led to believe; they embraced Shakespeare, Gorky's overtly political plays, and Symbolist plays by Maeterlinck and Hamsun, for which Stanislavski developed some enthusiasm. Joshua Logan, the writer of the Foreword to Sonia Moore's *The Stanislavski System* (Viking Press, 1960), observed the workings of the MAT and Stanislavski's direction in 1930/1 and was greatly surprised by the nature and variety of the work: 'a racy, intense, farcical spirit' in *The Marriage of Figaro*; 'an underlying earthy humour' in *The Cherry Orchard*; 'the exaggerated style of a children's fairy tale' in *Three Fat Men*, a political cartoon.

Yevgeny Vakhtanghov, another MAT director, used Stanislavski's 'system' but created what he called *fantastic* or theatrical realism, a more heightened reality, in productions such as Strindberg's *Erik XIV*, in which the very unnaturalistic and bold actor, Michael Chekhov, Anton's nephew, played the lead. Chekhov, himself, extolling the virtues of truth and imaginative transformation, ran the Second MAT. So we need to explode both the myth of a pervasive 'slice-of-life' Naturalism and the myth that the Organic Stanislavski approach is exclusively wedded to it.

Also, plays by Shakespeare, Bond, Brecht or Schiller may be written in different styles but they fall within a broad definition of realism because they portray recognisable human beings. Whatever the academic literary definitions people choose to opt for, actors, unless they are to fall into unbelievable mannerism and formalism, must grasp the realist content and play people fully and truthfully within the demands of the particular language and style of each play, and so Stanislavski's approach has a place here too. Even Brecht, formerly hostile to Stanislavski having seen the American application of his approach, changed his view when he read his books and saw the MAT productions. In his 1951 *Letter to an Actor* (quoted in *Brecht on Theatre* by John Willett, Methuen Drama, 1964), he makes clear that some of his statements on critical objectivity in acting have been misunderstood: 'Of course the stage of a realistic theatre must be peopled by live, three-dimensional, self-contradictory people, with all their passions, unconsidered utterances and actions.' People were struck by the realism and inner content of the Berliner Ensemble's work when they came to Britain in 1956: the famous 'alienation effect' doesn't demand alienating acting!

- How we are presented and seen doesn't help, either. Whatever the reservations people in the UK have about Stanislavski, long rehearsals and ensemble companies, when an ensemble such as the Maly visits Britain critics, actors, directors and drama school practitioners and students are stunned and amazed by the superb, truthful quality of acting. Ah, the Russians! Well, actually, Russians weren't born great actors. It's not 'in the blood'. They become great through their acting culture and training. We all have something in common beyond nationality and conditioning. We're all human beings, and nothing is stopping our actors from achieving a similar quality of sustained depth and truth to that of these Russian actors, other than, of course, the development of ensemble theatre companies, links between them and complementary training schools teaching the organic approach, and sufficient funding for long-term acting contracts! This is possible if the will is there, but the will is only there if there is understanding of the importance of drama as a vital social force and of actors as artists on a par with any professional dancers or musicians.

This is a very relevant comparison because at the moment the sort of respect we might give to Russian actors from the Maly or MAT is like the respect the British public awards opera singers, ballet dancers, or orchestra musicians. There is respect for their years of training, dedication, hard work, and clear abilities. They are seen as hugely skilled artists. Actors, on the other hand, in public perception, are too frequently viewed as 'luvvies': lightweight, certainly not serious, a bit self-regarding but also self-effacing; the talented amateur, concerned about things but not *over*-committed. Outspoken rock stars are awarded more gravitas. Acting is seen more as personality promotion than an artform, and the fashionable cult of celebrity just reinforces that. Extreme images start to form of actors in fedoras and trailing scarves, Dames in layered shawls, and worst of all, *The Stage* newspaper's cartoon actor, Hamlet the pig, continually 'preparing' by propping up the bar with a pint of ale in his trotter! Often in the past, well-known British actors have been dismissive of 'seriousness' in acting, highlighting rather how they've 'corpsed' onstage, or never prepared before going on, or don't bother with research and just like a director to tell them where to stand – none of this improvisation lark, thank you! After all, it's just a bit of fun and pretending, not a job for a grown-up person at all really. Of course, they may not really mean all this stuff, but it's what young actors hear and it reinforces a particular view of acting. And then, of course, some critics further reinforce it: an actor's drama teacher or director may be saying, 'Be real. Go for the truth', but some witty, urbane drama critic may be flicking out reviews complimenting actors for being deliciously mannered, delightfully over-the-top, and full of wonderful ticks and twitches. The actor facing a possible bout of unemployment and poverty may think twice about truth and integrity.

## Training

To a large extent drama courses reflect the business and seek to help actors to gain work of a high standard. My impression is that some also have their own pioneering agenda and want to change and improve the quality of work in the industry, and not just service it as it is. Most acting students will have been taught some aspect or exercise of Stanislavski process. A number of courses, for example, at Drama Centre, East 15, the Royal Academy of Dramatic Art (RADA), Rose Bruford College, Arts Educational, profess to use the Stanislavski approach to a significant degree, and I'm sure others use it to some degree. Stanislavski is *the* most renowned theoretician and practitioner of acting, and specifically of Organic acting. There is no corresponding, relevant Representational theorist who is similarly taught in schools. This isn't accidental. Stanislavski has survived because of the demonstrated value of what he has to offer us. However, I don't believe any school would claim to be running courses to parallel the length, consistency, and comprehensiveness, in terms of Stanislavski-based process, as those in Russia and Eastern Europe, which run for four or five years and are steeped in that tradition.

A number of factors – and all of these may not apply to all schools – can get in the way of students sustaining a confident, absorbed organic approach, some of which I'll enlarge on in Chapter 16.

- The length of the courses – a fourth year would allow for a sustained period of applying technique to a selection of plays.
- Too little time allowed for each project.
- Too many tutors/directors with different terminology and approaches that can confuse students before they have a firm grasp of a process. Consistency in training may be a greater virtue than mirroring the variety of the business.
- Seeing the use of 'specialists' in a particular field – Shakespeare or Restoration, for example – as more important than applying a consistent process of character creation through different theatre genres, so the students end up playing 'style'.
- The influence of role models in the Representational style in the industry.

Further, there isn't a tradition in the UK of continuing training after drama school. American actors always seem to be doing classes. In Russia, training continues in the ensemble companies and doesn't stop. The RSC under Michael Boyd's directorship has introduced regular classes. There are Actors' Centres in London, Manchester, Birmingham and Newcastle providing courses and one-off classes. Various other workshops and courses often flourish in London. It's random, though, and only a small percentage of actors are involved. Again, belief that we really are the best actors in the world so we don't need to improve. Of course, we need to be working, but inside and outside our work there should be a continuing process of training and exploring technique. Having organised a number of acting workshops myself, I know that some participants' main concern was often a showcase presentation at the end and the possibility of getting an agent and work, not the process of learning something new and improving as an actor. This is a result, not of some defect in the British actor, but of a defect in the circumstances in which we train and work, or don't work. People get desperate, they need to pay the rent. The same phenomenon can be seen in the final term of drama courses when the showcase of speeches, scenes and songs comes around, in which the students display themselves anxiously to representatives from the industry. The pressures of the business – of getting an agent, meeting casting directors, getting the job, competition between actors – intrude and can damage the mutual respect and trust that has built up between teachers and students in the work that follows. Ego and acting to please can predominate over the potential and ability of the actors, their real selves, and further damage the absorption of an organic process. This has prompted one drama course leader not to allow showcases on his course at all.

## In pursuit of clarity

Actors have a role to play as artists in society; we need to interpret and communicate a script fully to an audience not only to entertain but to elucidate our world and affect people on a number of levels and encourage change for the better. I believe the most appropriate form of acting to serve this need is Organic acting based on Stanislavski's principles. Misrepresented and misunderstood, this approach is not the most accepted form of acting, but when seen at its best in certain ensemble companies and film acting it is universally acclaimed, and has been a key influence in the work of many leading and varied practitioners such as Augusto Boal, Jerzy Grotowski and Peter Brook, not to mention Chaplin and Maria Callas. To make this approach more widely accepted, for example, in Britain, ideological and economic objections have to be overcome.

There are also misunderstandings and confusions about Stanislavski and the Organic approach which I want to tackle in this book. The *essential* notion of recreating human experience and producing truthful, affecting performance is often lost. Particular aspects of technique aimed at freeing the intuition are misunderstood and turned into intellectual exercises. Contradictory messages are given in training and companies.

Often Stanislavski is completely misrepresented and one has to remember that he gave different emphasis to aspects of his approach in different periods; he didn't see it as a formula set in tablets of stone. For example, apart from the erroneous tag of 'Naturalism', he's sometimes attributed with:

*not caring about language* – when his *Building a Character*, in particular, is emphatic about the need for clear, flexible voices and precise verbal expression as a vital means to convey the all-important message of the writer;

*advocating that the actor 'must be wholly immersed in his character'* – as Simon Callow critically maintains in his Foreword to the new edition of Michael Chekhov's *To The Actor* (Routledge, 2002), when, in fact, Stanislavski believed, just like Chekhov, that an actor had to exercise control onstage through an internal monitor, and that actors who thought they actually *were* a different character were suffering from a pathological delusion.

*blocking off the audience* – to contradict Callow again, Stanislavski's invention of the imaginary 'fourth wall' in front of the audience didn't mean he believed the actor should be completely cut off from the audience but that their main focus should be on the *action* onstage. Equally, though, the audience should inform and affect the actor as 'a huge mirror reflecting the actor's creativity ... the actor must act as the character and listen as an actor'. The presence of the audience could enhance the actor's involvement and inspiration: 'Because to act without a public is like singing in a place without resonance ... The audience constitute the spiritual acoustics for us. They give back what they receive from us as living, human emotions' (*An Actor Prepares*). Many more examples can be found.

For those acting students and professional actors who may have become mystified and frustrated by what appeared to them as the Stanislavski approach, or by misleading and contradictory things said about it, I want to make it accessible and comprehensible. I also want to offer a more comprehensive and integrated view of his approach than we're used to by examining the content of all three of the books we know as *An Actor Prepares, Building a Character* and

*Creating a Role*, as well as records of his training exercises with actors and of his directing process.

In addition, I want to relate to Stanislavski's legacy and successors, especially Michael Chekhov and his emphasis on the role of the imagination and psycho-physical work in character transformation, and to reclaim him from those who wish to present him in opposition to Stanislavski. While accepting there were differences of approach and opinion between them, Chekhov's work came out of the Moscow Art Theatre (MAT) and Stanislavski's experiments around the relation between psychology and physical action, truth and imagination. His later incorporation of some techniques influenced by Rudolph Steiner was an attempt to further the full physical and inner expression of one's life as the character, and was not a rejection of those roots or flight into a theatre of formalistic gesture. As Chekhov says of Stanislavski's teaching in his autobiography, *The Path of the Actor* (Routledge, 2005): '... I placed it at the foundation of my subsequent and, to some extent independent, experiments in the art of drama'. I shall also look at the views of teachers such as Uta Hagen, Stella Adler, Lee Strasberg, Sanford Meisner, and David Mamet to highlight their likeness or difference to the Stanislavski approach to throw it into sharper relief.

The book is structured as a step-by-step guide to key elements in the process of how we create truthful performance: the first three parts deal with developing basic faculties, action, and an imaginary world; the fourth part focuses on applying that to text, character, rehearsal, and performance; and the final part looks at how we organise ourselves to work effectively. I also place this in the often unfavourable context of working in British theatre and suggest some ways of dealing with that conflict. For example, Stanislavski rehearsed for long periods. We don't. That doesn't discount his approach, but rather forces us to make adaptations, such as looking more closely at the independent preparation of the actor before joining a company.

I have opted for terminology that I find clear and that is in most common use, and which may not coincide with the latest translations of Stanislavski's works or win the approval of academics. This book is a practical guide for *actors* and other theatre practitioners. However, it is not intended as a comprehensive training manual in the sense of a full acting course curriculum – the place for that is in a school offering a full-time training course.

My main aim is to clarify and demistify the Organic acting process associated with Stanislavski and his successors, remove confusion and misunderstandings, and in the process, I hope actors will be inspired to look to our common humanity in order to produce the truthful and transformational performances of which we are capable and which our audiences deserve.

**Konstantin Stanislavski 1863–1938**

Stanislavski was born Konstantin Sergeyevich Alexeyev into a wealthy textile family. He spent much of his youth making theatre: creating puppet shows, circus acts and music. He briefly attended the Imperial Dramatic School and considered opera as a career, but finally committed to drama. Embarking on his career as an actor, he adopted the stage name, Stanislavski, and collaborated on establishing the Society of Art and Literature in 1888, playing his first major role at twenty-five. His early acting attempts were based on external imitation of actor role models and personal vanity. Much of the acting of the time was stereotypical, poorly-rehearsed and within a star-based theatre focused on vaudeville and melodramas. His lessons in the need for ease, control and sense of truth were hard-learned, but he set out 'to destroy the ancient hokum of the theatre' and revolutionise both the nature of theatre and of acting.

In 1898, he and Vladimir Nemirovich-Danchenko, a prominent writer and teacher, set up the Moscow Art Theatre. Stanislavski was to be actor and overall director, and the plays were to have serious and psychological content: Chekhov's *The Seagull* was in the opening season and was ground-breaking in its rounded characters, subtlety, and inner life. Stanislavski explored the psychology of the writing, not through an Organic rehearsal process, but through a production plan with naturalistic visual detail and a soundscape. Since the actors had no psycho-physical technique, he told them what to do autocratically, and this persisted through other Chekhov productions. Theatre production was changing but acting technique clearly wasn't.

After Stanislavski endured the despotic treatment himself, playing Brutus in Nemirovich-Danchenko's production of *Julius Caesar* in 1903, he turned his focus on how the actors themselves could make creative contributions, and began the process of detailed company study of each play. He also set up the Theatrical Studio in 1905 to explore psychology and physicality and new theatre techniques. Under Vsevelod Meyerhold it concentrated on the physical but there were financial problems and the first Revolution forced it to close.

In 1906, depressed over the state of his theatre and the inadequacies of his own acting, he set about examining all his past observation and experience to arrive at the new approach to acting required by his search for theatrical truth. He looked at all the natural processes that create spontaneity and life onstage and concluded that the way to a creative mood and inspiration lay in freedom and ease, concentration, imagination, and belief in the action. He proposed work on the inner and outer self, and work on the role and play through the round-the-table analysis he'd already initiated. By 1910, he'd identified some key elements of a process: given circumstances, units and objectives, emotion memory, inner motive forces, radiation and communion. 1911 saw the legendary productions of *The Brothers Karamazov* and *Hamlet*. Outstanding experimentation took place in the First Studio of 1912, involving his most brilliant student, Michael Chekhov; Yevgeny Vakhtangov, the director of 'fantastic realism'; and the great teacher, Leopold Sulerzhitski, who introduced Hatha yoga into training.

After the First World War, the MAT toured the US where people were eager for knowledge of Stanislavski's approach, and two company members, Richard Boleslavski and Maria Ouspenskaya, remained behind to establish the American Laboratory Theatre and training in the Stanislavski process and inspired the creation of the Group Theatre. By this time, Stanislavski was emphasising given circumstances and the right actions as a route to the inner life rather than emotion memory.

His production of *Dead Souls* in 1928 led him to question long periods of analytical discussion. He moved towards his final stage of development with its emphasis on 'analysis through action', improvisation of a text, and uncovering the physical and psychological actions to fulfil objectives. This now was the means of creating 'the life of the human spirit' and real feeling in acting: the Method of Physical Action. He experimented with this at the Opera-Dramatic Studio with a selected group of actors between 1935–38, and it was during this innovative work that he died of a heart attack in August 1938.

**Michael Chekhov 1891–1955**

Chekhov was the nephew of Anton Chekhov and, for Stanislavski, 'my most brilliant student'. Along with Vakhtangov and Meyerhold, he became one of the most influential actor/teachers of the twentieth century. He joined the Moscow Art Theatre in 1909, was prominent in the First Studio, and appeared as a lead or supporting actor in twelve MAT and independent productions between 1913–23, creating both excitement and controversy with his imaginative characterisations. Stanislavski approved of his results, but not always, at this time, of the means. In 1918, he suffered mental, drink and marital problems and found relief in Hindu philosophy and Rudolph Steiner's Anthroposophy, whose experimentation with gesture in speech and movement (Speechformation and Eurythmy) now influenced him. He operated his own experimental studio in Moscow from this period until 1922. Perhaps his most famous roles came in 1921: Strindberg's *Erik XIV*, directed by Vakhtangov, and Khlestakov in Stanislavski's production of *The Government Inspector*, in which he produced extraordinarily imaginative characterisations combined with emotional truth: imagination and transformation were the very bedrock of his ideas. In 1923, he was entrusted with the directorship of the Second Moscow Art Theatre and experimented with movement and imagery. However his work was condemned by Stalin's regime as 'alien' and 'idealist' and he emigrated in 1928.

Chekhov had seven difficult years failing to establish a training school and company. He worked for Max Reinhardt and in films in Germany, set up a company in Paris, and performed in Latvia and Lithuania. In 1935, he took the Moscow Art Players to New York where he impressed members of the Group Theatre like Stella Adler, Sanford Meisner and Robert Lewis, and presented his ideas to them in the form of a lecture and demonstration, an exercise he repeated in 1941.

In 1936, the actor, Beatrice Straight, invited Chekhov to set up a training centre on her family's estate at Dartington Hall in Devon. The Chekhov Theatre Studio ran from 1936–39 and continued experiments in gesture, atmosphere, and sensation and qualities as an alternative to emotion recall, an emphasis on which Stanislavski himself was now replacing with imagination in given circumstances. With the war, Chekhov reorganised in Ridgefield, Connecticut. After an initial Broadway failure, his company successfully toured a number of States. In 1941, he organised a second Studio in New York and worked to refine his technique, especially relating to Psychological Gesture. Finally, he established a Hollywood film career between 1943 and 1954 and received an Academy Award nomination for his psychoanalyst in Hitchcock's *Spellbound*. During this time he taught his techniques to actors including Monroe, Jack Palance and Anthony Quinn. He died of a heart attack in 1955.

# Part 1

## Starting from nothing

# 1 Awareness

> *All actors must be character actors*
>
> Stanislavski

When you first encounter the Organic acting process based on Stanislavski's observations and conclusions about what makes great performance, you are inevitably influenced by contemporary actors and current versions of the original theory. When I attended what was possibly London's first acting school based on the approach of Stanislavski and Michael Chekhov, the Actors Workshop, the emphasis of myself and my colleagues was very much on 'being emotionally involved' and 'feeling the part' because we were impressed by the American role models like Marlon Brando, Eva Marie Saint, James Dean and Paul Newman, and although critical of 'the Method' were nevertheless influenced by it since it was a tangible manifestation in our time of at least part of the famous Stanislavski approach. As our training developed, though, and I read Stanislavski's books, *An Actor Prepares* and *Building a Character*, and Sonia Moore's classic text, *The Stanislavski System* (Viking Press, 1960), it became clear there was a surprising difference of emphasis.

## Action

I was confronted not by a Method of Emotions, but by the *Method of Physical Action*. Since *drama* itself means action this is very appropriate. Stanislavski examines a script by what *happens* in it, by what the characters *do* and *why*.

What motives or objectives will an actor perceive through the lines and events, and what verbal, psychological and bodily actions will they develop to bring them to life? Contact with others in dramatic interaction will bring new actions which are reactions or adaptations to changed circumstances. A dynamic develops and through that atmospheres and emotions will emerge, and a whole new imaginary life – but the basis is *action*. From conscious work on the text and action, from playing why I do something and what I do to get it, as we do in life, and from believing in the *imaginary* circumstances created, the actor is led into contact with the *subconscious* and the working of creative intuition. From structure comes spontaneity, from discipline comes freedom, from preparation comes inspiration. The central aim of Stanislavski was to find a conscious process to enable actors to reach inspiration more often: that state in which an actor appears totally in the moment and in control, in the character and connected to the audience, moved by a creative consciousness not the conscious intellect, recreating truthful human experience. *The life of the human spirit*, Stanislavski called it – flowing from a commitment to the action. The more this occurred the more audiences would be affected and made to think and feel. It all comes from simple action – what an audience actually sees, and what an actor can truthfully perform, not mechanically, but arising from inner psychological impulse and justification. 'On the stage', says Stanislavski in *An Actor Prepares*, 'you must always be enacting something', and it is this which will produce the feelings which are 'not subject to direct command'.

## Awareness

What do we need to perform actions within their context, to reproduce human activity? We need ourselves obviously. There isn't anybody else in the performing space. The characters are created in the writer's imagination, but we are bringing them to life off the page through our imagination and action. They become us, and whether that diminishes them or whether they are fully realised through us depends on our awareness and understanding of ourselves, others, and the world we live in. When we come to rehearse and perform we have to play the action clearly and economically in order to communicate it, and we do that as we are at our current state of development. To understand a wide range of characters – who they are, why they do what they do, what forces are acting on them in different periods and places – we need to widen our awareness of life generally, and to increase our capacity for understanding; that is, of course, if we want to play a range of characters beyond a narrow type, to be transformational, as I believe most actors do.

*Awareness can be heightened through observing, understanding, and sensing.*

## Observing

- **People we know**. Examining closely what we really see or may have taken for granted. Their actions, habits, mannerisms and appearance and how these relate to their backgrounds, their class, education, family, job, position in the community, religion, nationality, and the psychology we've experienced. Imagining ourselves in their circumstances and how they must sense and feel things.

- **Strangers**. Taking someone we see frequently – in a news kiosk, shop, or at the gym – and examining in close detail their face, body and clothes, and then imagining what sort of life they lead now, what they do alone and with others at leisure and work, what sort of person they are and what their history is. Imagining yourself in this other life. Michael Chekhov, in *To the Actor*, suggests taking characters from a history book or novel, and from other countries, to get into the experience of people from other periods and cultures, to penetrate their specific way of life, thinking and morality, so we don't simply fall into playing different people like ourselves. We could take a character from a painting by, say, Caravaggio or Edvard Munch, observe their face, physicality, clothes and circumstances and construct their life.

- **Nature**. Observing plants, trees, animals, a spider's web, or frost on glass, and seeing their distinct forms, and then all the detailed constituent parts that make up their whole, imagining how they came to this state and how they may change with time and the seasons.

  This use of observation and imagination to increase our awareness of other people and nature will sharpen our ability to understand imaginary characters through their actions and flesh out their psychology and physicality. We discover what Chekhov calls the 'inexhaustible fund of originality, inventiveness and ingenuity you are capable of displaying as an actor.'

## Understanding

- **Ourselves**. How have we become what we are through our own family background and relationships, our environment and education, our class and community, our choices and experiences? Where do our preferred actions come from? How have our feelings, vocal and physical characteristics developed? What were key formative influences on political and religious views, and the development of hobbies, sports, and skills? Do we have conflicts and contradictions in our makeup? Do we want to be liked, but repel people? Do we want to be great actors, but spend too much time in the pub? How do we behave when we are alone, at work or leisure? How do we behave when with other people either at work or leisure? How do we act differently when we're with family as opposed to close friends? How do age and gender make a difference to our responses? How are we with total strangers of different age and sex? There are so many permutations to our actions that we can appear completely different people according to whom we're with and where. That gives an indication of how much we can transform even within the limits of our own lives, and, therefore, the range of different characters we may be able to play using ourselves as the basis.

- **Society**. To understand an individual and their choices and actions we have to know the sort of world they are living in. People don't act the same way in different countries and different epochs, under different economic systems, social structures, and cultural mores. We know this to be the case because we may have read books on history, economics, and anthropology, but at some point someone will state 'Hamlet was just a guy like myself', as quoted by Michael Chekhov, or 'All the knowledge in the world of the Elizabethan era will not help you play Mary Stuart', David Mamet's similar comment in *True and False* (Vintage Books, 1997). There is some truth in the first statement, at least, in that the Hamlet of Shakespeare's play existed within the modern historical period when our world was changing from a fixed, hierarchical feudal system based on the land to an early form of capitalist economy developing trade, industry, financial institutions and much greater social mobility. The changes and resultant tensions are reflected in the play, for example, in the opposing figures of old Hamlet and Claudius. A similar conflict is evident between Lear and Edmund. We can relate to these characters, their ambitions and struggles, their intellectual dilemmas and emotions better than we can relate to a feudal serf's life or to courtly, Platonic love because our world is a more developed form of Shakespeare's world. We recognise the economic drives, the political and financial institutions, and the emotions that come with greater freedom, possibilities and responsibilities and erotic love, uniting both love and sexual passion. Nevertheless, the Court of Denmark in that time is not a New York college of education in the present. We need to know the specifics of the time and place to understand the context in which action occurs in order to fully understand what is happening. For example, is Hamlet simply 'a man who could not make up his mind', as in Olivier's interpretation, or is he living, like Shakespeare was, in a society full of plots, conspiracies, and challenges to the monarchy, of changing values, a world in a great upheaval containing potential for good and bad, and trying to understand the meaning of everything and decide on the most productive course of action? Different interpretations based on different understandings of the world produce different actions, and reading widely, both generally and in terms of specific research, will enhance our understanding and ability to interpret what characters do in an informed and imaginative way.

**David Mamet b. 1947**

Born in Chicago, he is a playwright, screenwriter, theatre and film director, acting theorist and founder member of Atlantic Theatre Company. He has written, among many plays, *American Buffalo*, *Glengarry Glen Ross* and *Speed-the-Plow*. His films include *House of Cards*, *The Spanish Prisoner* and *Heist*.

## Sensing

We need to open our senses so that we are always receptive to information and stimuli from the world outside us, absorbing and processing it. We can test and train our senses by focusing on simple exercises.

- **Seeing**. Sit opposite another person and take in their face, body, and clothes. Look at the fine detail: the nature of forehead lines, their depth, length and number; the exact shape, width, and length of the nose, aquiline or snub; the form and colour of a necklace; the nature of the hands and how they rest in the lap. Turn away and see how much you have really absorbed by describing it out loud.

- **Hearing**. Sit still in a room and focus on all the sounds inside and outside: the breathing of others, the rustle of a shirt, a cough, the shifting of a foot, birds, traffic, distant laughter, the movement of wind through trees. Recall how many sounds you took in.
- **Smelling**. Walking on a beach or along a city street, be conscious of all the different smells: seaweed, sun lotion, wet sand, hot drinks or traffic fumes, cooking, wet paint, rubbish. Recall how many there were.
- **Tasting**. On your way through a wood what can you taste? Possibly tree bark, rainwater from leaves, smoke from burning wood, elements in addition to what we may have actually put in our mouths, like a sandwich or chewing gum.
- **Touching**. Lying in the park, what do you feel? A rug and lumpy grass under the back, a bag under the head, a book in the hand, a water bottle resting against a foot, sandals rubbing the skin, a fly brushing the hair, sweat trickling down the neck?

  Try taking one situation and focus on all the senses. For example, what are you seeing, hearing, smelling, tasting, touching as you sunbathe in your back garden?

All these elements of awareness, understanding, and sensory openness will assist our development as informed, sensitised and integrated people. Michael Chekhov highlights three basic requirements for the actor, one of which being *richness of the psychology*. The other two, *sensitivity of the body to psychological creative impulse* and *control of both body and psychology*, I'll address in the next chapter.

# 2 Ease and focus

> *What we need are simple, expressive actions with an inner content*
>
> Stanislavski

To act, to perform action creatively, imaginatively and effectively, we need to find our centres. We often hear the term *centred*. It's become common modern usage to describe an essential state. When we're centred we feel connected to ourselves, integrated, in control, undistracted and in the moment, energised, easy and confident. Stanislavski referred to this as *self-possession* and *repose*, which enables the actor to 'forget all about himself as an individual and yield his place to the character in the play' (quoted from his lectures to opera singers at the Moscow Bolshoi Theatre, 1918–22, in *Stanislavsky on the Art of the Stage*, translated by David Magarshak, Faber and Faber, 1960). This is what Michael Chekhov meant when he emphasised the need for *control by the actor over psychology and body*, and *sensitivity of the body to psychological creative impulse*. To bring about this state the actor has to aim for ease and focus, which, because of their mutual connection, I express as a *focused ease* or *relaxed concentration*. The two need to be considered together, because we don't want to be so relaxed we're floating and floppy, or so focused we're like a coiled, tight spring. Lev Dodin, the Maly Drama Theatre's Director, in *Journey Without End* (Tantalus Books, 2005) talks of the liberation Stanislavski was striving for as 'liberation through tension. Only by trying to achieve the topmost heights can we achieve genuine freedom'. This means that all art involves some struggle in the same manner as a sport. A horse-rider needs to be relaxed in the saddle but with alert, engaged muscles, and there may be a few hurtful falls in the process of learning as there will be with acting.

**Lev Dodin b. 1944**
Born in Siberia, Dodin studied theatre as a child at the Leningrad Young Viewer's Theatre and then entered the St. Petersburg Academy of Theatrical Arts and studied under Boris Zon. He freelanced as a director in Russia and abroad, and first worked at the Maly Drama Theatre in 1975. He became the Artistic Director in 1983 and staged productions including *Stars in the Morning Sky*, *Claustrophobia*, *The Possessed*, and *The Cherry Orchard*. He has received numerous awards and also runs a course at the St. Petersburg Academy.

## Ease of body and focus

For Stanislavski and any other theorist and practitioner, 'freeing our muscles' is important because of the limitations imposed on an actor by muscular spasm and physical tightness, which block energy. Voices become hoarse and inexpressive. Legs become stiff. Faces become like stone. Breathing becomes clavicular and short. Lesser tensions can produce unconscious mannerisms and twitches in a little finger or eyebrow. What may go unnoticed in everyday life, is highlighted in performance as in the lens of a camera. If an actor looks tense and wooden then their whole inner life looks wooden. To prove the debilitating effect of tension on the mind and creative state Stanislavski famously urged his students to lift a grand piano while multiplying numbers or visualising stores in the street outside the theatre. They couldn't do it, with the conclusion that in a state of tension 'how much less possible must it be to express the delicate emotions of a complicated role' (*An Actor Prepares*). Stanislavski's physical training regime involved gymnastics, to improve the flexibility, muscle tone, and expressiveness of the body; acrobatics, for developing 'the quality of decisiveness' so that an actor can release and act on impulse more; and dance, for alignment and clarity of form. These disciplines, to varying degrees, will be evident in many acting schools.

There are now other types of physical exercise available: the Alexander technique for improving alignment, and yoga, t'ai chi, and pilates for posture, muscle toning and integration of mind, breathing and body. Stanislavski was actually interested in yoga from 1906 and owned numerous books on it. In the First Studio of 1912, he and Leopold Sulerzhitski, its leader, regularly used Hatha yoga and Raja yoga. The first aims for calm and relaxation through working on physical postures and balance (*asana*) and breath control (*pranayama*); and the second focuses on mental control through concentration (*dharana*), visualisation, observation and meditation. Both also have an influence on Stanislavski's techniques for communication and visualisation of images, which we'll look at in Chapters 4 and 6.

This interest in yoga relates to the concern of Stanislavski and Chekhov for the connection between the psychological and the physical at all stages of the acting process. At the most basic level, the psychological contains the physical and vice versa. For example, if I want to control and restrict you, I may press my hand on your shoulder to prevent you from rising from a seat. If I guide you by the arm in the direction of the door, it could be because I'm disturbed by you and want you to leave. Emotional experience has a physical manifestation; for example, something very upsetting may make a person weak and dizzy. Whatever the value of the contribution gymnastics and dance can offer to the actor, an actor is not a dancer or gymnast and should not rely on a set pattern of movement and gesture, an *external line of movement*. The actor needs movement that is more spontaneous, wider ranging and which has an *inner line of movement*, an inner flow of energy that is unbroken, as in a piece of music, and which prompts a sensitive and corresponding response from the body. This *psycho-physical* connection may not come easily to people given the organisation, pressures and stresses of modern life and the way our intellectual, physical, and imaginative experience may be split during our working lives in the factory, office, or school. We can become dualistic, head cut off from body, thoughts from emotions, desires from action, alienated from others and from ourselves, rather than wholly integrated. This gets worse the more we rely on technology and sedentary tasks centred around computers, the faster life gets, and the greater the emphasis on sensory titillation in TV and film drama rather than on a deeper intellectual and emotional understanding of life. As actors, we need to remove blocks and disconnections so that we operate much more as we did as a child, when thoughts, wants, emotions and physical expression were unthinkingly integrated. The acting process and acting training should focus on regaining this state which opens us to sensitivity and creativity. Physical exercises to achieve a focused ease are central to this.

**Leopold Sulerzhitski 1872–1916**

Close friend and collaborator of Stanislavski, he was a singer, artist, writer, fisherman, shepherd, pacifist, revolutionary and Tolstoyan. He became Stanislavski's assistant by 1907 and head of the First Studio in 1912, where experimentation took place with Michael Chekhov and Yevgeny Vakhtangov and he introduced yoga into the training.

Between 1935 and 1938 Stanislavski worked with a group of selected students at the Opera-Dramatic Studio in Moscow. He created a course of exercises and rehearsals which would define his approach practically, in addition to its record in the famous three books published in Britain after 1936 (see *Stanislavski and the Actor*, Jean Benedetti, Methuen, 1998). Stanislavski's exercises on physical ease from the classes and the books focused on:

- Awareness of tension (particularly as a result of performing in public) and its effects on the mind as well as the body (as in the piano-lifting example above).
- Release of tension in particular muscles: Stanislavski's instruction to students to 'Relax more!' was replaced by Michael Chekhov with the advice to create a *sense of ease* because he believed any exhortation to feel something can be guaranteed to promote resistance and tension – the opposite effect desired!
- Development of an *internal monitor*: the inner awareness that detects and releases tension and identifies what the body needs to do to accomplish actions.
- Isolation exercises: control of different muscles and limbs – fingers, arms, chest, pelvis, legs, head, spine – so they can move independently of each other.
- Economy of movement: without straining or excess effort, using only whatever muscles and energy are necessary to achieve a goal, like a cat that is easy, clear, focused, energised and powerful.

- Balance and co-ordination: what is required of the different parts of the body to perform difficult actions while maintaining balance and shifting the centre of gravity.
- Co-operation: working with others to complete a task such as tidying a room.
- Conflict: finding the muscles needed to physically subdue someone or escape from their grasp.
- Justification of an adopted action and position: assessing what the body needs to do to sustain it, releasing excess tension, and then giving a reason for it through creating an objective and action, e.g. I'm standing stretched upwards because I'm reaching up to pick an apple, change a light bulb, paint the ceiling.

Achieving physical ease and control will help the actor to

- gain suppleness and co-ordination
- become more open and responsive, decisive and spontaneous
- develop a neutral, balanced alignment
- concentrate energy economically
- remove blocks to expression
- eradicate personal habits and mannerisms
- find a sense of inner ease and strength
- communicate objectives and actions
- adapt to different characters' physicality and tempos
- create sensitivity of the body to psychological creative impulse.

This last point now demands more attention. What is clearly evident so far is that all the physical work referred to has an immediate relevance to the process of acting, as opposed to being simply an end in itself. In addition, Stanislavski stresses that whatever we do as actors has to be justified. 'There is no place for theatrical conventionality in true creative art' (*An Actor Prepares*). Whatever we do physically, unless it is to be empty posing, has to have an inner justification that corresponds to something we want and are doing in a particular set of circumstances. Pursuing this will 'naturally and unconsciously put nature to work' and make our movement more controlled and easy. In *Building a Character*, Stanislavski elaborates on the connection between the inner impulse and physical expression, the *psycho-physical*, and asserts that 'external plasticity is based on our inner sense of the movement of energy' and that only movement and action coming from inside are fit for creating the physical form of a *character*.

To illustrate this a movement instructor demonstrates to student actors the power of using an imaginative impulse to produce ease and energy flow in the body: a 'drop of mercury' is poured into the index finger and runs through the whole arm, first through the finger joints, and as they straighten, into the palm and wrist and forearm, then past the elbow straightening the whole arm before it runs into the shoulder, and then back down into the arm and fingers making each part drop as it goes. Then the mercury is sent from the top of the head down the spine and into the legs and back up to the head. This imaginary 'unbroken line' of energy activates and moves the actors in a way that creates a fluid *plasticity of motion*, and which can be used both to relax points of tension in the muscles arising from blocked energy, and also to radiate out to affect other people. This relates to references to *prana*, the yoga concept of vital energy and life force, in some of Stanislavski's rehearsal notes from around 1920; he describes *prana* as 'like mercury, like a snake' running through the body (see *Stanislavski in focus* by Sharon M. Carnicke, Routledge, 1998).

To many people, for whom Stanislavski erroneously signifies low-key mumbled naturalism, this emphasis on movement, fluidity and ease (and his teaching on speech and voice also) will come as a surprise.

Michael Chekhov developed further the psycho-physical approach and devised a number of exercises which relate to the 'drop of mercury', and aim to create control over mind and body and sensitivity of the body to inner impulse. These are to be found in *To the Actor*, first published in 1953 (Harper & Row) and republished in 2002 (Routledge).

## The basic movements

These movements – often called archetypal gestures, gestures typical and representative of particular actions – are only in *To the Actor* not in the later version entitled *On the Technique of Acting* (ed. Mel Gordon, Harper Perennial, 1991). Chekhov outlines actions known as growing bigger or opening, growing smaller or closing, reaching out, dragging, lifting, and throwing. These employ full body movement exercised with strength but not strain, and at a sustained and moderate tempo. They are performed with an inner impulse, an objective of 'I want to wake my muscles by growing bigger, smaller, reaching out, etc. using maximum/minimum space around me.'

**Growing bigger** involves standing with the legs far enough apart to feel a pull on the leg muscles, hands and arms along the thighs. After giving yourself an impulse in the form of the the inner command, 'I want to wake my muscles by growing bigger, using maximum space around me', spread your fingers and raise your arms and hands wide until they reach up to the sky, palms facing up, and head and eyes lifted, so you are fully opened out. Stay in this expanded and energised position for a few seconds, experiencing the sensation of having grown, then end the action cleanly. Adopt the original position and do it again, only beginning once you have given yourself another strong inner impulse. The movement, and the others below, should have a clear beginning and end, a clearly defined form, and a sense of ease. Don't hold your breath, but rather exhale on the movement and then breathe normally. Keep trying the action until

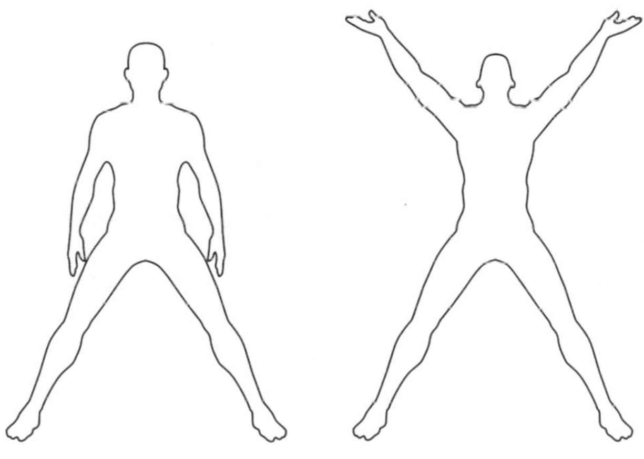

you have created as perfectly formed and executed a movement as you can. The instructions in the book are much less detailed. I learned this and the following movements as part of my own acting school training from a tutor who'd been taught Chekhov exercises. There may well be equally valid variations on the actual form of each movement according to different teachers' own experiences and actors' imagination, but the aim and principles of them will remain the same.

**Growing smaller** involves standing feet together with your arms crossed over your chest. On the impulse, 'I want to wake my muscles by growing smaller, using minimum space around me,' bend to your knees smoothly, dropping your head and curling down to the floor, closing and disappearing into a shrinking space. Hold the position again to really experience the sense of having grown small, then start again. Observe all the other instructions as above.

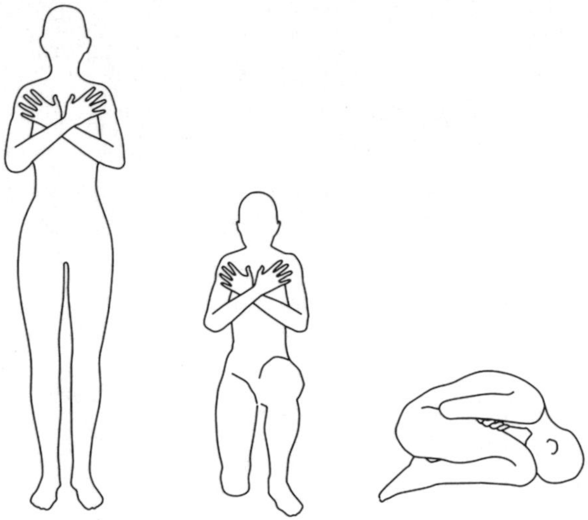

**Reaching out** involves standing with your feet slightly apart and arms thrust back, fingers spread. On the objective, 'I want to wake my muscles by reaching out, using maximum space around me', thrust your body forward on one knee as far as possible and swing your straight arms through, reaching as far forward as possible, with the other leg fully extended. Hold the position a few seconds, then try on the other leg.

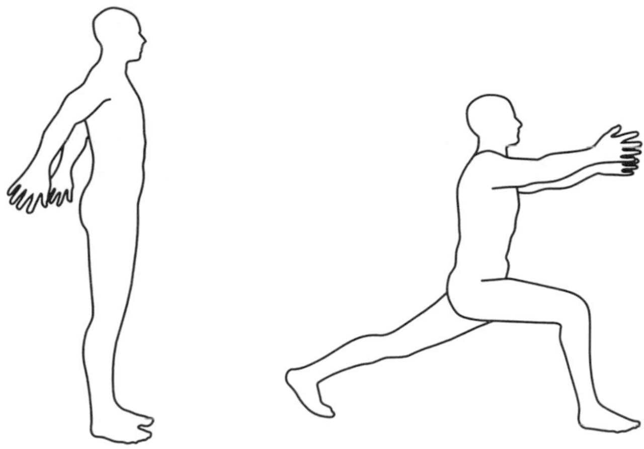

**Dragging** involves the same starting position as *reaching out*. On the impulse, reach far out and down towards the floor with your front leg bending and back leg stretching straight, then pull back an imaginary object between your spread fingers, and drag it to your back foot as the front leg straightens and back leg bends, with both feet flat on the floor. Hold the position, then try the action on the other leg.

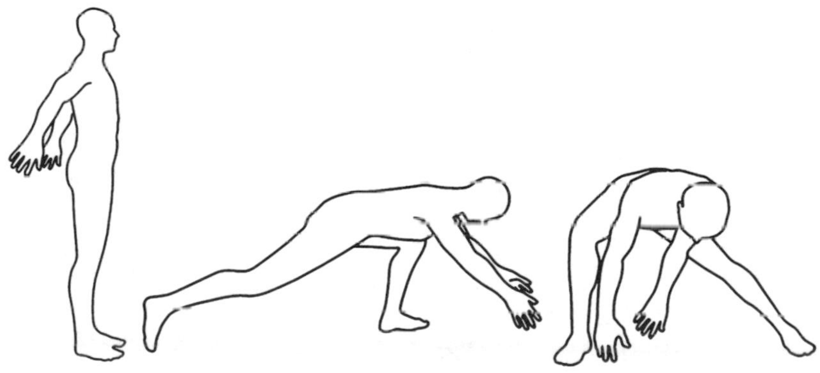

**Lifting** involves standing with your feet apart, legs straight, and arms held out parallel to the floor with your fingers spread. On the impulse, lower your body from the pelvis, swinging your arms down until your fingers touch the floor, then lift an imaginary object and hold it above your head.

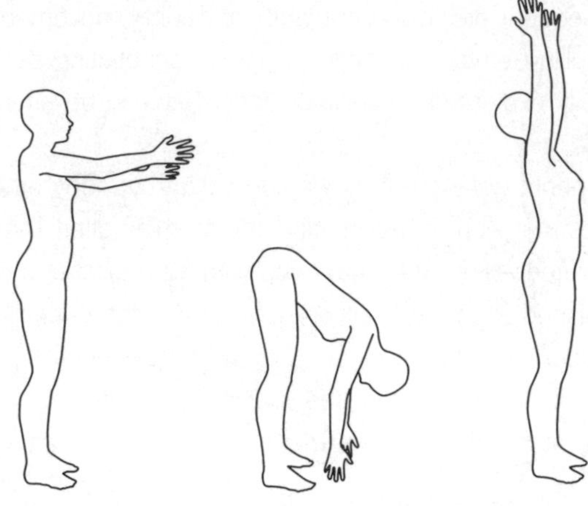

**Throwing**, the most complicated movement, involves standing with your legs apart at a right angle, and arms outstretched forward and behind, parallel to the floor and along the line of the front leg, and your eyes looking forward along the front arm. On the impulse, with ease and control (not stiffness or floppiness), swing your front arm bending across your chest and the back arm as far behind and straight as it will go, while your front leg bends forward. Then, swing your back arm over in an arc in a straight arm bowling action finishing parallel to the floor with your hand facing down; the forward arm simultaneously swings horizontally round in front of your body to behind it; as the arms move, the front leg straightens, and back leg bends. Try with the other leg facing forward, and your other arm throwing.

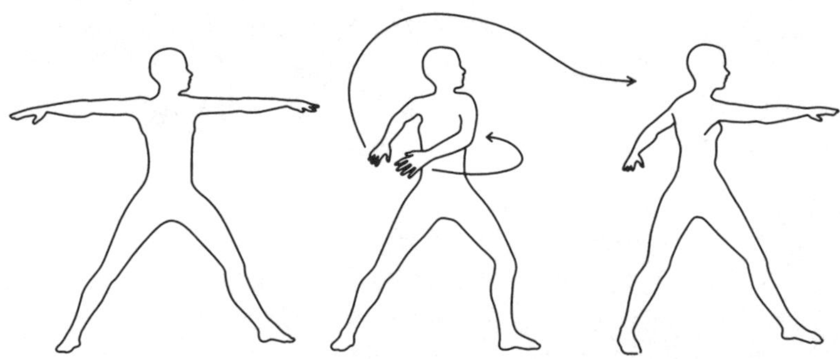

Chekhov and subsequent practitioners suggest additional movements such as beating, pushing, pulling, embracing, tearing, wringing, penetrating, slashing. Once tried out in their fully expressed, archetypical form they can be attempted with different tempos.

All these movements *will* wake muscles not woken by many other forms of physical exercise, as many an actor can affirm the morning after! They link inner impulse to an executed action. They leave you with a physical and inner sense of having accomplished a particular action. They demand the clarity, economy, freedom, co-ordination and sense of form, completeness and creative sense summed up in Chekhov's concept of the *four brothers*, the four qualities he believes to be present in any great piece of art: *ease*, *form*, *entirety* and *beauty*.

**Ease** is what makes a performance appear to be not performed, an actor seem as though they are the character and not acting at all. Heaviness, awkwardness, coarseness, physical tension may be qualities or themes to be portrayed, but the *actor* has to avoid being heavy, awkward, coarse and tense in the communication of the character. We are not presenting everyday reality and its problems literally, but a recreation of this in theatre, film, radio and TV reality in a manner that enables an audience to understand and learn from it. So, we are not justified in showing how well we can sweat, shout, declaim, stomp and mug to demonstrate grossness, energy, intensity, etc. Conversely, we shouldn't demonstrate how wonderfully light and easy we can be: both are examples of overblown egotism as opposed to the apparently effortless creativity which an enormous amount of work, time, and commitment will have gone into producing. 'I'm acting, look at me and admire me' is not the motto of the artistic actor.

**Form** is the shape and style, physical appearance and expression of a content: I grow bigger with wide, sweeping, direct, light and sustained movements, appearing uplifted, energised and confident. Everything else I do in performance needs a similarly defined and clear external appearance, arising from an inner impulse and desire to express and communicate it fully.

**Entirety** is the sense of the whole, seeing how each action fits into the overall movement, and to what purpose, just as each bar is part of a whole concerto, or each brushstroke part of a whole painting. In acting we need to start an action clearly, execute it with full definition, and finish it clearly, and then move on to the next action. Seeing everything in terms of the sum of its parts will give greater significance both to the parts and the whole thing. In a whole play, what you do in scene three will be influenced by what you've done in scenes one and two, and what you will do at the end of the play. What you want in one part will be influenced by what your character wants most in life as a whole. If I want to reach out as in the movement above, I know what I must do physically and with my will to fulfil the movement. I start with a clear impulse, I perform the actions to achieve this end, and then finish clearly. So, a sense of entirety means we focus on our aim and what we need to do to achieve it, and that will help to focus the attention of the audience.

**Beauty**, seen not as on the outside, but coming from inside; a combination of a number of elements including harmony, form, ease, sincerity, simplicity, originality, strength, feeling, truth and humanity, but which has to be experienced intuitively rather than analytically, and without vanity and sentimentality. Can we find beauty in something which appears ugly? Even violence and hopelessness can be presented in a way that uplifts rather than depresses. Samuel Beckett's plays may focus on the absurdity and barrenness of life, but they do it in language full of imagery, rhythm, and humour, and attest to our common humanity and endurance. In *King Lear*, the barbaric blinding of Gloucester should horrify, not through indulging in the gruesome physical aspects, but by throwing light on the callous ruthlessness of Regan and Cornwall and the subsequent deprivations and self-destructiveness of Gloucester; his loss of sight also relates to the blindness in the character of Lear and the greater understanding he gains at the end. Ugliness is only ugly if it's indulged for effect, not if it's part of a whole in which there are affirmations of humanity and contradictions that produce revelations and alternate courses of action.

We should now go back to the basic exercises and try them, not only with the inner impulse to wake the muscles by an action using maximum space around us, but also trying to accomplish them with a sense of ease, form, entirety and beauty, all the time monitoring how obedient our body is to the inner impulse.

## Radiation

We start by imagining that we have a centre in the chest, from which come all the impulses and energy for our movements. Rather than place this in the chest above the sternum (see Leonardo da Vinci's anatomical drawing of Vitruvian Man), I always imagine it to be in the *solar plexus* where we have a complex of nerves, our breathing centre, and which is also what Stanislavski identifies as the radiating centre of *prana*, the energy stimulated by breath. This is also the energy centre or *chakra* associated with feeling and consequently he calls it the 'seat of emotion' (*An Actor Prepares*). I also imagine this source of inner energy and power to be literally like the sun, a revolving ball of golden fire, lighting up and energising the body.

Once the imaginary centre is strongly experienced, send this golden current of energy (like the 'drop of mercury') down into an arm, whose different sections are activated as the current flows through them. Then try the other arm, your legs, your head and whole body, so that each individual part of your body responds with ease to the imaginary impulse. Next, bring all the body together in walking: from a standing position, imagine the centre of energy again, and that it is emerging through the solar plexus to a position just in front of you, smoothly and easily pulling you forward and up so that you are gliding over the floor as on a cushion of air. Imagine the centre burning and radiating with lesser and greater power so that your movement slows and quickens. Moving from this centre will help you to become more easy and responsive, to release normal tensions, make you aware of where your own personal centre is (the shoulders, head, stomach, etc.), and to experience this new centre as the *ideal* one for an actor, assisting in the development of a neutral, centred, relaxed body.

Come to a standstill and sustain this sense of radiating. How do you feel? Actors invariably say *energised, free, relaxed, powerful, light, warm, focused, strong, centred, happy, confident*. This feeling also creates the actor's *presence* on stage or screen. *Presence* is often referred to as something mystical or a gift you either possess or you don't, but it really comes down to the inner energy experienced and radiated out to other actors and the audience; the space you fill inside and outside of yourself. Whatever centre may belong to the character you're playing (and we look at this in Chapter 13), actors will benefit from developing this radiating centre as their own natural one, the basis from which they work and adapt to create other centres and types of body for different characters.

Now go back to the basic exercises and execute them under the influence of this imaginary radiating centre, so that the impulse for each movement is coming from this centre of energy and power. Experiment with doing everyday movements under this influence, making sure that every action is powered by the inner energy, but done with truth and simplicity: walk at different tempos, run, sit, lie down and get up. In real life we get an impulse to sit down – to rest or read, for example – and psychologically we continue to sit down once seated, we *radiate* sitting. So, do natural movements, sending out the energy through your body and its various parts – hands, arms, legs, head, back – and into the space around you and continue to radiate the movement when you come to a static position. Try different actions using objects: pick up a cup, close a window, open a door, put on a jacket, pack a bag. Finally, select an everyday activity you commonly do, and perform it under this radiating influence: put on shoes, clean windows, wash dishes, polish furniture.

Often what we see in acting is either purely external movement, mechanical and cerebrally determined, or vague, inexpressive 'naturalistic' movement. These Chekhov exercises are designed to create expressive, formed action that is full of the inner life and energy of the individual actor.

## Moulding

Here we focus on the creation of form by moulding shapes in space as if it were made of earth or clay. From the impulse: 'I want to create a perfect circle, oval, square, figure of eight, etc. in the space around me', you define that shape using one part of the body – finger, hand, elbow, head, leg, pelvis, foot – and mould the shape against a resistant space. As with the basic movements, start cleanly after the impulse, execute the action, and finish cleanly, aware of the sense of ease, form, entirety and beauty. Keep searching for the most clear, perfect, expressive form. Imagine different levels of resistance giving different tempos of movement as with moulding through oil, sand or moist earth.

Try moulding with the radiating centre. Next, move in the space picking up objects and moulding shapes with them as a controlled extension of you. Then work with only the hands or fingers separately, creating forms as they pick up, put down, move around objects.

This creates physical movement that is easy, clear, strong and a response to imaginary impulse, as opposed to vague, shapeless, uncontrolled and generalised actions.

### Flying

Imagine you are flying like a bird, gliding, soaring, hovering, swooping above the clouds, while maintaining physical control and strength. As you move, your body should feel weightless. Experiment with different tempos and levels of resistance in the air. Next, do the natural movements of walking, running, sitting, lying, etc. under the influence of *flying*; and finally, use objects and perform tasks and an everyday activity. As a result of the flying movement, actors say they feel *light, easy, joyful, exhilarated, free.*

### Floating

Imagine now that the air around you is water and you are immersed in it, walking on the seabed, floating and slowly moving through and on the surface of it. Feel the resistance of the water and currents, and how they move you slowly and support your light body. Avoid tension, but keep the muscles alert; the movements should be clear, controlled, and formed but flowing and merging, like waves. As with all the other exercises, aim to make this a little piece of art. Try everyday movements under its influence. With *floating*, actors experience a sense of *calm, warmth, peace,* and *poise.*

All these *psycho-physical* exercises start with an inner impulse – coming from the will and imagination – which is then translated into easy, formed, complete action, which in turn has an effect on how we feel. Using them in our training will increase our sense of ourselves as integrated, sensitised, centred individuals, improve our control over our bodies and minds, and sharpen the receptivity of our bodies to every inner creative impulse. This is why they are most useful to, and specially designed for, actors.

## Ease of mind and focus

As made clear earlier, ease of body and mind are completely interrelated, one directly affecting the other. The easier and freer the body, the more likely the mind will be in an easy state, although this is not automatically the case. We need to look at what can create inner ease in public performance in addition to physical relaxation, which can easily disappear through inner tension and anxiety.

Being in front of an audience, or technical crews in studios and on set, can make us nervous and anxious, and cause us to lose focus and even panic. That can have all sorts of physical effects like sweating, the mind going blank, neck tension, and so on. One student I worked with was regularly sick before each performance. Although the audience is a vital part of any stage performance and can productively affect it, in order to be open to that creative relationship you have to feel confident and at ease. This requires us to focus on what is actually happening on stage, on microphone, on camera, on the action with other actors, and not to let our attention wander to what's happening elsewhere. This isn't about cutting off the audience. It's about clearly focusing on the task in hand to give the audience the best result and establish a strong relationship with them. This is exactly what a sportsperson would do. Before a race a good athlete will be concentrating totally on the race ahead, loosening up, perhaps imagining the race as they want to run it, keeping to themselves as centred, self-contained individuals. Once the race has started, they may be spurred on by the encouragement of the spectators who enter into the spirit of the race, and find greater speed. Another parallel is that athletes will prepare consciously, mapping out a training programme and preparation for a race, as we train and rehearse, but to be most effective in the race, they will go from moment to moment, action to action, and perform from impulse and intuition developed from what they've learned, rather than consciously tell themselves how to move while they are actually running.

To gain an easy focus in performance involves many elements, not least a belief in the imaginary circumstances within which we act in a fully committed manner. Nevertheless, there are simple things we can do now to acquire this ease and focus in public; what Stanislavski called *public solitude*, the state of being alone in your attention but in the presence of an audience. This is different to the notion of *private moments* in the 'Method', where the tendency is to act out something in a private bubble divorced from other actors and the audience.

This simple means is to focus on something arising from the action, an *object of attention*. This can be a book, a flower, a photograph, a computer screen image, which is made interesting by the actor fully understanding or imagining its relevance and history. You then really see this object for a particular reason, but without tension, strain and over-effort: the book might have been a present from an absent and problematic lover, and the actor remembers the circumstances on holiday when it was received, wonders how the relationship might be improved in the future, and writes a loving note to him; or the computer image is a vital piece of research on the internet the actor needs for a project, so he prints it off and reads it; or the flower is the last of a bunch given by a father who is now seriously ill in hospital, and she presses it and puts it in a personal notebook. If you see and experience these objects in this way, your whole attention will be focused and it will attract the total attention of the audience who will be interested in what *you* find of interest. The more our attention is focused *outward*, and the more it leads to action, the more interesting we become. The smallest action done with conviction will be of interest: note the fascination of watching a craftsman painting letters on a shop sign, a person in the street trying to put up an umbrella in a wind, or as Brecht noted, a man trying to get a knot out of his shoelaces. An exercise that further demonstrates this is for actors to stand in front of others, doing nothing and with no focus of attention. They then concentrate on something simple like counting the lights in the room or the marks on the walls. In the first case they feel self-conscious and awkward. In the second, confident and easy. The difference being that in the second case they had a clear object and purpose to focus on.

This ease and focus helps enable actors to arrive at the inner creative state Stanislavski calls '*I am*': where you act in the moment intuitively and imaginatively, spontaneously and unselfconsciously.

The opposite of this is the type of performance demonstrated even by some of our most famous actors. Objects are not really seen, actions are not really done, but an excess of effort is put into *showing* that something is happening. Attention is drawn to the actor, not the character and the action. We see a lot of huffing and puffing and theatrical trickery, as opposed to economy, truth and the beauty of an action simply executed.

From the *object of attention*, Stanislavski developed *circles of attention* as a means of holding, expanding or regaining concentration. The *object*, let's say a diary, is the first point of focus and is within a *small circle*: maybe a table in front of the actor with papers, books, and a lamp on it. The *medium circle* could be some chairs, a table, and other people further away. The *large circle* would extend to the edge of the stage and side and back walls; on a film location it would extend to the horizon beyond fields or the seashore. To focus attention, he recommends you start with the object, then expand through the small and medium circles in turn and end with the large one. If concentration wavers as you're doing this, go back to a smaller circle. If you lose concentration in performance – although this shouldn't happen if you are fully committing to the action – you can regain it by refocusing on the object, then the small circle and expanding outwards to the largest.

There are many exercises for sharpening concentration, for example:

- Study an object – a leaf, CD, banana – and then look away and describe its form, colour, dimensions, special characteristics.
- Examine a person sitting opposite you – turn away and describe their face, body, clothes in exact detail.
- Observe the layout of furniture in a room. Turn away while others rearrange it. Look back and put the furniture as it was.
- Tell a story while counting the number of matches in a box.
- Set up an object of attention and three circles containing numerous objects. Tell a story while changing focus from the object to each circle in turn. Turn away and see how many objects you can remember from each circle.
- Read a newspaper while people make a lot of noise around you and then answer questions on the content. Read it out loud during noise without being distracted.

How ease and focus will be channelled is the subject of the rest of the book.

# Part 2

## Imagination and action

### – creating the foundations

# 3 Acting in circumstances

> *Action, motion, is the basis of the art followed by the actor*
>
> Stanislavski

## Acting action

The word drama is Greek and means t*o do an action.* To base a process of acting on *action,* as Stanislavski has done, makes a lot of sense. The action we address is not the action of everyday life. It is a recreation of that in imaginary circumstances. Not an imitation, illustration, demonstration, or pretence of action, as in the representational approach, but a reproduction of genuine human experience. We *really* do things as *if* we are in a real situation. We *make believe* the circumstances are real. We *believe* we are in an imaginary situation in the sense that we *imagine* we are. This is not the same as really believing we are Ophelia or Macbeth in real life. That would mean we are in a pathological state. We aim to *be* in the circumstances of a character while we are acting, to imagine we are the character for that time, using our own being, experience, and intuition to do that. So, any action on stage, screen or radio has to be a combination of doing and imagination.

As in life, all theatrical action has to be continuous. You must always be enacting *something.* Even if you sit still in a chair, something must be happening *inside.* We need a flowing line of action, as referred to in the last chapter, which is also inwardly motivated. We don't act for the sake of it. It has to be for a purpose, to be justified because all action in real life is goal-directed. The essence of art, Stanislavski maintains, is not in its external forms but in the inner content which creates them. So actions will be unbelievable if simply determined and executed mechanically. To be credible and understood we have to see where they come from.

Neither should action be given the purpose of arousing a feeling. 'Never seek to be jealous... or to suffer, for its own sake' (*An Actor Prepares*). Feelings are the *result* of action and what has gone before. Mamet, in his *True and False*, appears to equate Stanislavski and the Method, tarring them with the same brush. He says, 'Actors are told to learn how to "be happy", "be sad"...'. This may be the case in some Method classes, but it is the opposite of the Stanislavski approach as outlined here, and Mamet's own emphasis on the importance of action is at the core of the real Stanislavski approach.

So, action must be continuous, have a reason, be happening outwardly or inwardly, and must not be aimed at creating an emotion. Also, to be communicated to an audience, it requires precision and clarity, ease, and a sense of form and entirety, as with the Chekhov exercises above.

## Types of action

Most actions are simple. The complexity in a character and circumstances comes from why and how the actions arise, the combinations of them, and what they lead to. We can't play the whole complexity of a character all at once on every line and action, and to attempt to do this, as actors sometimes do, leads to playing a general state and manner, obliterating the complexity and producing something one-dimensional. The depth, range and contradictions of a character will only come through by playing each action simply, economically and truthfully. That will affect our body and psychology, stimulate our senses and emotions and create a gateway into the whole inner life of you as the character.

As I said in the last chapter, all actions have a mix of the physical and the psychological, but one aspect may predominate. Also, they may be expressed verbally or silently.

### Physical action

**I arrive at my flat and put the kettle on for a drink.** That is a summary of what I do often. However, I can't do that all in one go, *in general*. I actually do a number of *specific* actions to achieve that, which will vary according to whether I'm in a good or bad mood, in a hurry or not, in need of stimulation or relaxation. For example, I walk to the back door of my flat. I get out my keys. I open the door. I enter the hall. I pick up a couple of leaves brought in by one of my cats. I check letters left on the hall table. I close the door. I walk into the living room. I stroke a cat on a chair. I progress into the kitchen. I put the dead leaves in the waste bin. I turn on the radio. I take off my coat. I hang it on a hook by the front door. I pick up new post lying on the floor. I rearrange a bike that's slipped down the wall. I check messages left by my partner in a pad on the breakfast bar. I walk to the kettle. I fill it with water at the sink, which involves opening the kettle lid, turning on the tap, putting the kettle under the tap, turning off the tap, closing the lid. I put the kettle on its stand and turn it on. I sit on a stool. I open the mail, reading or discarding it according to importance, as I wait for the kettle to boil.

If I have to do these actions as part of a script, I have to do them with the same justified sequence, belief, and clarity as in real life. I need to *really* close the door, *really* check for messages, *really* fill the kettle, and not just play-act and indicate. I must also give myself a clear reason why I do each of these actions. There is an impulse behind them. For example, I close the door because it's very cold out and there's a breeze that could sweep in more leaves, and I want to keep the flat tidy and warm because a friend is coming round. I stroke a cat because she is reacting to my arrival and looking totally beautiful. I turn on the radio to catch the news, not having read a morning paper. I hang my coat on a hook because I dislike clutter. I open the post now because it doesn't arrive first thing in the morning anymore and there may be something demanding action. I boil the kettle because I want to try a new tea my partner bought. When all the actions are done with a complete sense of truth as if it is real life, you reach the state of 'I am' in the circumstances.

Actions that we perform without thinking and/or have to be done in a particular order are called *organic actions*, for example, putting on trousers or hanging wallpaper. I have to make sure the buttons or zip on the trousers are undone first. Then I put in each leg. Then I do up the zip and buckle the belt. There's no other way to get them on. To hang paper, I have to cut a length from a roll, and put paste on the paper. Then place it on the wall. Then trim it. Of course, this seems obvious, but in performance things can get missed out because it's not treated as real. To get used to dividing an action into all its constituent parts, it will help to break down some simple everyday activities such as cleaning a window, printing a document from a computer, polishing shoes. Do all this with a sense of ease and form and of the entirety of each action, with clarity and an awareness of how one part of the action finishes and leads onto the next, that is, of where the *impulse* comes for the next part, e.g. when the computer has fully started up, only then can I click up a document, and only when that has fully appeared can I print it. An action has to be started, executed, and fully completed before the next action can take place.

A situation may well have a line of *logical action*. A boyfriend is coming round for the evening: you need to clean the dirty flat, make something to eat, get changed, sort out some music, open the wine. Each main action will involve a series of smaller ones, some of them organic, some of them requiring thought as to the order. Opening a bottle of wine is clearly an organic action, but cleaning the flat may involve choosing priorities such as tidying away magazines and books from the living room floor and seats, straightening the bed covers, then dealing with cleaning surfaces.

## Psychological action

All the above physical actions will have some psychological content because they must be done for a reason. Examples of predominantly psychological actions, performed verbally and/or physically, are as follows: I attack, I accuse, I embrace, I manipulate, I reject, I reprimand, I bemuse, I convince.

'I attack' can involve hitting someone out of anger or resentment, or verbally abusing, or both. 'You stole my wallet' could be said with an action of accusing, and a corresponding gesture of a clenched fist with pointing forefinger. 'I embrace' would normally involve wrapping someone in my arms. 'I manipulate' could be the action on a line like, 'Of course I may be persuaded to give you the money you need – if you'll just do a little favour for me'. If I express an explosive 'Ha!', sweep my arm away from my body and walk away from someone, I'm rejecting them. 'You shouldn't have done that. It was quite the wrong approach and you mustn't do it again,' might be a reprimand accompanied by a shaking head and wagging finger. 'I bemuse' might be enacted simply through a silent raising of an eyebrow. 'I convince' could involve a direct thrusting gesture with open hands on a line like, 'I care for you more than anything in the world, you've got to believe me'.

The nature of psychological actions and their physical manifestation will depend on *circumstances and relations* with other people; for example, 'You stole my wallet' could equally be said with an action of shaming, reminding or imploring, depending on whether you're talking to your child, a neighbour, or a friend. If your child has stolen your wallet to get money for fireworks you might shame them with the line. If they've stolen it for a second time, you might condemn them. If a neighbour once took your wallet and wants to know why you don't trust them, you might remind them with the line. If they are a hostile 'neighbour-from-hell', you might punish them. As you can see from these examples, *previous circumstances* come into play. If you've had a stable and happy childhood, you might acknowledge and return a strange man's smile. If you've been attacked and abused by a stranger, then you might block out another stranger's smile. I'll look at this again later in the chapter. We will also be affected by *future* circumstances. If I disagree with the views of someone I meet for the first time, I might contradict them. If this person is a director who is going to employ me, I might humour them. This really makes nonsense of Mamet's contention that '...you should discard the idea of "the situation" altogether'.

The situation will determine not only what you do but *how* you do it. *I sort papers*. If I'm sorting my own acting files I check letters quickly, discard old ones I don't need, discard old photos, order chronologically more recent documents, and so on. If I'm sorting the documents of my dead mother, I handle old letters to her very carefully, some from admirers; try to fit names to people in photographs; assess the emotional impact on her of having to get married to my father away from her home town; consider the difference between the person I knew while growing up and the person she was as a young woman. One set of actions is *simple*, one is much more *complex* psychologically. Preparing a meal for myself is a much quicker, more perfunctory affair than preparing a meal for friends visiting for the evening. Writing a card to a friend I haven't seen for two years and whom I miss, will involve different content, care, tempo, and emotion to writing a card to someone I see every day and with whom I have less warm relations.

## Given circumstances

So when we come to work on a text or a devised improvisation, it's only once we have considered the events and circumstances surrounding us or our characters that we can know what we actually *do*. Stella Adler, one of the most influential American actor/teachers, writes in *The Art of Acting* (Applause Books, 2000) about her studies with Stanislavski in Paris in the thirties and of his emphasis on the importance of the circumstances: 'He said that *where* you are is what you are and how you are and what you can be. You are in a place that will feed you, that will give you strength, that will give you the ability to do whatever you want.' So, as in real life, I enter a set of circumstances, these set the framework for what I do, and my actions and those of others set off a dynamic that triggers organic responses and emotions, a process that is spontaneous within a created structure, intuitive and subconscious as a result of conscious preparation. Stanislavski gives an overall description of given circumstances in *An Actor Prepares*: 'It means the story of the play, its facts, events, epoch, time and place of action, conditions of life, the actors' and regisseur's interpretation, the *mise en scène*, the production, the sets, the costumes, properties, lighting and sound effects – all the circumstances that are given to an actor to take into account as he creates his role'.

Specifically though, for an actor entering each scene, we can hone them down to the following:

**Who am I?** As myself the actor, or as the character in the script. My name, sense of identity, what has formed me in terms of background, family, environment, class, education, key events.

**Where am I?** Where have I come from, where am I now, where am I going? What is the specific place, the district, town, country and what is in the space around me (animals, plants, objects, furniture)?

**Why am I here?** What events, people, relationships and reasons bring me to this place?

**What time is it?** Time of the day, day and date, season, year, epoch.

I've kept these 4 Ws succinct because they are not only a form of analysis of what circumstances comprise, but crucially a means of providing an imaginative springboard for actually *entering* the circumstances and *engaging* with them.

You can't just step into imaginary circumstances freshly as if for the first time without any preparation. However, you often see actors just walk from the wings onto the stage or the set, not from one imaginary reality into another. They drift on bringing nothing imaginative with them, nothing behind the eyes, warm up on stage, then exit into the wings. Or, alternatively, they 'make an entrance' and 'make an exit' theatrically, thinking of the effect they might create rather than the truth of what they're doing. They might also joke, laugh, tell stories and generally fool around offstage before entering, or quietly recite their first lines. There often isn't much respect for preparation. On the other hand, if you do prepare you don't want to do too much. Imagining the character's whole life up to the point of entrance, or going over all the events of the day and all your detailed relations to a particular situation or person would be too much. All these details are for preparation at home and they need to be imaginatively absorbed and drawn on without much conscious thought and effort in rehearsal and performance. All you initially require to enter and engage with circumstances are these 4 Ws. These will focus your attention and help you to find stillness and ease and avoid self-consciousness.

**Stella Adler 1901–92**

Born in New York into the famous Adler acting family: daughter of Jacob and Sara Adler and sister of Luther. She toured in over a hundred plays in vaudeville and Yiddish theatre, then joined the American Laboratory Theatre under Richard Boleslavski. She joined the Group Theatre in 1931. In 1934, she spent five weeks studying with Stanislavski in Paris and returned to disagree with Lee Strasberg over Stanislavski's emphasis on given circumstances, action and imagination, as opposed to emotion recall, as the path to truthful acting. From 1937, she acted in Hollywood and Broadway theatre, and in the early '40s began teaching at Erwin Piscator's New York Dramatic Workshop, which for some, was a bridge between the Group Theatre and the Actors Studio. In 1949, she set up her own school, now known as the Stella Adler Studio of Acting, and ran it over five decades. She taught Marlon Brando, Benicio Del Toro, and Warren Beatty, among many, and emphasised not just development of acting technique but of the actor's sense of culture and humanity as well.

# 'If'

You need now to imagine you are in the circumstances and to respond to them, so they *work on you* rather than *you work on them*, and push for something to happen. A key word to prompt this is *'If'*: *'If* I am in these circumstances what would I do?' is how Stanislavski presents this. I think in a country where the representational approach is predominant this could be misunderstood. It could be interpreted to mean: 'If I am in these circumstances what do I *think* I would do?', which may lead to an actor forming a mentally-determined idea of what they would do, or would like to think they would do, and then imitating it. I'm absolutely sure that what Stanislavski meant is: 'If I am in these circumstances, imagined as if they are real, what *do* I do intuitively, spontaneously, unpremeditatedly, in *response* to them?' The actor then draws automatically on past experience, knowledge, and observation and what is created will be *organic* as opposed to *cerebral.*

'If' then is a prompt to the imagination and action, to the inner and outer life of the actor. It's a very small word with a great impact, which is why Stanislavski called it 'the *magic* if'. It doesn't demand that the actor believes something is *actually* happening, only that we imagine ourselves in circumstances as *if* they are real, just as children have always done with great commitment. Stanislavski offers the example of how to react if a violent psychopath has escaped from a hospital and is now trying to get through your door. To *act* this could involve the creation of false panic, histrionics, dramatic actions: what we would like to think we might do according to our (possibly romanticised) view of ourselves and in order to make the action interesting and 'entertaining'. To really make it interesting and entertaining we need to *make believe* and truthfully respond. *If* there is a psychopath behind the door what do we do *here and now* in this moment of imagined reality? Stanislavski's students, presented with the problem in this way, stopped thinking about how to act, of the external form of their activity, and began to focus on the actual problem: How far away is the door? What are the means of escape? Grabbing means of self-protection. Barricading the door with furniture. Phoning the hospital to get assistance. They did actions that were logical, coherent, real and justified by the situation.

Below are some examples of given circumstances and 'If' to try alone, in pairs, or as a group. Act as yourself. I think it's very important first to develop a sense of truth and belief as yourself before moving on to yourself as a character in particular circumstances.

## *Alone:*

**Example 1**

*I'm on a London tube train that stops in a tunnel and doesn't move.* What are the given circumstances?

- *Who am I?* I'm me as in everyday life at my current stage of development, with my real hopes and fears, ambitions and frustrations, qualities and failings. This applies to all the following examples.
- *Where have I come from, where am I now, where am I going to?* I've come from a friend's house to the Piccadilly line station at Finsbury Park, I've boarded a train and travelled for ten minutes, and I'm going to Leicester Place in the centre of London.
- *Why?* Because I have a job audition in the Spotlight office in Leicester Place at 11.20a.m.
- *What time is it?* It's now 10.40a.m. on Tuesday, 4th March, 2007

The train stops in the tunnel.

*If I'm in these circumstances what do I do?*

*What I shouldn't do*: play an emotional state like frustration, fear, anger; indicate anxiety over the time by constantly looking at my watch (unless that is justified by a unique personal obsession with time!); anticipate and premeditate what will happen; create dramatic moments and imaginary conversations with people (on the tube?!); represent and demonstrate a theatrical version of me in seeking to entertain; do a lot of superfluous 'business'.

*What I should do*: respond truthfully to the imaginary situation; live moment by moment, allowing my actions to unfold; find the impulse behind the actions; let each action be justified by the circumstances; allow any emotion to arise from the action; use economy, only doing what I need to do on any particular action.

*What might happen*: I might assess recent stoppages, accidents, bomb scares and how likely it is that the train will move soon, how many stops are to go and how long it will take to arrive, what time of departure would make me late and how much of a problem this might be; I don't like the tube and closed spaces so I drink some water and take some deep breaths to calm myself; I focus on the audition, remind myself of the director's name, their experience, the nature of the job, look through passages of the play I might be required to read; I can't prepare fruitfully anymore, so I put the play in my bag; I become conscious of silence, the motor isn't making that usual clicking sound, so maybe there's no intention of moving off – this makes me feel more claustrophobic, so I drink more water, get up and walk up and down the carriage, then sit back down, and try to focus on my newspaper to find some ease.

What emerges through these actions is also *what I want in these specific circumstances*, my fifth W, my *objective*. Objectives emerge organically from circumstances and they are always there in life. My objectives on the train, as defined by my actions, are to assess the likelihood of arriving on time, to calm myself, to prepare for the audition, and to overcome claustrophobia. You'll note that at no point am I simply *waiting* for the train to move, and doing nothing. I have inner action (assessing, estimating, reminding, concluding) and outer action (drinking, walking, reading and preparing).

Other people in this identical situation might have done a completely different range of actions motivated by different objectives such as wanting to amuse themselves by doing a sudoku puzzle, catch up on rest missed during a sleepless night, or learn their audition speech properly. In a script, too, we find out what someone wants by looking at their actions, and I shall focus on objectives in detail in Chapter 5.

For an audience observing such an exercise, the criteria for judgement should not be, 'Did the person do it like *I* would have done it?'. We need to look at each individual person and assess what they do objectively, not subjectively; to ask if we believe and understand what happens; if it is natural, justified and truthful; if what the person wanted in the circumstances came over.

**Example 2**

*I'm about to leave work, I check my jacket for my car and house keys and they are not there.*

Create the given circumstances as in Example 1 – Who am I? Where am I? Why am I here? What time is it? – and again ask, 'If I am in these circumstances what do I do?'

Avoid demonstrating your response and theatrical displays of emotion, and just do what the situation demands.

You might *really* check all your pockets in your jacket and trousers, *really* search your bag, maybe more than once; check around the room; retrace your steps to see if the keys have dropped anywhere. If you are working with someone, they may place the keys somewhere where you may actually find them. If not, you may go on to make sure you can leave your car overnight and find out if someone can let you into your home. If you make mobile phone calls, only make real ones with another person on the other end, e.g. to directory enquiries. Don't fake calls and imagine someone talking to you; this immediately breaks belief.

What you want here is clearly to find your keys or some other way of getting into your home.

If your keys have been placed by someone try the exercise again with the keys dropped in exactly the same place. This simulates actual theatre performance: you the actor know what will happen and where objects are but you have to put that out of your conscious mind and come to the situation *as if for the first time*, so that actions unfold with freshness and spontaneity. Don't simply *repeat* what you did last time – *recreate* it so that the exact order and manner of doing the search might be different but you still end up finding or not finding the keys as before.

**Example 3**

*I arrive home late at night having been chased along my road by a group of men.*

Create the circumstances including the imagined reasons why you are under threat, the number of men and what they look like.

Don't play a fearful, tearful state. Let any emotional and physical condition come through the run into the house and what you do after arriving.

You might rush to put the key in the door and fumble it as a result, enter and close the door very quietly in order to be less noticeable, draw the bolts, keep the lights off, draw the blinds, then peek through them inconspicuously; make sure the danger is passed; sit and try to recover; make a cup of tea or something stronger; check the window again to make sure they've really gone; decide to ring the police.

What you want here is to make yourself safe.

### *Pairs*

The same guidelines apply, but now try some improvisations with a partner. The given circumstances will vary to some degree for each of you, for example, *why* you're in a situation. Also, you don't *have* to engage in conversation because someone else is there. Act as you would if the circumstances were real.

**Example 4**

*I am in a hospital waiting to get results of a test for cancer.*

What are the specific circumstances for each – type of suspected cancer, whether it's occurred before, etc.? If I am in this situation with another person present what do I do?

**Example 5**

*I am in a cafe in the centre of a city and there is a bomb scare down the road and the police are arriving.*

Create good reasons for you both being there – you're meeting a friend, it has great coffee, you're early for the cinema. What do you do?

**Example 6**

*I am in a police cell following arrest at an anti-capitalist demonstration in the City of London.*

One of you might have been unwittingly caught up in a clash between demonstrators and police as you were passing through the area. The other might have been conspicuously protesting. Create your specific circumstances. If this is happening to me what do I do?

### *Group*

The same guidelines apply if there are more than two of you. With a number of people present, the temptation will be to engage in general conversation, to regard the group members as the individuals you know rather than as strangers, and to create high drama and present yourself in a particular way. Resist it. Imagine yourself in the circumstances: Where am I? Why am I here? What time is it? If I'm in this situation what do I do?

**Example 7**

*You are in an airport arrivals lounge waiting for friends or family to arrive from Florida. One of you is an airline staff member. A hurricane has struck the Southern States, the plane is delayed and you have just learned that contact with it has been interrupted.*

Each person must have their own circumstances including where you've come from, where you are going to, why you are there, who you are meeting and how important to you they are. Decide on the exact place and time. What do I do?

**Example 8**

*You are in a large lift in a London tube station and it stops between floors.*

Decide on a specific station and time. Imagine the rest of your own circumstances. What do you do?

## Previous circumstances

What I do in the given circumstances is also affected by what happens before: where I've come from and what has happened to me there. If I'd just heard my best friend had been run over I am likely to act differently in that situation to how I would act if I'd just received a cheque for £300. If I enter a situation direct from an exhilarating swim I might do different things to what I would do had I just had a sleepless night. My actions at a party might vary according to whether I've just argued with my partner or had a lot to drink.

Try Example 1 and 2, keeping the given circumstances as before, but imagining the different previous circumstances below.

**Example 1**

First, I have been phoned by my agent at 10a.m. to tell me I haven't got a job I really wanted (excellent part, pleasant director, good money). This might intensify my determination to prepare fully for the audition, or alternatively, increase my anxiety over the tube stoppage and focus my attention more on dealing with the discomfort. Alternately, I have been offered the fantastic job. I don't need this other job as much now. I'm calmer and more confident. I may concentrate on relaxing and saving my energy and quickly reassuring myself that I've done my preparation.

**Example 2**

First, I have arranged to have dinner with a friend and stay over. The need to find my keys and get into my flat is not so urgent: they might turn up before morning, and I have longer to deal with the practical issues. This may well affect the content of my search in terms of the tempo, urgency, and repetition within it. Alternatively, some relatives are coming two hundred miles to see me and will meet me at my flat in an hour, so the thoroughness, urgency, and speed of what I do will be affected accordingly.

Try experimenting with other situations to see how previous circumstances alter what you do and how you do it:

- You're in your rehearsal room before work on a key scene having just lost a lot of money/met an old friend by chance.
- You're on holiday and discover an eagerly anticipated church, castle, Greek temple having had a fascinating walk through the local market area/an argument with your companion.
- You're outside a theatre waiting for a friend having just won a free holiday/been knocked over in the street by fighting drunks.

Try a group improvisation – at a restaurant, in a pub, at a party, in a Green Room – where everyone has different previous circumstances and see how your action and interaction change.

## Entrances and exits

So, for any situation I establish the basic given and previous circumstances and ask myself, 'If I'm in these circumstances what do I do?'. *What if I'm required to actually enter and leave the circumstances?* As stated earlier, in real life, I don't enter a room from behind a curtain in the wings of a theatre or from behind a flat surrounded by electrical cables. In the imaginary reality of theatre, screen and radio I need to imagine the world around me as if it were real in order to prompt my imagination and action when I'm in the circumstances. I know who I am, where I've come from and what happened to me in the previous circumstances, where I am and where I might be going to, why I'm here, and what time it is.

To effect my entrance into these circumstances I can create an extra imaginative impulse by asking these questions:

What do I do just before entering?
What am I doing as I enter?
What do I want first?

So, I come from the past, into the present, and with a future. What this will give me is greater focus, immediacy and involvement – and this especially will be the case if I enter once I have begun the action, *in the middle or at the end of it,* as opposed to right at the beginning. Equally, once I have accomplished what I want to do, I will exit and I can address similar questions:

What do I do just before exiting?
What am I doing as I exit?
What do I want first once I've gone?

This can prevent me from just drifting offstage, doing a big theatrical exit, or giving the impression that my life stops dead on the other side of the door.

**Example 1**

*Previous and given circumstances.*

I've come from town on a day off. I've been to an art exhibition and a film and had a very enjoyable experience, enhanced by a visit to my agent who has put me up for interesting projects. I'm now approaching my flat and intend to stay in because I want to see a particular TV documentary. It's 6.50p.m., Thursday 12th July, 2007 when I arrive at my front door which I open out of view of the audience.

*What do I do just before I enter?*

In the hall, I pick up post, which I check. I see a bank statement. I open it nervously because I'm overdrawn, but in a good mood to deal with any problem.

*What do I do as I enter?*

As I enter the kitchen in view of the audience I am already unfolding the statement and see that I've exceeded my overdraft limit and am being fined. I react to that in the doorway and as I'm closing the door.

*What do I want first?*

To make sense of it because I don't understand it and to work out what to do to stop any further fines being levied on me!

I might then pour a glass of wine, make a sandwich, weigh up the problem further, then check the rest of the post and read the paper. I might deal with the problem quite optimistically because, after all, my agent has been positive and I had a good day.

*What do I do just before exiting?*

I refill my glass with wine, pick it up, and pick up the paper.

*What am I doing as I exit?*

I am sipping the wine and re-examining an article.

*What do I want first once I've gone offstage?*

I intend to sit and turn on the TV in preparation for the documentary I want to see.

**Example 2**

*Previous and given circumstances.*

Last night I worked late and on the way home my car broke down. My breakdown service patched it up and I arrived home around 11p.m. I had a restless night and woke up tired and irritable. I got up late and rushed off to work in the repaired car. I am now at work and heading for my office where I'll be staying till 6p.m. It's now 9.15a.m., Tuesday 10 November, 2007. I'm late for a 9.00a.m. appointment with a difficult, unpredictable boss.

*What do I do before I enter?*

I rush up the stairs to my office with a file under my arm. I can hear my phone ringing on the desk. I take out my keys and in my haste they drop to the floor. I pick them up and as I put the right key in the lock and turn it my file drops to the floor and papers spill out.

*What do I do as I enter?*

I bend down to gather the papers and put them back in the file, as I push open the door and enter taking the key from the lock, and kick the door closed.

*What do I want first?*
I need to answer the phone. I get to it but there's no-one there now. I assume it was the boss checking where I am.

I now put my file down, take off my coat and hang it up. I check my diary to see what else I have to do today. I then gather together whatever documents I might need for my appointment. I take a swig of water and calm myself.

*What do I do just before exiting?*
I pick up the documents and put them in a folder. I tidy my collar under my jacket and head for the door.

*What am I doing as I exit?*
As I open the door I brush some bits of fluff off my jacket and smooth down my hair.

*What do I want first once I've gone offstage?*
Before closing the door I turn in the direction of the office where I am now going for my appointment, and head off there once the door is closed.

This refining of the circumstances adds reality and interest to what you do – doing actions on entrances and exits is, after all, a common occurrence in everyday life. It prompts the playing of a variety of actions, not just the most obvious ones devoid of detail. It focuses attention on the immediate circumstances, not on 'making an entrance/exit', and so will help you to avoid nerves, self-consciousness, fear of the audience, and find ease, confidence, and engagement. Whatever you do on an entrance or exit must, of course, be justified by the previous and given circumstances, and not done simply for effect, so the suggestions above are just examples of what might happen *if* you are in these circumstances.

## 'If' with a character

All these examples of circumstances and 'If' have related to ourselves. Can we use 'If' when we are playing another person? Stanislavski also saw 'If' as a means of enabling the actor to identify with a character in particular circumstances. So the question could be asked: 'If I am in the circumstances of this character what do I do?' On first consideration, you might look at a whole range of characters and say, 'Well, I wouldn't do what they do, I'm a completely different person with a different background, drives, qualities, and relationships!' If you stuck with this view then you would end up simply pretending to be other characters and representing them superficially.

The organic approach to acting assumes we can change physically and psychologically. The characters of individual people are not completely determined genetically. Some may believe that biology is the main determining influence, but I think the more convincing argument is that the circumstances in which we are born and develop are the crucial determining factor, although the body and genetic structure with which we're born have an influence. So, we are not born what we are now. We are our past actions and experiences. As the French philosopher, Jean-Paul Sartre, believed: existence precedes essence. Karl Marx put it as: social being determines consciousness. You don't have to believe this to be an actor – but it may help belief in our ability to change! If I thought Hitler was 'evil' or a 'monster' and born like this, how could I play him as anything other than a caricature? I wouldn't relate to him as human, so how could I understand his actions? If I can't understand him, how would an audience? And that is very dangerous. If we present people as totally genetically determined or born with a given personality or soul, then the inference is that none of us can change, which is manifestly not true. For an organic performance of Hitler see Bruno Ganz's brilliant performance in *Downfall*; for representational versions, see just about every other characterisation before.

The even more constraining, bleak and widely-believed conventional wisdom on human personality is that dreadful things will always happen, the world will always be like it is, no significant improvement will ever be made because of human nature! So Nazism, Stalinism, Hutu massacres, Balkan wars, and State and individual acts of terror in Iraq will all recur because we're simply like that, always have been and always will be. We're all intrinsically programmed with some awful virus of genetic or God-given characteristics like greed, acquisitiveness, selfishness, competitiveness, violent aggression, sexual predatoriness, restless dissatisfaction, bloodlust, hatred of the foreign, possessiveness, jealousy, and so on. If any people manifest qualities such as love, generosity, creativity, co-operation, or cosmopolitanism we then have to assume this is a freak aberration or that these individuals aren't actually human! Why aren't *these* characteristics presented as human nature? There is, of course, plentiful evidence of people revealing these qualities throughout history, and of people acting in radically different ways socially, culturally, politically, economically, emotionally and sexually according to the different natures of the societies into which they were born and the different epochs in which they lived. What we *have* had in common for thousands of years, and which represents a real but very basic human nature, is our need for food and water, clothing and shelter, and the capacity to work together to attain them, which has produced language, a highly-formed consciousness, culture and artistic creativity. *How* we satisfy our needs and organise ourselves is constantly changing, however.

Let's look at a few fundamentally different ways in which humans have operated. People in early primitive societies organised co-operatively. In modern capitalist society we are in constant competition with each other. It's believed the oldest form of family was based on group marriage, with mutual sexual intercourse between different men and women and also between blood relations, so there was little room for jealousy. Monogamy is the approved modern form of marriage and sexual relationship so that jealousy is often seen as natural and a sign of love. Under feudalism, families were small units of production. Under capitalism the family became a basic social unit producing labour for industry and consumers for the market. People's experience of life is different in all these different forms. Relationships and emotions, customs and lifestyles, work and pleasure change. The Native Americans believed private ownership of land to be unnatural; to the new European settlers it was a basic human right. The !Kung San people of the Kalahari still hunt, gather and share collectively; Rupert Murdoch makes private profit. To the ancient Greeks homosexuality was a high form of love; to the Victorians it was the basest. Some Hindus and Muslims believe in arranged marriages; most Christians don't. There is no common human nature here. Human beings are infinitely changeable according to social conditions. We become different according to circumstances like water flowing into differently shaped vessels. We are adaptable and that helps us to survive. So it's quite logical to expect an actor to adapt their makeup and potential to the circumstances and character of someone else.

*If I am in the circumstances of this character what do I do?* If I were in Macbeth's circumstances would I choose to kill Duncan, the king? Of course not, I might say initially. But probing more, what would I do if I were in a childless marriage in this period with an ambitious, powerful and possibly younger wife; if I were given supernatural encouragement to my advancement in a society that believes in God, the Devil, and spirits; if I were a conquering and respected soldier who had already discussed the possibility of becoming king with my wife – then I can start to understand imaginatively why and how I as Macbeth could commit this act. Asking 'If' brings us into empathy with a character – not the same as *approval*, it must be emphasised – and helps us to perform the character's actions truthfully. It prompts us to imagine ourselves more fully in the circumstances and mind of this person, to make conscious or unconscious associations with our own experience, relationships, frustrations and ambitions.

If at any point in a script you find it hard to make such empathic connections with a character, you can use the idea that a situation is *as if* you are in real or imagined circumstances from your own life that *can* connect you. If I can't see Duncan as a justifiable candidate for murder I might look at him *as if* he is a very unpleasant senior teacher at my secondary school whom I would cheerfully have despatched – at least in my imagination! Giving in to Lady Macbeth's persuasion might be *as if* I am yielding to my own partner's reasonable and forceful urgings on certain issues of importance at home. An *as if* is also called a *substitution* or *transference* by, for example, Uta Hagen and is a means of using 'the past to make the present real' (*A Challenge for the Actor*, and *Respect for Acting*). Whatever example you take it has to be specifically related to and equated with a particular experience in the script, and its effects must be imaginatively absorbed in rehearsal so you are not continually experiencing something from *your* life as opposed to the character's. Also, like some other conscious acting tools, *as if* need only be used if you are failing to find the truth in particular actions through the exercise of your imagination in the given circumstances alone.

So, in conclusion, action is the basis of acting, within an imaginary framework; 'If' stimulates the imagination, inner and outer action, and the 'creative subconscious', as Stanislavski terms it; and the given circumstances 'build the basis for *if* itself'.

**Uta Hagen 1919–2004**

Born in Germany, raised in Wisconsin, but trained at RADA, her first role was Ophelia, followed by Nina in the Lunts' production of Chekhov's *The Seagull*. She won awards for the *Country Girl* (1951) and *Who's Afraid of Virginia Woolf* (1963), and taught for forty years at the school of her second husband, Herbert Berghof, in New York. Among many, she taught Sigourney Weaver, Al Pacino and Jack Lemmon, and created an array of exercises, sometimes called Object Exercises, to find truth in imaginary circumstances and identification with the character's actions.

# 4 Acting with others

> *... the nature of theatre ... is based on the inter-communication of the dramatis personae*
>
> Stanislavski

In life we encounter other people. We are linked to them within a social framework: the 'social animals' of Aristotle. We relate and respond to each other according to our personalities, goals, relationships, social customs and taboos and, crucially, what they do to us. In life, we are in constant interaction with each other on some level – looking, listening, touching, reacting. If that communication is not present in performance you just see disconnected actors going through lines and moves mechanically, acting in separate worlds. It's unbelievable. It's also not entertaining or enlightening because there's no real energy, dynamic and life. How many times have we seen wooden acting by people who seem alien to the human race? How many times have we seen actors talking at each other, being unaware of each other, or simply playing out to the audience? How many times have we heard and seen words and actions delivered as though they have no relation to what's gone before? I know I've witnessed this many times, usually in the theatre. I know from the first few seconds of a performance whether I'll enjoy it because I can tell right from the opening moments whether the actors are focused on truthful experience and communication or not.

## Communion

Stanislavski believed you should be in total *communion* with everything around you in performance. There should be awareness of and connection between you and objects, the setting, your clothes, other people, yourself, and the audience. If communication is important in life for all sorts of necessary social reasons, not least the need to organise together to accomplish our actions and objectives, it is even more important in performance, because here we normally only see people in action with a functioning inner life, and not in states of unconsciousness or sleep as in life. Even in plays by Pinter or Beckett where characters may be distanced from one another through loss, betrayal, alienation, age, pain, violence or hopelessness, for example, they are nevertheless usually still in contact and communicating, however indirectly and defectively. If one actor creates an unbroken connection with another through thoughts, feelings, actions and silences, and another takes in what the first is doing and then responds so that there is genuine communication, the audience will also be drawn in and interested. There will be an indirect communication with them through the direct communication of the actors with each other. This is the most usual form of audience communication, although of course we sometimes *directly* address the audience: with asides and certain monologues in Shakespearean and Jacobean theatre; through archetypal characters in *commedia dell'arte* and melodrama; with narration in plays like Arthur Miller's *A View from the Bridge* and Peter Schaffer's *Equus*; and in the political challenges of Dario Fo's agitational satires.

We can divide Stanislavski's areas of concern into communication with self and communication with others.

### Communication with self

This must be the starting point for any communication with other people. If we are unfocused, unsure and uneasy our communication with others will be unclear and disjointed. We need to start from the state outlined in Chapters 1 and 2, one in which we have a heightened awareness and understanding of ourselves and the world around us, a mental and physical ease and focus, sensitivity and receptivity, inner and outer stillness and openness. In this state we feel centred, in *communion* with our whole self. This enables us to receive and process all the signals and stimuli from outside us, and then to transmit clear tuned signals back.

What if we actually have to communicate with ourselves in performance, either silently or through lines and whole monologues while alone? Some would say that talking to oneself is the first sign of madness, but most of us do it on numerous occasions: to *express feelings* of, say, anger, protest, frustration or pleasure about oneself or others ('You idiot, John.' 'Well done!' 'How can people do that?'); to *establish an order* (as in verbalising a shopping list, a mechanical procedure or reasons why something has happened in order to fix them better in the brain); for *amusement* (doing an imitation of someone, or commenting on one's appearance or behaviour); to *resolve problems* (weighing up options, working out means, resolving exactly what to do). All these reasons are essentially means of dealing with circumstances, and exerting some *control*. Utterances should not be *illustrations* of a perceived inner state, but genuine responses to inner impulses prompted by external conditions and events. For example, the supermarket I use has changed ownership and been reorganised. I wasted time hunting for items during my last shop and want to avoid that annoyance again, so I talk myself through a shopping list, putting down items in the order in which I think I'll now find them. A well-known actor has said something fatuous to me about what's important in acting. I find her intensely annoying and wish I'd said more to counteract her view, so on the way home I imitate her to deal with my frustration.

Stanislavski suggests that to speak to ourselves in performance we need to set up a conversation between different parts of ourselves, and he focuses on two connected centres: the head and heart, or more specifically the brain, our centre of thought and consciousness, and the solar plexus, our nerve and emotional centre. This, of course, actually relates to the sort of internal debates in which we have to engage with Shakespeare's monologues. When we argue with ourselves over issues and the course of action we should take, as frequently occurs in these, we may be setting up a dialogue between reason and feelings, or reason and will. Often monologues are recited and pushed out by actors rather than made an expression of an inner understanding, crisis or conflict. They are also invariably treated as a report on something already decided, rather than a process of decision-making, which is what they more commonly are; but even reports on the past need to be delivered for a particular reason in the *present* and not just declaimed.

In *Othello*, Iago's speech in Act 2, Scene 3, beginning 'And what's he then that says I play the villain?', is arguably Iago impressing the audience with the fiendish audacity and plausibility of the plan he has already made to ensnare Othello, Cassio and Desdemona. But when we look at earlier speeches he is planning what to do within the speeches. In his speech at the end of Act 2, Scene 1, beginning 'That Cassio loves her, I do well believe't;' he is working out *in the moment* how to bring down Othello. This process of working out matters, of resolving what to do, is perhaps even more evident in his first monologue at the end of Act 1, Scene 3:

I hate the Moor,
And it is thought abroad that 'twixt my sheets
H'as done my office. I know not if't be true,
But I, for mere suspicion in that kind,
Will do, as if for surety. He holds me well;
The better shall my purpose work on him.
Cassio's a proper man. Let me see now:
To get his place, and to plume up my will
In double knavery. How? How? Let's see.
After some time, to abuse Othello's ears
That he is too familiar with his wife.
He hath a person and a smooth dispose
To be suspected – framed to make women false.
The Moor is of a free and open nature
That thinks men honest that but seem to be so;
And will as tenderly be led by th'nose
As asses are.
I have't. It is engendered. Hell and night
Must bring this monstrous birth to the world's light.

Note also the broken line, 'As asses are', where Shakespeare may be indicating a pause for silent thought. In this speech, Iago is working out in the moment how to take revenge on Othello for appointing Cassio as his lieutenant and to replace Cassio with himself. It's an internal process involving his intellect addressing his will for power and his own jealous and resentful feelings: in Stanislavski's concept, Iago's brain might be talking to his solar plexus or even a lower stomach full of bile. Iago's speeches are also some of the best examples of monologues that need to be addressed directly to the audience, drawing them into an uncomfortable complicity involving both revulsion and admiration.

Other examples of this internal process abound in Shakespeare: for example, Macbeth, in the speech in Act 1, Scene 7, beginning 'If it were done when 'tis done, then 'twere well/It were done quickly.' is not reporting on his decision to kill Duncan and worrying about it, but weighing up, now as he speaks, whether he should do the deed; Helena in *All's Well That Ends Well*, alone after Bertram's departure, isn't just stating her love and his attributes, but trying to come to terms with her loss; the severe Angelo in *Measure for Measure*, shaken by Isabella pleading for her brother's life, tries to work out what's happening inside him, addressing his feelings, conscience, and notion of self; Isabella, when threatened by him, has to work out what she can do in response and addresses first her feelings of helplessness and then her will to overcome the problem – this could involve the head addressing the solar plexus and the lower body associated with the will. Another good example would be Launcelot Gobbo's speech at the start of Act 2, Scene 2, of *The Merchant of Venice*, in which he tries to decide whether to leave the employment of Shylock or not. He addresses both his conscience 'hanging about the neck of my heart' and his will because the 'fiend' is tempting him to 'use your legs, take the start, run away.'

Stanislavski called thought, feeling and will *the inner motive forces*, and Michael Chekhov associated these and other character qualities with different *imaginary centres* in the body. These are ideas I'll look at in more detail in Chapters 11 and 13.

## Communication with others

To communicate with someone else we need to be clear what it is we want to communicate – a thought, feeling, or want, and have various means with which to do it – speech, gesture, eye contact conveying thought and feeling. Essentially, we need to try to make a two-way contact with the whole, living person in front of us, to experience their individuality and convey our own, and not just talk words at each other. This applies just as much if we are playing characters. It is we real human beings who are using our own tangible humanity to present new versions of ourselves, and we must continue to communicate as real people. The cast *are* the characters. A different cast would make different versions of the characters. We have to communicate with whoever is actually in front of us, not with something imaginary we would prefer to see.

The vital means of establishing this communication is through the eyes. We listen with the eyes as well as the ears. They create a continuous flow of contact and energy between us that prompts words, actions, thoughts and feelings, some of which may be expressed, some of which may only be experienced while the other person is talking. Stanislavski called this process of genuine communication *radiation* (linking to the inner flow of energy referred to in Chapter 2): one person *transmits* and the other *receives*, but the process never becomes interrupted by one closing off and shutting down, for example, while the other is talking. There is an unbroken line of communication, with your senses taking in every nuance of what the other is saying and doing, how and with what intention, every subtlety of verbal intonation, physical movement, and emotional expression; you then react to those impulses in a natural manner that is a direct response to what has been done to you and *only* that, just as we do in life. He described this communication as 'like an underground river, which flows continuously under the surface of both words and silences'. In *To the Actor,* Chekhov also puts emphasis on giving and receiving: 'True acting is a constant exchange of the two. There are no moments on the stage when an actor can allow himself – or rather his character – to remain passive ... without running the risk of weakening the audience's attention and creating the sensation of a psychological vacuum'. On the importance of receiving he says: 'To actually receive means to *draw toward* one's self with the utmost *inner* power the things, persons or events of the situation'. Stanislavski puts the whole giving and receiving process in a similarly muscular way: we must be like a bulldog and 'seize with our eyes, ears and all our senses' to achieve *grasp*, the strength of our ability to remain totally connected with each other, and which needs to increase in strength according to the power of a role and play.

A simple exercise that reveals this radiation of giving and receiving involves throwing and catching a ball among a group standing in a circle. People often start by throwing the ball carelessly, tentatively or aggressively at someone else who may catch it – or not – and then immediately chuck it back to anyone as though it's a hot potato. So the exercise often brings actions such as dismissing, intimidating, and apologising in the way the ball is thrown or received. However, the essential nature of throwing and catching in this context is *giving and receiving*. To achieve *real* giving and receiving we need to start from a position of alertness and ease in which we are open to each other and ready to receive. Someone gives the ball to someone who is *chosen*, and then continues to give, to radiate giving, until the other person has *fully* received the ball and decided to give it to someone else. They then resume the alert, open, ready to receive position, and so on. Chekhov also refers to this process as one of preparation, action, and sustaining (*Lessons for the Professional Actor*, Performing Arts Journal Publications, 1985).

The mutual transmitting and receiving in our communication creates an alive, spontaneous and dynamic interaction, which is so sensitised that it could go in different directions given a different thought, feeling or action at a particular time, and it was this freshness and truth that Stanislavski was seeking within the structure of a production. How ironic that Mamet in *True and False* attacks what he calls 'the Stanislavski "Method"' for not aiming precisely for this organic result. He says quite correctly, though, 'The truth of the moment is another name for what is actually happening between the two people onstage. The interchange is always unplanned ....'. Again, an unpremeditated, spontaneous interaction, albeit within a planned production such as Mamet himself creates, is precisely what Stanislavski searched for. Mamet also goes on to say, '... and it is to the end of concealing that interchange that most acting training is directed'. Now I wouldn't say there was a clear *aim* in training to conceal real communication between actors in performance, but I believe that this essential element of the Stanislavski approach is not emphasised and that techniques are often used that do block interaction: externally driven characterisation, intellectualised approaches to choosing actions, overemphasis on creating emotion, or telling actors *how* to do something and forcing them into production 'concepts', and so on.

Communication between actors can break down for a number of reasons:

- **Not really seeing, listening and reacting**. This is the overall reason behind all the reasons for faulty connections in the transmit/receive wiring. Each actor has to be easily but totally focused on the other actor to absorb the message they are being given by *listening and seeing*. They need to make eye contact and be open, sensitive and responsive to the signal from the other's eyes and face, gestures and words, and give back a spontaneous and clear signal that is a specific and unique response to that, and not a calculated and described response. A stone thrown into a pond creates ripples. A sudden physical threat to a person creates an immediate reaction of self-defence. An old friend appearing unexpectedly provokes a spontaneous reaction of surprise. Most things people do cannot be predicted, and so provoke consequent unpremeditated responses. Even if you know certain people very well and can predict how they will behave in a particular situation and you have planned a strategy to deal with them, you still respond to what they do as each moment unfolds but in a manner determined by prior knowledge and expectation. Even if you have very bad communication with a person in the sense that you don't understand and empathise with each other, nevertheless there is action and reaction between you albeit based on confusion and unease; you still work off each other. Even if someone is locked off and passive, you still respond to their incommunicability and silences as they inwardly respond in some way to you. Good communication as actors does not imply or demand good communication and sympathy between characters. In performance you have to connect and interact. The other person gives you what you do next.

- **Waiting for cues**. The old 'my turn, your turn' habit of acting is still out there. I speak my lines, then you speak and I turn off, then you finish speaking and I speak again, and so on. Some actors do it deliberately because they think listening and reacting to their partner will distract and 'pull focus'. This view, I suspect, derives from the old star system in which the 'star' demands centre stage and special lighting and that the focus be on them at all times, so that when they are speaking all others shall be still. Of course, this is very old-fashioned and doesn't promote dynamic productions. Another reason may be the emphasis on getting the 'spoken word' right because of our very British emphasis on the importance of the language. Of course, the language is vital but it has to be seen as a means of active communication and not treated in an arid academic way. Language is usually in the form of *dialogue*, what one person says comes out of what the other says, it's responsive. It's absolutely essential then that, by our connection and responses to the speaking actors – our *grasp* – we make sense of their lines and present our lines as a direct response so that they appear to be the *only* response that could be made and could *only* be spoken at this precise time. When you're speaking the other actor responds in the same manner to everything you're saying, keeping the current of energy flowing. This is working from *impulse*, not mechanically from cues. It produces genuine interaction, dynamic, and excitement in performance and the audience. When this occurs it's usually, in my experience, a result of good actors clicking with each other, but it isn't often emphasised and strived for by a director, whose emphasis is more likely to be on getting the lines stated in a particular way within a production concept. This concern with the director/design concept has been prevalent for years and it takes theatre away from the actors and the audience: the actors remain frustrated, although no doubt pleased to be working, and in such a prestigious production, etc.; the audience, having probably paid vast sums for their tickets and suffered huge inconvenience and discomfort to get to and in the theatre, will be determined to enjoy themselves, but may feel a creeping sense of dissatisfaction, or even sadder, will not realise the uplifting excitement they are missing. Without the actor there is no drama. We can do without everyone else – directors, designers, stage management, administration, marketing, publicity, casting directors, producers – but they can't do without us. Of course performance is a collaborative artform – or should be (how often are actors consulted?) – and all of the above have a role to play, but essentially drama is about actors doing.

- **Remembering lines**. Any effort that makes us conscious of ourselves as actors in performance will hinder our being in the moment and making spontaneous reactions to another. One of the most common obstacles is created by thinking about the lines, going over them before they appear and while the other person is speaking. You can't possibly be responding to your partner fully and truthfully because your focus is somewhere else. We must trust in our preparation, assuming it's been done thoroughly, and then put it out of our conscious minds when actually rehearsing and performing. Once absorbed, all the words and action, the understanding of the script and character, knowledge of circumstances and relationships will all remain with us without having to think consciously about them every time we get up to do something. Actors who never seem sure of what they are saying or doing either don't prepare properly because they're lazy or lack process, or they don't understand or trust creative processes which require them to give in to the imaginative and intuitive part of the brain after conscious preparation. From the conscious to the subconscious, as Stanislavski put it.

- **Speaking for effect**. Equally, if you try to say the lines in a particular way, to create a certain effect as you're saying them, this will stop them being a genuine response to what's gone before. They will be a practised speech, calculated in isolation without contact with other human beings. This cannot create a real dynamic. Your words will be stilted and empty. *How* to say the lines has to come from why you say them, what you want to achieve by saying them, and what means you use to achieve that. These means or actions will largely be determined by what the other person is doing to you. They will be *adaptations* to the other which should not be planned in advance. I'll say more about this later.

- **Speaking from habit**. Increasingly in the industry, actors are typecast. I once sat in on a mock audition at a leading drama school and I heard an associate director from the Royal National Theatre and a prominent agent tell students that playing something different to yourself is out-of-date, something from twenty years ago, and that 'all we want to see is you'. And this was a mock audition for theatre! Under this sort of pressure it becomes understandable that actors give up on why they probably started acting in the first place: the urge to transform. Instead we see the development of *the actor persona*. This is neither the actor as they are in everyday life, nor a separate character, but a phoney version of the actor which they wheel out for every part offered, fully fitted with ticks and tricks, intonations garnered from popular television stars, facial and vocal mannerisms copied from leading actors, and all held together by the glue of self satisfaction. Nothing creative here, but it's safe and may gain employment for as long as it's fashionable. However, this habitual persona will also block real communication because it won't fit the specific circumstances, action and characters of every script and, again, it will obstruct spontaneous responsiveness.

- **Words not sense**. If we intently listen to each word someone says, we most likely won't take in the overall sense. We might as well be hearing 'elephant, wallpaper, battery'. In life, we take in whole sentences, the meaning within and behind them, and form visual images from what is being said, and we need to reproduce this in performance. Again, we should be attentive in the moment in an easy way, not a forced, effortful one.

- **Creating a substitute**. The actor playing opposite you is the character for this production. If you imagine that they are someone else behaving differently, 'the real character', you won't be interacting with what is *actually* happening because you'll be putting this figment between you and the other actor. The same applies if you react to how you think your partner *should* be speaking or acting instead of to how they actually are speaking and acting. Actors often compensate for what their partner isn't doing, so their response to what they *are* doing becomes unbelievable. Of course you may try to put the offending actor right, to encourage them to say or do something in a particular way so that *you* can say or do something else in a particular, calculated way. 'Could you just say that line more aggressively, then I can hit you because I think she would hit him at this point?', or 'Could you possibly pause longer here then I can get this bit of business in and we'll get a laugh?', etc. etc. This turns the other actors into what you want them to be for your sake and it's clearly very egotistic and doesn't produce organic performance. If there's a problem with the dynamic at a particular point then the actors and director have to deal with it co-operatively, but from the point of view of the actual nature of the writing, its meaning and structure, and the agreed interpretation of the play. Then action and reaction can be adjusted to create genuine interaction and realisation of the demands of the script. This is one of the differences between working as an *ensemble* and working selfishly.

*Communication with others may also take unusual forms*. Stanislavski raises the problem of communion with something unreal like an *apparition* – the ghost of Hamlet's father, for example. Rather than trying to delude yourself into believing it is actually there onstage or that a present actor *is* a ghost, you should focus your energy on the key question: what do I do *if* a ghost appears before me? That will depend on all your circumstances: your relationship to the dead person, your system of beliefs, what it requires of you, your relations to other people it refers to, and what you want to achieve by talking to it. Within this framework, you then interact with this unreal presence.

We may also have to communicate with many people in the form of *crowds*. Our focus may be on specific individuals. Stanislavski worked in a detailed way to individualise his crowds onstage, making sure each person had a specific character and life history. He may himself have been inspired to this approach by his experience of Kronek's disciplined direction of the Meiningers Company, the ensemble company of the Duke of Saxe-Meiningen, who had pioneered this type of work from the 1870s and also inspired André Antoine at the Paris Theatre Libre. Clearly, the presence of identifiable personalities in a crowd might well attract the address of certain lines in a speech to them in particular. At other times, it might be more appropriate to address the crowd as a whole. Stanislavski makes the point that, even in this instance, the varied emotions and thoughts of the many individuals present in the crowd and the effect of the crowd atmosphere on each individual will intensify the communication for all involved: crowd, principal actors and audience.

As I mentioned earlier, we may have to communicate with the *audience* directly. I never find the approach of generally speaking out to one place somewhere in the darkness of the auditorium believable or involving for the audience. It's a token offering lacking in conviction. If you opt for the idea of direct address, then the audience, like a crowd, becomes a mass of individuals and we need to personalise them. A speech should sweep the whole audience as if one is making contact with a number of people in a large room at a party, in a lecture hall, or a rehearsal studio, with different parts of the speech going to specific areas and groups of people. How this is determined may depend on your focus: if you are searching the past you might look into the stalls; if you are envisioning the future or presenting ideas, you might look into the circle and gallery. You could imagine different groups of people – young, old, male or female – sitting in particular areas, who might appreciate in different ways specific parts of your speech or narration. You might even create a few imaginary individuals and place them in different parts of the audience to act as specific listening partners.

We must also decide on *who* this audience is and what we want to achieve with them. Most direct address comes in period drama. It may help the actor to keep belief in the circumstances of the play by imagining the audience to be of the period and circumstances being presented onstage. For example, Iago might be addressing an audience of Venetian or Cypriot townspeople or soldiers who are his social equals and potentially sympathetic to his cause of ambition and revenge; or on the other hand, they may be his social and moral superiors. His objective could be to draw them into his plotting and impress them, or on the other hand, to shock them. De Flores, in Middleton and Rowleys' *The Changeling*, set in Alicante, is a gentleman servant deeply infatuated with Beatrice, his master's noble daughter, who loathes him. In Act 2, Scene 2, in order to persuade him to murder the man to whom she is betrothed so she can marry another she suddenly starts to compliment him and show concern. His consequent and numerous asides of surprise and pleasure could be expressions of inner thought and feeling, but equally could be addressed directly to the audience as if to a group of Spanish bourgeois men who, like him, have unfulfilled financial and sexual ambitions, and whose support and understanding he hopes to win.

Of course, a problem appears when you can see most of the audience clearly, as can be the case with thrust stages or theatre-in-the-round. If you choose not to make direct contact with individuals, you could take the approach of addressing imaginary individuals positioned between or above the real members of the audience – not a problem in a large theatre with the audience at a distance in a darkened auditorium. However, a close audience will become aware of this technique and it may well seem an unreal form of contact, and contact is necessary with direct address because you are effectively entering a dialogue with the audience as a partner with no lines. The alternative of selecting individuals to address who are visible to you the actor and probably the rest of the audience might prove intimidating for some people, but I think it's worth the risk in an intimate theatre where the audience has come to accept proximity to the stage action. You can, of course, first get a sense of which members might be open to this sort of contact and focus on them.

We might also address the audience as if they are a part of the imaginary reality we create onstage, as characters actually in the circumstances onstage with us, particularly if we're playing in an intimate space. For example, at the start of Brecht's *The Mother*, Pelagea Vlasova, the mother of the title, is complaining about her poverty which prevents her from feeding her son properly. The actor could imagine that the audience are neighbours and poor mothers just like her and who have come to visit her in her home. The lawyer, Alfieri, in Miller's *A View from the Bridge*, who acts as a narrator explaining the tragic events in the life of Eddie Carbone, speaks from the desk in his office and the actor might imagine the audience as lawyer friends or writers who have asked him to relate the story.

Any of these techniques for relating to the audience aim to personalise our contact with them, give it conviction, reality and range of expression – and also, some spontaneous responsiveness to audience reactions since they are our partner, sometimes silent, sometimes clearly audible.

## Interaction exercises

### Silent reaction

Sit opposite a partner and radiate a chain of reactions silently, only using eye and mental contact and minimal facial and body movement. One begins with an action towards the other, e.g. I accuse. The other starts in a neutral state and then reacts precisely to what the first has done and no more, so their action might be, e.g. I challenge. The first responds to that action by, for example, scorning. These are only examples to illustrate a process of action/reaction – all reactions must be spontaneous, not consciously determined. They shouldn't be mime, gestures substituting for words or indicating feeling in a silent movie manner, or an attempt to entertain or create a story, although the latter might be a by-product of the exercise. They should be an unbroken current of transmissions and receptions arising from initial eye contact, and subsequent thoughts, actions, feelings, attitudes, facial expressions. The chain reaction should continue only for as long as it is organic, truthful, and justified. It is difficult not to force responses and pull faces, but the exercise is only seeking to reproduce the continuous reactions we produce in everyday life, and highlights the sort of responsiveness and interaction which should be evident in performance, not only during silences but before, during and after spoken words according to what the other person is doing to you.

Once truth and spontaneity have been achieved in this interaction, try standing and doing the same exercise without pushing but allowing full bodily responses, movement and gesture which correspond to the actions/reactions enacted. The aim here is to create the integration between mind, will, feelings and body Michael Chekhov has emphasised.

### Adopting positions

This and the next exercise are inspired by ones recorded by Benedetti from Stanislavski's training course at the Opera-Dramatic Studio, 1935–38 (*Stanislavski and the Actor*). Again, they are without words.

Two actors stand opposite each other and spontaneously adopt a physical gesture, not necessarily 'naturalistic' and possibly extreme and grotesque. They try to justify personally what they are doing in relation to each other, move while observing each other, justifying and understanding the actions, and then come to a conclusion about what they may both be actually doing together and co-ordinate their actions to complete the task. And it should be a *task*; a physical activity with a beginning, middle and end that requires interaction, co-operation and co-ordination to be accomplished, and not a competitive game of tennis, a fight, or a dance. For example, the two actors might be mending a puncture, wallpapering or planting bulbs.

**Completing the improvisation**

One actor begins to improvise an activity silently, e.g. washing the dishes, cooking a pie, preparing to paint a room. The other observes, decides what is happening and then joins in to complete the task.

This can become a group improvisation. One starts an activity that can be shared by a number, e.g. putting up a tent or exploring an archaeological dig, the others decide what is happening and then each take on a particular function to complete the job.

You could decide on a specific occupational activity, e.g. a surgeon in an operating theatre is joined by an anaesthetist, nurses, orderlies and operating assistants.

The first person could focus on *where* they are, e.g. by looking at rows of shelves in a library, and others enter the place and adopt library functions. The place could be a supermarket, restaurant or train station.

**Word repetition**

After the impros with no words we move on to using words, but only to the extent of testing our responsiveness. Word repetition is an exercise devised by Sanford Meisner, a former member of the famous Group Theatre in the 1930s, which included Luther and Stella Adler, Elia Kazan, Lee Strasberg, Harold Clurman, and Robert Lewis, who all became notable acting teachers or directors. Each teacher emphasised different aspects of the Stanislavski approach: for example, Strasberg, emotion memory; Stella Adler, creating varied and truthful actions; Uta Hagen, the detail of creating reality.

Meisner focused on interaction and *the reality of doing* (*Sanford Meisner on Acting* by Meisner and Dennis Longwell, Vintage Books, 1987). Like the other practitioners, Meisner is misunderstood if his techniques are seen as the latest fad and indulged in as techniques per se. He proposes an approach to the work and certain exercises in order to achieve a result which is firmly bedded in the Stanislavski tradition: *living truthfully in imaginary circumstances.* The basic word repetition exercise is aimed at getting actors to respond to what the other is doing to them, without 'acting', exaggerating, or consciously determining what to do and how to do it. It is an exercise in spontaneous reacting in which we work from *impulse* and *we only do what the other makes us do.* We focus *outward* on the other person, not *inward* on ourselves. It forces us to really *listen and respond.*

One actor makes a simple observation about another sitting opposite. The other responds by *repeating the line from their point of view* and this repetition continues until there is a clear impulse to change the line, until the other *makes* you change it by what they do. Either can change the line but only as a *response* to the other. Avoid pausing, consciously determining what to do, anticipating what the other may do, or doing line readings to create variety. The lines must be a truthful and spontaneous verbal response to what the other is doing on the lines, their intonations, their facial expressions, eye contact, feelings, body language and gestures. The actual line and its meaning are not important in this exercise. The delivery is everything.

**A.** You're wearing a pink sweater.
**B.** I'm wearing a pink sweater.
**A.** You're wearing a pink sweater.
**B.** Yes, I'm wearing a pink sweater.
**A.** But you're wearing a pink sweater.
**B.** Yes. I am wearing a pink sweater!
**A.** You don't have much taste.
**B.** I don't have much taste?
**A.** You really don't have much taste.
**B.** I don't have much taste.
**A.** No. You don't
**B.** You are very rude
**A.** I'm rude?

B. Yes. You are *rude*.
A. I am?
B. Yes. You bloody are!

This type of dialogue can go into more personal and emotional areas as well, but essentially it's about real interacting. Meisner says, '... it plays on the source of all organic creativity, which is the inner impulses'. It can also be done in different forms.

**Pinch and ouch**

One person makes a physical contact with the other, for example by pinching them with a reason, e.g. to tease, provoke, flirt or silence. The other responds because they've been *made* to respond, and the first responds to that in repetition form, as above:

A. Hey, you hurt me doing that, you idiot!
B. I hurt you doing that?
A. Yes, you hurt me!
B. Well, you deserved it.
A. I deserved it?
B. Yes, you did deserve it.
A. I deserved it?
B. Yes. You need shaking up.
A. I need shaking up?
B. That's right. You need shaking up.
A. I need shaking up!
B. You need shaking up!
A. You're sick.
B. I'm sick?
A. You're sick!

**The knock on the door**

This elaboration on the same theme of repetition gets closer to a real situation.

One actor is in a room involved in an independent activity which is sufficiently difficult to really focus their concentration, e.g. solving a mathematical problem, learning lines, mending a broken plate. Give yourself a compelling reason why it is important to do this. The other knocks on the door for a clear, simple and specific reason, e.g. they need milk, help with the electrics, or herbs for a meal, but the reason isn't given out unless it's made to come out. The first knock is done under that influence. There is no response initially because the first person is focused and busy. The second knock is a response to no response. The third or final knock is a response to the previous ignored knocks. It must be real and not theatrical, but has to be sufficiently arresting to *make* the first person drop their activity and answer the door. Once the door is opened, the first person goes to resume their activity and the repetition dialogue can begin:

A. You took your time.
B. Yeah, I took my time.
A. Yes, you certainly took your time.
B. So, I took my time?
A. Well, you took your time, that's all.
B. I took my time.
A. You seem in a bad mood.
B. I seem in a bad mood?
A. You seem in a bad mood of some sort.
B. Of some sort?
A. Of some sort.
B. You're bothering me
A. I'm bothering you.
B. Yes, you're bothering me.
A. So you want me to go?
B. OK. I want you to go.
A. You want me to go, really?
B. I really want you to go ...

### Reacting on text

We now look at using words which constitute dialogue with more meaning and context. Take a page of modern text preferably, one with sequences of duologue in the form of one-liners – Clare McIntyre, Pinter, and Patrick Marber are good for this. Read the text with a partner and focus on reacting to each others' inflexions, meanings, actions, objectives, eye contact, and body language. Let what the other person does affect you vocally and physically. After the first time through, do it again under different influences, allowing these to affect what you do in different ways: for example, start the dialogue with a different action on the first line, e.g. I demean you as opposed to I confront you; begin with a different overall attitude towards the other person, e.g. hostile instead of appreciative; work under the influence of a different personality quality, e.g. scornful rather than generous; try a different atmosphere, e.g. tense rather than peaceful; adopt a different spatial relationship, close or distant, direct or indirect; use a different physical state, cold or heat, and so on. Responding truthfully to these varied influences will reveal how differently any one piece of dialogue could be played, will free you from having a rigid interpretation of a text, and increase your transformational ability and versatility.

**Sanford Meisner 1905–97**

Born in Brooklyn, New York, he originally studied music, but at 19 joined the Theatre Guild as an extra and found his passion for acting. He studied at the Theatre Guild of Acting and met Harold Clurman and Lee Strasberg. In 1931, Clurman, Strasberg and Cheryl Crawford set up the Group Theatre, with Meisner as a member. He acted in Group productions through the '30s, then became a teacher at the Neighbourhood Playhouse in NY where he developed his 'Meisner Technique' based on Stanislavski's emphasis on responsiveness and truthful actions in imaginary circumstances. He taught many renowned actors, such as James Caan, Gregory Peck and Jeff Goldblum. In 1995, he opened the Sanford Meisner Centre in California.

**The Group Theatre 1931–41**

Its aim was to develop an 'American acting technique' based on Stanislavski. It was an ensemble of actors, directors, and writers, and included Elia Kazan, John Garfield, Lee J. Cobb and Frances Farmer. It specialised in realistic plays of a radical nature by, for example, Clifford Odets and John Howard Lawson, and many Group members were blacklisted in the 1950s by the House Un-American Activities Committee in Senator Joseph MacCarthy's anti-Communist witchhunt. The Group ended in 1941 due to financial problems and artistic and political disagreements but its legacy was enormous.

## Adaptation

Another form of responsiveness is *adaptation*, referred to earlier. Stanislavski defines this as both the *inner and outer means that people use in adjusting to one another in a variety of relationships and to effect an objective*. If a friend we visit is unexpectedly ill, we respond by adapting to the new circumstances and demands of the situation. If I'm going on holiday and my water tank starts leaking, I have to adapt and change my plans. If I've bought tickets for a rock concert but my partner has a headache and wants a quiet meal, I have to adjust.

How we react and adapt to such circumstances will depend on their specific nature and the range of possibilities available to us. We adapt in a way that corresponds to place and time, for example, whether we're at home or abroad; with friends, family or strangers; during the day or at night. Also our own makeup determines how we adapt. It is advantageous for an actor to be flexible and summon up a wide range of qualities and tactics enabling the achievement of what we want or, at least, a suitable compromise.

Stanislavski makes the point that 'if people in ordinary walks of life use a large variety of adaptations, actors need a correspondingly greater number because we must be constantly in contact with one another and therefore incessantly adjusting ourselves'. Our adaptations should encompass the vivid and colourful, the bold and the subtle, but should always be focused on the action and not on trying to get cheap laughs or impress the audience with our cleverness.

*Adaptations are made consciously and unconsciously*. We have concentrated so far on the need for spontaneous reactions to achieve truth in performance and most adaptations should be spontaneous, unconscious, unexpected. 'The most powerful, vivid and convincing adaptations are the product of that wonder-working artist – nature.' They come through constant unbroken contact with each other, through being in the moment. This is worth remembering the next time actors bring out their lists or books of 'actions' and start writing in their scripts a cerebrally worked out action for each line before any organic process of interaction has taken place in practice!

Some adaptations are consciously determined. The ones to avoid, completely devoid of artistic content, are those mechanical and self-conscious actions repeated out of habit – what Stanislavski calls *rubber stamps*. However, an adaptation may be *suggested* by a director or another actor that is suitable; you then have to justify it and find the impulse behind it so you make it your own and not enact it mechanically. There are also what he calls *motor* adaptations. These are adjustments discovered organically and which have become a part of the character but are now conscious and habitual, for example, it may be a frequent characteristic of you in your role to look around to see if anyone's looking at you. This might have developed organically out of the character's insecurity and paranoia and is now a habitual element, something you as the character are aware of doing.

### *Exercises*

Try these three exercises in adaptation with a partner.

1. One of the examples Stanislavski gives in *An Actor Prepares* is that you have to find the adaptations necessary to get out of an acting class early when your tutor is ignoring you and is unsympathetic.
2. You want to go to see a film with your friend but they are upset over a relative's death.
3. You want a relaxing evening but your flatmate is full of anger and reproach and needs to talk it through.

As a group exercise:
You are in a cinema queue, on a bus or a tube and a provocative person – drunk, clownish, racist or otherwise insulting and intimidating – gets on and starts addressing everyone individually and as a whole. React and adapt to this truthfully as part of a group.

Different imaginative influences may be used to increase your range of actions, reactions and adaptations, such as I've noted above in the text exercises, and which we'll look at in more detail in later chapters.

# 5 What do I want?

> *Every objective must carry in itself the germ of action*
>
> Stanislavski

I start to enter circumstances through my imagination and action. I interact with others. The third essential element in creating the dynamics of action is engaging the will: what do I want? What is my *objective*? I've unavoidably mentioned objectives in earlier sections – they clearly emerge through any action and they influence how we interact – but I'll now focus on this practical and creative element in some detail.

## What are objectives?

Objectives are also variously called intentions, the action, goals, motivations, aims, tasks and wants. I prefer *objective*, not just because it's the term used in the Elizabeth Reynolds Hapgood translation of *An Actor Prepares*, which has been known to us for decades, and is the most commonly accepted term, but because, according to my *Oxford Dictionary*, it means *something sought or aimed at*, and so, for the English speaker, involves immediacy and action and encapsulates all the other terms. Benedetti, in *Stanislavski and the Actor*, uses instead the term *task* as a translation for *zadacha*, which Stanislavski used at the Opera-Dramatic Studio, but the meaning of *task* for us as *a piece of work to be done* does not carry the same sense of immediacy, drive, inner impulse and personal engagement associated with *objective*, and which are the qualities

Stanislavski demands should be present when actually executing an objective. The numerous terms and alternatives Benedetti includes in his appendix on terminology are no doubt valid translations, present in Stanislavski's workshops and writings, and of academic interest, but they can be a bit confusing. I'm concerned with what Stanislavski was actually aiming for so I prefer to simplify and emphasise whatever stimulates the will and action of the actor. In different countries with different languages the most appropriate terms for concepts may be completely different. I'd go further – it doesn't *matter* what terms you use as long as they help you to *act*. If you prefer other terms to the ones used in this book – and some practitioners do – and they help you more to grasp the principles and processes being described, then use them!

Objectives are what we have in life, at every moment of every day, in some form. When we think, we think about something. Our behaviour is purposeful, goal-directed. We have needs and wants that we try to satisfy through our actions. Even if our objectives are clear or unclear, conscious or unconscious, weak or strong, they are there. We will have immediate objectives and also medium and long-term ones. Overall in life, we also have a *Superobjective*. For example, my immediate objective might be to persuade my bank to lend me £10,000 for a mortgage deposit, because I want to buy a larger house. I want to install all my family there, because my Superobjective is to reunite my family who are split up around Europe. Or, I want to convince my parents that acting is a worthwhile occupation, because I want to go to a drama school. In the long term I want to establish myself as a versatile actor working in varied fields, and my Superobjective is to fulfil my creative artistic potential and social role as an artist in society. This sort of structure will be evident also when we come to look at objectives on text in Chapter 12, and forms what we call *the through line of action*, the linking of all our objectives towards the fulfilment of the Superobjective.

*Objectives, in order to be creative, truthful and alive as opposed to mechanical, theatrical or academic must:*

- **Be active**: every objective must have a *verb* and begin with *I want*. For example, 'I want to get him to support me' *not* 'I want to be supported'. The verb *to be* is static and passive, involves wish-fulfillment, and does not have what Stanislavski calls 'the active germ necessary to an objective'. Or 'I want to find a way of escaping from this prison' rather than 'I want to be free'. The first you can play actively, you can find actions to achieve it. The second is a state of mind. Objectives must move the action forward.

- **Address the action**: unless we're involved in direct address to the audience we should try to affect the other actors and not focus directly on the audience. For example, 'I want to calm your fears' *not* 'I want to get the audience to see my softer nature and get them on my side'.
- **Be clear and specific**: 'I want to take control of people in this room' rather than 'I want some power', which is too *general*, vague and descriptive. Even as a wider Superobjective, this should be made more specific and active, e.g. 'I want to win the office of Prime Minister by any means necessary'. To get there 'I want to reassure big business of my support, to conceal my long-term plans from the electorate, to win people over with my charm.'
- **Be do-able**: 'I want to make amends with you' *not* 'I want to make everything beautiful'. The first is clearly achievable, and the second is a bit of a tall order, general and abstract.
- **Stir and engage**: 'I want to make you admit you love me' rather than 'I want to express my feelings of concern and the hope that you might have the feelings for me I have for you, so we may one day possibly ... etc. etc.' The first expresses a need and urgency and is directly focused on action towards the other person. The second is discursive, weak and concerned with feelings and not the action prompted by the feelings. We have to find objectives that really galvanise us to act and appeal to us *personally* as the actors. It's no good choosing an objective that seems right intellectually but doesn't connect with your will. You need something to hit your gut! As Chekhov says in *To the Actor*, 'Your emotions, your will and even your body must be entirely filled with the objective'. You need to feel 'possessed' by it and 'see' it being fulfilled as you pursue it.
- **Be testable in the action**: 'I want to persuade you to lend me £20'. This is something that is aimed at achieving something concrete and we will know whether it's been achieved or not. This is not the case with ' I want to inform you of my problems, tell you I care, deliver you my message.' Inform, tell, deliver are weak actions not strong objectives, because they require no

response from the other person and no result is actively sought. Objectives seek to change things.

- **Do not presuppose physical or emotional states**: these should develop through the action and not be imposed on the playing of an objective. For example, 'I want to get you out of my life' should not presuppose a weakened, crumpled physicality or a heightened anger. To make such impositions is to decide intellectually what should happen rather than allowing physical and emotional responses to emerge organically through action and interaction.
- **Be consistent with the author and the part**: sometimes actors and directors decide to make a play more 'interesting' by inventing odd objectives that have nothing to do with the play, the author's intentions, or the true nature of a role. Whatever we decide on, we have to be able to justify it in the text. It would be absurd, for example, to give Madame Ranyevskaya in *The Cherry Orchard*, whose main concern is to preserve her way of life, an objective like 'I want to find religious fulfilment'; or to make Hedda Gabler, who wants to instigate courageous and beautiful acts, play out 'I want to get Eilert Loevborg to take Tesman's place as my husband'.

*Objectives may be simple or complex, conscious or subconscious.* A simple objective would be to welcome a guest into your party and make them feel at home. A more complex one would arise if this guest were a current lover of whom your husband is unaware, so the objective might be to put the person at ease or to convince everyone you're just good friends. You might then join your husband and enter a conversation with his potential employer, an established theatre director, and try to convince him of your husband's abilities and suitability for a job. Subconscious objectives here might be to convince your husband of your love and loyalty, to erase any suspicion he might have of your affair, or to assure him of your support and that everything's fine so it's safe for you to go and talk to your lover. The conscious objective involves behaving in a constructive, well-meaning, loyal and decent manner towards your husband, which is how we mostly want to believe we behave. The subconscious objective stems from deeper desires and stronger impulses and involves deviousness and deceit.

Both your lover and the theatre director now take a keen interest in a very attractive young actress and your lover actually appears to be flirting with her!

The director tells you he's looking for someone just like her to play a part in his production, and you take him over to her and introduce her, referring to the wonderful work she's done recently and draw your lover away so they can talk privately. Consciously, you want to promote her and get her work. The subconscious objective is to remove temptation from under your lover's nose. The conscious objective involves consideration and helpfulness. The subconscious one, jealousy and possessiveness. You can only consciously play one objective at a time, whether you have this sort of subtext or not. It may help to focus first on the subconscious objective and fully explore your actions towards achieving it, allowing your hidden feelings to come out into the open. That can only be done in rehearsal, of course, and the results have to be concealed in performance so that the conscious objective and relevant actions are played. Or you may find it more helpful to focus first on the conscious objective and then allow the subconscious elements to exert an influence.

The pleasure you may find in doing something will determine the objective as well. If you want to make a meal for an anniversary with your girlfriend, your objective may be 'I want to make this meal really special to please her'. If you hate cooking but have to eat something before going out to do what you really want to do like see a film or play football, then your objective will be 'I want to get this meal out of the way as quickly and easily as possible'.

To satisfy all the points above on what an objective should be, you will find you need to change the wording sometimes for it to really affect you. For example, 'I want to avoid contact with him' might not give you as strong a drive as 'I want to keep him at a distance'. 'I want to make you change your mind' might engage you more than 'I want to convince you I'm right'. 'I want to make you admit what you did', might fit your forcefulness better than 'I want to find out what happened'. How you frame the objective then will be determined by your character, the circumstances and the nature of the other person and your relationship to them, the emotions involved, what's at stake and what you have to overcome to achieve what you want.

## What is at stake?

How important is it to fulfil your objective – life and death, or not very important at all? John Proctor, in Arthur Miller's *The Crucible*, has to convince the Salem judges that his wife, Elizabeth, is innocent of the witchcraft charges brought against her. If he doesn't succeed she may be executed, he and others will be accused and executed, and the whole society will descend further into lies, treachery, and revenge. So he has a personal and social matter of life and death to deal with. The stakes are the highest imaginable. This demands strong, clear, direct objectives. In Ibsen's *The Lady from the Sea*, the sick artist, Lyngstrand, wants to attract the committed interest of Bolette Wangel in order to feel inspired while he's away making his career as a sculptor. However, he'll go off and try his hand at being an artist anyway. You feel her interest would be a bonus to boost his unselfconsciously large ego. So his aim is important to him at this point, but not life-threatening if he fails to achieve it – there may be other young ladies around on his travels after all.

Of course, the most dramatic and intense action will occur where the stakes are high, and your objectives will gain energy and conviction by making their realisation important. I don't think it would ever pay to make them lacking in *any* importance. When you do see action played without any drive it makes deathly dull viewing. Even if a point is being made that a character appears to lack any goal in life and lives like a vegetable, you may find they have a strong objective to keep as they are and not be interfered with.

## The counteraction

What is primarily in my way to achieve my objectives, through line of action and Superobjective, is people and circumstances in opposition to me. As Stanislavski says in *An Actor Prepares*:

> *Every* action *meets with a* reaction *which in turn intensifies the first. In every play, beside the main action we find its opposite* counteraction. *This is fortunate because its inevitable result is more action. We need that clash of purposes, and all the problems to solve that grow out of them. They cause activity which is the basis of art.*

So, the other person's objective will invariably be in opposition to mine; this is essentially what creates dramatic conflict. For every protagonist there is an antagonist. Stanislavski gives Ibsen's play, *Brand*, as an example. The protagonist, Brand, is an uncompromising 'all or nothing' preacher determined to bring people to God through will. Typical of this in one scene, he wants his wife, Agnes, to give away the clothes of their dead child but she resists out of love and attachment to the baby. She provides the counteraction to his action: love wrestles with duty, the mother with the preacher, the female with the male. In Chekhov's *The Cherry Orchard*, Lophakin sets up the main action by trying to persuade Ranyevskaya to convert her cherry orchard into profitable holiday homes to save her from losing the whole estate. Ranyevskaya provides the counteraction by totally opposing the plans and resisting any change. It is out of such conflicts that the main themes of plays will emerge.

## The obstacle

In addition to the basic conflict we face, there are other obstacles, taking a variety of forms, that we need to overcome with our objective:

- **An inner psychological state**, e.g. low confidence, a complex or phobia, respect for the other person, fear of rejection.
- **Something in the previous circumstances leading up to the action**, e.g. you owe the other person favours, they've argued with you, you've acted selfishly towards them, you've had a rupture in your relationship
- **A physical condition**, e.g. you have a headache, flu, period pain, exhaustion.
- **Something external**, e.g. freezing cold weather, suffocating heat, shortage of time, problematic clothes or objects.

By identifying one or more obstacles you enrich what you do to get what you want. Because there's more to overcome, your resolve may well strengthen, but what you do to get what you want may also become more clever, subtle, penetrating and varied. This is one reason for *always* finding an obstacle in each situation. Further, in addition to the basic conflict in the action, you are also creating an *internal* conflict and dynamic which intensifies the dramatic nature of a situation.

This conflict is often wrongly interpreted by actors to mean you can play more than one objective at the same time but if you try this you end up with a muddle. What one *does* do is to allow the objective to be *influenced* by the bigger objectives running through a scene or a larger episode in the script, or by the Superobjective, and you have to deal with your obstacle. For example, 'I want to convince my husband I love and desire only him' but I have an internal obstacle worrying me, my sense of guilt and hypocrisy over my infidelity, which makes me want to get a mile away. That obstacle will influence how I play my objective, but I can't actively play reassuring my husband *and* trying to get away. You must play what you want and try to overcome obstacles of feeling and desire. Doing this will communicate a contradiction and complexity clearly. Trying to play more than one objective will communicate the confusion of the actor. Ambivalence and ambiguity will come through the complexity of inner conflict; we can't act the alleged 'ambivalence of art', only the action.

## Actions

As we saw in Chapter 2, actions are what we do to achieve what we want. For example, if my objective is 'I want to stop you leaving me', I might restrain you, block the door, implore you, contradict you, reproach you, embrace you, reassure you, tease you, instruct you, entice you, etc. etc. Many of the actions will arise spontaneously, if you allow them, through playing your objective and interacting, and they will change according to how the circumstances alter, what's at stake and what the obstacles are. In Stanislavski's work on *Hamlet* (recorded in *Stanislavski and the Actor*), he examines the scene where Gertrude and Claudius hold court. Gertrude's objective is to *present her husband in such a way that he is accepted*. Stanislavski says that her important actions here are to fawn, cajole, bribe. These produce adaptations such as calming Hamlet, giving an affectionate look, etc. but these are spontaneous. He stresses that *the most important thing is to create the impulse to action*. All actions should not be planned and contrived because that creates mechanical, clichéd acting. We should not think about *how* to act either, because invariably here it's a hallmark of Representational acting that means adopting a manner or 'style': actors deciding to do something sadly or irritably, gracefully or eccentrically, so we see a 'sad' or 'eccentric' scene as opposed to the clear telling of a story and enactment of action. The process of creating a score of actions that are responses to impulses was explored by Stanislavski in his 'Method of Physical Action', which we look at in Chapter 12, and later by Grotowski in his montages of actors' experiences (see *At Work with Grotowski on Physical Actions* by Thomas Richards, Routledge, 1995).

## What do objectives give us?

Objectives create an essential part of our *inner life* in imaginary situations. They engage our will and give us a *drive* through the circumstances, stopping us playing moods and general emotional states. They prompt our *imagination* and a range of *actions*. They give us an *inner* structure because we link all the things we want. That structure creates a confidence and real *security* that enables *freedom* because we are working from an inner impulse to create words in an improvisation, or recreate lines in a script – this is totally different to the false security of knowing how you will say every line and do every move in a mechanical, predetermined fashion. They enable you to *react spontaneously* to other actors and events while keeping the inner structure and the interpretations agreed with the director. So whether you are improvising or working from a script, every take on what you do is effectively a *fresh improvisation* rather than a stone tablet. Because objectives help you engage in the moment and promote dramatic conflict they also help to *access and release emotion*.

Actors who don't play objectives will usually end up playing generalisations rather than specifics, which for Stanislavski is the enemy of art: general moods, attitudes, emotions and external gestures and business, as frequently encouraged by directors. This will create one-dimensional, dull, unstructured, undramatic, boring, indulgent, posturing deadly theatre. Need I go on? Objectives are one of Stanislavski's most important and creative tools.

Of course, they can be misused, like anything. If I use my telephone as a hammer it won't help me to communicate. If objectives (and other aspects of this approach) are seen in an intellectual way, they will not have the described effects. 'If I am in these circumstances what do I do and what do I want?' I imagine myself in the circumstances. I identify with them, or with another character in them. I don't intellectually deduce by some mathematical process what I want. I'm human, I empathise to understand on a range of levels. When

I get a sense of what I may want in a situation, I follow that impulse with my *will* and *feeling*, spontaneously create actions to achieve what I want against certain obstacles, also engaging my voice and body to that end. If I do it all cerebrally and 'my objective' just sticks in my head like a piece of calculus, not descending below neck level, and I try to implement it in a self-conscious and over-controlled manner, thinking the words I've used to define it all the time I'm trying to play it, it will of course be worse than useless. Some practitioners reject objectives because they perceive them in this light, as intellectual and a block to real involvement, the opposite of what they are intended to be and can be. They are essentially about the will, and once we have put the objective in mind we must trust in it and pursue it. When we're actually performing we don't necessarily have to get into our heads a whole sentence like 'I want to convince them I'm innocent'. We may just get a flash of particular words like 'convince innocent', or a particular visual image associated with that, and that gives us the impulse to engage. If it's wrong to determine and think the objectives intellectually and drily without them entering one's whole being, it's equally wrong not to be aware of them in performance at all, relying on the fact that having created them in rehearsal they'll just be working away for you automatically. They need to be kept alive organically as you as the character, as we experience them as ourselves in everyday life. Each time we perform, we have to rediscover and re-experience all the impulses behind the action – thoughts, objectives, images, sensory elements, emotions – without which the action will be unjustified and mechanical. There is no point where we can or should go onto automatic pilot.

### *Exercises*

**A.**

Try playing opposing objectives in pairs, as yourselves, keeping the stakes high.

Don't be premeditatedly rigid – 'I'll never let this person overcome *my* objective!' – but be responsive to what is actually done to you. As in life, and in scripts, someone will achieve what they want sometime.

If you don't succeed at first, don't get stuck in one set of tactics. Try other actions – adapt!

For all exercises you must create for yourself the given circumstances, including good reasons why you want what you do.

1. A wants to get B out of their small flat for the evening because a boyfriend is coming round. B wants to convince A she has to stay in to get important work done.

2. A wants to make contact with B who is sitting on a park bench alone. B wants to study her book, keep to herself and other people at a distance.

3. A wants to find out what is worrying B. B wants to steer him away from the issues.

**B.**

Try doing the same impros again but with an *obstacle*, and see how it changes what you do.

For example:

1. A has already asked this sort of favour before. B is a very compliant, obliging person.

2. A has bad body odour. B recently rejected a friend who ended up killing himself.

3. A is worried about a leaking ceiling. B is feeling nauseous.

**C.**

Now try the same impros and pursue your objective using ten *actions* you would not commonly use given your personality. Select these in advance but allow them to come through as organically as possible according to what the other does to you. This will encourage you to find a wider range of adaptations and flexibility and not get in a rut.

**D.**

Now come to the same impros a fourth time. Try to keep them fresh and this time focus on finding a *fuller verbal and physical expression* for the actions. Allow your voice to respond to the dynamic between you in its tone, range and inflexions. Find gestures that fit the actions, e.g. the natural gestures associated with commanding, warning, begging, calming, dismissing, soothing, and so on. The objectives will then pervade your whole mental and physical life and be communicated to their fullest.

**E.**

If you have a number of people to work with, try a group exercise incorporating the above elements. For example:

You are all staying in a guest house in Australia and have become surrounded and trapped by a forest fire. You are gathered in the lounge to discuss the options. All have different objectives, e.g. to work out how to escape, to discourage this and get everyone to play safe, to cheer everyone up, to support whoever seems sensible, to get small constructive things done, to blot everything out, etc. You all have different obstacles, and will employ a variety of actions. Don't forget to listen and respond to each other as you pursue your objectives.

**F.**

Now take short pieces of text, no more than a page or two, and play a different objective each time you do it. Try it in pairs and in a group. You will see how different the script can be with each objective, how many readings are theoretically possible, how versatile you as the actor can be and how you needn't be constrained by a set of static line readings.

To summarise this part of the book: doing in circumstances brings being and experiencing; interaction creates communication and continuous flow; objectives produce drive and will, and connect to feeling. These provide the basic dynamics of action and the foundations of acting, on which the imagination and intuition can take flight and soar.

# Part 3

# Developing the imaginary reality

## – seeing, sensing, feeling

# 6 Visualising the action

> *Every movement you make on stage, every word you speak, is the result of the right life of your imagination*
>
> Stanislavski

## The role of imagination

What we have looked at so far is the creation of the backbone of our work on circumstances and character. We can now look at how to flesh this out. Michael Chekhov begins one of his chapters in *To The Actor* with this assertion: 'Transformation – that is what the actor's nature, consciously or subconsciously, longs for'. Transformation means a thorough change in form and character, so that one thing changes into another. To some actors transformation may mean adopting a mask or set of mannerisms and physical affectations. To Stanislavski, it meant you 'go from yourself', using your own individuality, organic nature and potential, but rearranging it into other permutations of wants and qualities to change into something different while you're performing. This is not the same as using your customary everyday personality, or a socially conditioned self, but harnessing the full range of your humanity and unique identity, the *essential self* with which playwrights like Ibsen, Miller and Shakespeare were so concerned. 'An actor must adjust himself to the role, not the role to himself' (*An Actor Prepares*). So, I become *myself as the character*. We aim to play a myriad characters but never lose ourselves as the basis for transformation. For many actors, transformation is not an issue: they will play themselves, or a regular *persona*, which the casting system increasingly encourages. Some Method actors may *bring the character to themselves* rather than *go from themselves to the character.*

Michael Chekhov emphasises the different roles of writer and actor. The writer has provided their creation in the form of a play. The actor's job is to discover 'the psychological depths of the characters given you in the play ... The true actor will not glide over the surfaces of the characters he plays nor impose upon them his personal and unvarying mannerisms. ... It is a crime to chain and imprison an actor within the limits of his so-called "personality"'. Another of Stanislavski's students, Yevgeny Vakhtangov, who became a renowned and brilliant director himself and ran the First Studio of the Moscow Art Theatre said: 'The character is the organic union of the life of the character and the life of the actor. An actor must assimilate the character's life'. This inner life then had to be given physical life through the imagination. 'The truth on stage is not what happens in real life, but what could happen' (quoted in Sonia Moore's *The Stanislavski System*).

What Chekhov, Vakhtangov and some of Stanislavski's modern-day advocates say, originate in his own writings, of course. The *If* 'lifts us out of everyday life on to the plane of imagination ... The aim of the actor should be to use his technique to turn the play into a theatrical reality. In this process imagination plays by far the greatest part'. The author provides words and actions and basic information on characters and circumstances, but not a full account of what has happened before the play or of the characters' life histories or what happens between scenes. In Shakespeare we're given the place and a time and very little else. In Ibsen and Chekhov, for example, we get a lot more detail but there are whole areas in the past events and relationships which may be suggested but need to be fully interpreted, *imagined,* before we can find all the actions for a scene.

Mamet, in *True and False,* sounding surprisingly like Michael Chekhov, puts the view that 'Your true creative powers lie in your imagination, which is eternally fertile, but cannot be forced, and your *will,* that is, your true character, which can be developed through exercise.' He also says it's the writer's job to make the play interesting and the actor's job to make it truthful. So far so good. Then in one of the glaring contradictions in the book he also says: 'There is no character. There are only lines upon a page'; and '... the words and their meaning are not your responsibility', but meaning 'is conveyed by the actor's intention'. What value is imagination if it is not used to interpret the words and action? While the actor playing a part has to be the basis of the character, the lines on the page plus imagination indicate a character yet to be achieved, and how can the actor come to a grasp of *intention* without considering *meaning*? To deny the actor as the basis of the character denies the reality of the acting process, but to deny that an imaginary character exists denies its evidence in the writing and in the will of the actor to transform.

As I pointed out earlier, there are practitioners who believe all this stuff about imagination and transformation is old-fashioned and not possible on screen. They must have missed the work of actors like Anthony Hopkins, Gary Oldman, Daniel Day-Lewis, Chiwetel Ejiofor, Meryl Streep, Daniel Auteuil, and Al Pacino, all of whom can be seen on film and who create distinctly different and believable transformations, psychologically and physically, and appear to have done pretty well for themselves. I suspect the directors, agents, and casting directors who enforce the stereotypical norms in casting and production don't have much respect for acting or an understanding of the great artistry of people such as those mentioned above, or they hive them off into the 'Oh, they're different' category. Instead, they perpetuate the safety of mediocrity and a desire to give the public something easy and ultimately unsatisfying. So, one of the excellent and succinct pieces of advice Mamet does offer actors is *Do not internalise the industrial model!* In other words, stick to your creative values and what's inspiring you as an actor, and then try to resolve the contradictory pressures of the industry.

A key emphasis then in Stanislavski's conclusions on acting and in the work of his most prominent followers is on *imagination*, and not arid intellectual reasoning, cerebral deliberations on *how* something should be done, or on habitual mannerisms as an attempt at 'naturalism', all of which might be present in what today sometimes parades as a Stanislavski-influenced approach.

**Yevgeny Vakhatangov 1883–1922**

Born in the North Caucasus, he trained as an actor with Leopold Sulerzhitski, greatly respected by Stanislavski, and joined the Moscow Art Theatre in 1911. As a brilliant student of Stanislavski he directed at the First Studio from 1913 and also developed his own studio, which was named after him following his premature death. Initially a strict adherent to 'naturalistic' principles, he developed his own heightened or 'fantastic realism', involving music, dance and mask. Renowned productions were *Turandot*, *The Dybbuk* and *Erik XIV* with Michael Chekhov. One of the influences on Lee Strasberg's Actors Studio in New York.

## Seeing the circumstances

In Chapter 3 we looked at given circumstances, previous circumstances and the action of making an entrance and exit, and the use of the 5 Ws and 'If' as imaginative spurs to launch us into the action. To give these *imaginary* circumstances extra life and belief we need to *visualise* what we've invented and to engage our other senses as well.

To look back at one of the exercises in Chapter 3, you've been out in the evening and have been chased home by a group of men. The previous circumstances are that your mother's developed a psychosis and was taken to a mental unit five hours' journey away earlier that morning. At 7.30p.m. you first went for a meal with a friend to an Indian restaurant, and then went for a drink in a local pub before making your way home. What was the name of the restaurant, what did it look like, what did you eat, who was your waiter? What was the pub, what is it like, was it crowded, empty, smokey, what did you drink? Were the men who later chase you there, how many were there, what did they look like, what interest did they show in you, did you or your friend do anything to annoy them, were they just looking for a fight or to pick you up? When you leave are you aware of the men leaving too? Where does your friend go – to get a bus or taxi, walk, to their car? When are you aware of the men following you and when do you start to run? Do they immediately chase after you? How long does it take to get home? Can you still taste the meal and drinks? Are there distinctive smells on the way back, for example, of trees or car fumes? Do your clothes start to stick to you because of the exertion and sweat? Are the men shouting at you? What does your home look like at the present time as you approach and enter it? This is all part of your preparation, of course. All you need to enter the circumstances is 'If I am in these circumstances what do I do?' and your basic 5 Ws: Who am I? Where? Why? What time is it? What do I want? However, once in the situation, the images and other sensory elements will affect what you do and how by creating a greater sense of an obstacle to be overcome by an objective such as 'I want to make myself safe'. An image of your mother may add to the horror of what's happening and affect your entrance into your home and cause you to fumble the keys. Seeing four burly skinheads will be more fear-inducing than seeing a couple of skinny weaklings and will prompt a more urgent drawing of the curtains and locking of the doors. Recalling images of the journey and of your friend might intensify your sense of isolation. So, working from the imagination in this way, not the intellect, will create a more detailed make-believe situation, prompt the actor to action, and help to create atmosphere and emotion.

What we are doing here is to create what Stanislavski calls *an inner chain of circumstances* which enriches and stirs our action. We create a series of images that are projected like a film onto the screen of our mind's eye. This reproduces what we do naturally in everyday life, and Stanislavski might also have been inspired to this idea by the use of visualisation in Raja yoga.

## Seeing the past

Our characters, just like ourselves, have backgrounds to be imagined. We see images of our own parents, pets, houses lived in, holidays taken, jobs done, friends met, and partners married, and so on. To reproduce human reality in the creative process we need to create not only an imagined life history for ourselves as different people, but also to create the images that go with this. These images also become part of the *inner chain of circumstances*, and can be incorporated into the action of the play to give greater belief and colour in what we do. If I mention my wife or father, as in real life I have an image of them in my head before or while I'm speaking and that influences how I say the lines. If I just learn my wife's name, say Julia, and only intellectually know that she has caused my character a lot of pain and resentment, I might say a line like, 'Julia didn't even bother to turn up to father's funeral' in a flat, stated way. It's more likely to be expressive and believable if I have imagined specific causes for my resentment, have images of them in my mind and see an image of Julia before I say the line.

The actor playing Hedda Gabler could have scores of images flicking through her head: of her father, General Gabler, of the house where she lived and talked with Eilert Loevborg, of what he looked like at that time, of the honeymoon with Tesman in the Tyrol, of the horse she used to ride, and her schooldays and behaviour towards Mrs Elvstedt, etc. All the images need to be suggested and substantiated by the text, but imaginatively elaborated by the actor's and director's interpretation of the action and previous events. In rehearsal and performance, the run images then prompt inner and outer action and help to give the impression of a life actually lived rather than described.

The Hamlet actor will have images of studies in Wittenburg, of his relationship with Ophelia, of his father and the nature of government before his death. The actor playing Willy Loman from Miller's *Death of a Salesman* will see the numerous stores where he sold or didn't sell goods, the highs and lows with Biff, the women he had affairs with, what Brooklyn used to be like, and so on.

This equally applies to events between scenes. The actor should have an unbroken *through line of action* as outlined in Chapter 5, and this should include what happens off stage, screen, or microphone. Instead of moving from one scripted scene to another, we need to shift from one life experience to another, absorbing in our imagination the events which have taken place in the intervening hours, weeks or years and bringing those back into performance with us. The incorporation of crucial images and other sensory experiences – of pain, or distinctive smells, or the sound of an orchestra – will enhance belief in this imagined inner life. We'll bring on the past life and increase the audience's own belief and involvement. This creation of the whole life of the character, past and present, as a continuous, unbroken chain is what Stanislavski's co-director at the Moscow Art Theatre, Nemirovich-Danchenko, called the *second plan*: something not indicated by the actor or seen by the audience, but experienced by the actor and sensed by the audience.

## Seeing the surroundings

We should be aware of everything in the performing space: the set, props, decoration and furniture, clothes, the effects of lighting and sound. We should also create an awareness of what is *not* there: on the so-called *fourth wall* or fourth side, the side in a proscenium arch theatre where the audience sits, as in London West End theatres; on two sides if playing in traverse; on three sides, if working in an amphitheatre space, as in a traditional Greek amphitheatre like Epidaurus or the Young Vic in London; on four sides, if working in the round, as in Scarborough's Stephen Joseph Theatre, or if the setting is outdoors in an open landscape.

As I said in the Introduction, Stanislavski's idea of the fourth wall is often misunderstood. It is created to focus actors on the action onstage, to sustain belief in the created circumstances and stop the audience distracting them, and to guard against glazed staring into the dark emptiness. It is not created for actors to face out to the audience and pose, nor to cut off the audience and indulge in 'private moments'. We will always be aware of the audience's presence since we perform for them, unless, of course, we consciously try to cut them off or are lacking our full senses.

So, on however many sides of the stage are not occupied by design, we have to complete the visual setting. In a room, we might place paintings or photographs on the imaginary walls, light fittings or cabinets, bookshelves or a home cinema unit. It's advisable to place these during rehearsal where they can be re-envisaged without effort, and then once in the theatre, to fix them in line with landmarks out in the body of the auditorium, for example, next to a box or in the middle of the circle's fascia. If creating an outdoor scene you will very likely have to create a panoramic view. A scene in Philip Osment's 1993 play, *The Dearly Beloved*, is set on a Devon moor. It's given that there is a river and a wood with deer. Both elements are imagined by everyone, and a group focus on emerging deer at the end of one scene so there has to be agreement on exactly where they and the wood are placed. In the production, the river was set upstage behind a rise, and the wood and deer were placed beyond the audience to the left. This is a *conscious* use of an imaginary side.

The filling in of other details and landmarks will be up to each member of the cast, or can be done by group agreement, but these elements will only be focused on *unconsciously* and spontaneously for the sake of the actors' sense of truth in the imaginary surroundings. For example, upstage beyond the river there might be a line of gorse, a road bending into the distance, and some rocky moorland. To the left, there might be a line of hills in the distance. To the right, a couple of pathways leading to another part of the river, a footbridge and a rocky hillock rising to two hundred feet. Out front, apart from the wood to the left, there might be a line of wire fencing, some grazing sheep, and a building on a hillside to the right. Of course, there is also the ground, which might be coarse and tufty; and there is the sky, which might be blue with small dabs of white cloud and a bright sun in the west, and the occasional buzzard or rook. Any of these elements might be seen while dialogue or thought is taking place, but without conscious attention given to them.

## Seeing the character

Michael Chekhov takes Stanislavski's emphasis on imagination and transformation into new areas and was renowned as an actor for his extreme transformations while remaining truthful and emotionally connected, e.g. his portrayal of Erik XIV in Strindberg's play, directed by Vakhtangov. He believed in the possible rather than the actual, and that actors will find intuitive insights into their characters by letting the imagination roam. He points to how at the end of a day we may simply close our eyes and see in an unforced way the events and places we've experienced pass before us, and then images from the past start to appear, and then images that are not real but imaginary. Suddenly you are seeing a performance created in your mind's eye.

He refers to writers and painters like Dickens and Michelangelo who were driven to create by images appearing to them. These images come to us as actors, too. We find at a certain stage of rehearsal that we are getting an image of the character that is not us. We are seeing a different appearance with a different height, weight, build, hair colour, posture, and walk. We may see the character in a particular scene doing various actions in a particular way. The character is unlikely to be completely formed and Chekhov suggests we prompt it by asking questions. I might see John Proctor returning from a long day's work out in the fields before his entrance in Act 2 of Miller's *The Crucible*, and prompt him to show me how he ploughs alone, plants seeds, where the pain and tiredness takes effect in his body, how he walks the long distance back to the house and enters with the weight of physical work on him and the anxiety over his tense relationship with Elizabeth, his wife. I see how he enters, listens to her singing their boys to sleep, tastes her food from the pot over the fire, and washes himself. I may see him first obsessed with the problems he faces. Then I may rewind the images and look at the same situation from a different perspective. Proctor this time is positive and determined to improve the relationship and I see him walk and enter with that intention. What I see is not just something external and physical as I might perceive strangers I see casually in everyday life. By this process I can see straight into the inner life of characters, their thoughts, feelings and drives. I can see into their relationships with others as well. These can't be determined intellectually and then simply enacted in rehearsal. Things begin to take shape over time with the specific people you are working with. Then we start to see our characters together with others in different situations and again we can prompt them to reveal what they do under certain impulses.

This is not the same process as intellectually deciding what your character is like, or imagining the character, and then representing it externally. This is a means for entering into the world of our characters directly and imaginatively and grasping aspects of their inner and outer life which can then inform our acting. It is also only one element in a wider process. Earlier chapters looked at placing ourselves imaginatively in circumstances through '*If*' and the 5 Ws, but this use of images of the character can remove obstacles that may block our way to the truth of a situation and enrich what we're doing. The different processes are not in contradiction. It's the same as reading a novel and seeing all the characters move before you, and empathising with the circumstances of particular ones, entering into their lives, feelings and desires, putting yourself compassionately in their shoes so that you actually start to feel what they feel, want what they want. Gradually you can incorporate the imagined experiences – that is, draw them into your own self and action – and find your feelings and will stirred effortlessly, without pushing and wringing out the emotions, and your physicality respond to these inner impulses.

## *Exercises*

We can do conscious exercises to stimulate the imagination so that it responds more automatically and subconsciously.

1. Chekhov suggests a number of exercises to make incorporation of images more flexible.
   - Open a book at random and catch an image of one of the characters. Look at it and wait for it to move, speak, change by itself. Allow it an independent life.
   - Next, ask it questions and prompt it to change. How does it sit down? Welcome a friend? Run for the bus? Deal with a rival? Laugh or cry?
   - Pick a play and imagine a short scene with a few characters. Then prompt them to do it differently – with a different atmosphere, tempo, quality, or individual feelings. You guide and also take suggestions from what you see.
   - Try to penetrate the inner life of the characters so that you become affected by their emotions and desires, and find a compassionate empathy.
   - See images transform, e.g. a young man into an old man, a hut into a castle, a winter landscape into a summer one.

- Create a character by yourself. Put it in different situations, develop its characteristics, follow its inner life and open yourself to its influence. When this becomes strong, incorporate, take on the character gradually, not all at once, and act out a bit of the character's life.

2. - You are sitting in a tree in a field in Suffolk in the 17th, 18th, 19th and 20th centuries. What do you see? What farming, animals, birds? How do people look? How do houses change? You might see Civil War, the effects of the Agricultural and Industrial Revolution, and air battles from World War Two.
   - You're a security guard at the doorway of a clothing department store. Imagine all the different people and types of clothes for sale, the size and decor of the store.
   - Imagine three different types of cat, e.g. a Persian pedigree, a moggy, a hairless variety. Imagine three different types of garden, e.g. an English country garden in Wiltshire, a garden in a quiet village on a Greek island, the extensive garden of a French chateau.

3. - Go on a journey. Improvise a walk in a wood, by a stream, through an old railway tunnel, or in a derelict house. What do you see, smell, taste, touch, and hear? Give yourself a reason for being there, e.g. to collect flowers, take photos, get exercise, and then allow your imagination to run and create new events in the moment, justified by what has gone before but on impulse rather than by conscious calculation.

   For example, I take a walk in a wood to take photos of sunlight through branches. As I enter I follow a wide, dry path. A raindrop falls from a leaf onto my eyelid. I wipe my face with a hanky. I see a good shot in the direction I'm now looking. The path is more narrow and wetter. I take a picture. I sit down on a tree root waiting for the light to change. I see wild mushrooms at the side of the trunk. As I look up I see a good shot to my right and head for a better position quickly. I trip over a creeper and scrabble in wet leaves. But I take the shot. The sky now quickly clouds over and it starts to rain. I hide my camera inside my zipped jacket and head back out of the wood to my car.

- Choose three very different objects and construct a scenario around them that makes psychological sense.

  For example, horseshoe, sewing-machine, and book. I might have a number of tasks to do. First, I'll sort out all my bills and write the necessary cheques. Having done that I place all the bills under a horseshoe acting as a paper weight, until I find time to file them away in order. I then mend the hem on my trousers with the machine. I wipe down the surfaces of the table and windows. I look at what's on TV. Nothing. So I sit down and read a novel I'm finding a bit slow.
- If you are part of a group, choose three disconnected words and weave them into a fantastical, surreal situation. For example, you have to say bodkin, syrup, and fetlock while making a meal on a cloud, or digging for oil on the moon!

4. – *The image exercise.* Learn a two-minute speech that is full of visual images and other sensory elements. This can be invented by you or be a piece of text. Do it as you, not as a character. It can be a story, e.g. of a robbery, a holiday, a journey; or a description, e.g. of a painting, landscape, sunset, or of an event, e.g. a party, wedding, funeral.

   See the images, run the film in your head, and describe what you see. Allow your voice, body and movement to respond to what you recreate.

   The audience should actually see clearly the images you see. We should feel the speech is being invented in the moment so that the descriptive adjectives are being freshly coined in response to the images, which draw you and us in.

# 7 Sensing

*Never begin with results. They will appear in time as the logical outcome of what has gone before*

Stanislavski

All the information and stimuli coming from the world outside us is taken in by the senses and processed by the brain. If we have no senses or deadened senses we stop being a full part of the world, we become alienated from others and ourselves, and more and more insular. We are living through a communications revolution but ironically we genuinely communicate less and less. We have more devices like mobile phones which link us to others and news and entertainment services, but whatever their value in terms of convenience and access to information, they often serve to block us off from the immediate world around us. 'I'm on a bus!' but you're not really, you're down a phone with a disembodied voice, and the world of the bus, the people on it, what's happening outside is not experienced. Equally the old Walkmans and current iPods draw all your focus into a set of headphones and a point directly in front of you creating a snug cocoon to insulate you from the world around. Emails enable quick contact, not like the old snail mail, but if you're getting twenty to a hundred a day you don't read them all, they become a burden, and important messages can be missed.

I'm not, of course, proposing we ditch this sort of new technology but if these means of communication stop us really communicating maybe we should adjust their usage and focus on how to make real human contact with each other. Our own thoughts, feelings and imagination about what's outside can't flourish if we're constantly bombarded with sounds in a headset or phone messages. Increasingly long working hours, low-paid, repetitive jobs, and greater stress also serve to break down any sense of being in a community. We're prompted to look for forms of escape: in rising alcohol or cocaine intake, obesity-forming foods, sensory titillation in violent films, 'reality' shows or Springer-style chat shows in which we see miserable people failing to communicate! Increasingly, people don't really see or listen to each other and connect.

'They all want to escape from the pain of being alive', said John Osborne's Jimmy Porter in 1956, and understandable though that may be, particularly in our increasingly violent, dangerous, and unstable world, it doesn't solve any problems. Actors cannot be allowed the luxury of escape. We have to understand humanity and express its experiences however awful. We need to sensitise not desensitise ourselves and go through life fully aware. How else can we follow Michael Chekhov's urging to enrich the psychology and increase the sensitivity of our minds and bodies? This process has to be constant so we have all the necessary resources ready at hand to be used in our work. The actor never clocks off!

## Opening the senses

In Chapter 1, I looked at how the senses were an important element in increasing our awareness, and there are exercises there for focusing on each of the five senses.

Stanislavski, in his Opera and Dramatic Studio exercises, requires the actors to recall actual experiences to sharpen sensory awareness.

For example,

- see a house where you once lived; an elephant, a camel, an earthworm; a wasp, ladybird, caterpillar; a starry sky; a famous building; winter snow, ice, mist.
- hear waves on the shore, wind rattling the window, dripping raindrops; a piano, guitar, trumpet, an orchestra tuning up; a barking dog, a cawing crow; sawing and chopping wood; heavy lorries, a motorbike, a train shunting into a siding; footsteps on stairs and in snow.

- smell the sea, smoke from a wood fire, rain on grass; roses, lilac, hyacinth; petrol, wine, coffee; an apple, orange.
- taste chocolate, ice-cream; a lemon, raspberries, an apricot.
- feel the touch of hot, cold, tepid water; a cat, dog; cotton, silk, wool, velvet, sandpaper; hot tea on the tongue; a pineapple, cabbage, wet fish.

Of course, there are hundreds more you can try. For most of us, seeing and hearing are probably the senses we find it easiest to recall, so smell, taste, and touch will require more effort and practice.

Also, one sense may well trigger other senses and memories. Charles Baudelaire, the mid-nineteenth century French poet, was very keen on these connections. Look at this very sensual extract from a prose poem called *A Hemisphere in a Head of Hair*, in which all five senses are triggered:

> *In the ocean of your hair I am shown brief visions of a port resounding with melancholy songs ... In the glowing fire-grate of your hair I inhale the odour of tobacco mingled with opium and sugar; in the night of your hair I see the infinity of tropical azure resplendent; on the downed banks of your hair I inebriate myself with the mingled odours of tar, of musk and of coconut oil. Long let me bite your heavy, black tresses. When I gnaw your elastic and rebellious hair, it seems to me that I am eating memories.*

## The physical score

When we look at all the senses functioning together we create a *physical score*. What am I seeing, hearing, smelling, tasting, touching at any point in performance?

For example, I am sitting at my computer. I see the keyboard, screen, my hands and watch, lamps and desk, books and notes, a seascape photo and water-colour painting on the wall in front of me. I hear the sound of the keys being pressed, the hum of the computer, loud voices and a car engine outside, and birdsong. I smell wool from my new sweater. I taste fruit tea in my mouth. I touch a hard chair with my bottom, the desk with my right knee, the floor with my feet, the desk top with my hands, and keyboard with my fingertips, and I can also feel my collar against my neck and trousers against my calves.

If I am one of the women out potato picking in Caryl Churchill's *Fen*, I see the dark earth with stones, a wire fence, and thin line of trees in the distance, other women to each side and ahead. I hear rooks cawing, the sound of potatoes pulled up and thrown in baskets, women talking. I smell the damp earth, sweat, smoke from a farm fire. I taste earth that's come from my hand, drinking water, and my sweat. I feel the ground with my knees, feet, and hands, and the weight of clothes on my back.

Every scene will have some sort of *physical score* such as this and identifying it through the facts the writer gives us and our own imagination will increase our sense of belief in the action and our involvement.

## Sense memory

Sense memory (also called analytical memory by Boleslavski at the American Laboratory Theatre) is the recall of particular physical sensations so they are re-experienced and not crudely described. This recreation can produce truth, richness, and subtlety as opposed to clichéd illustration, and can also tap into emotions which may be triggered by memory of an image, sound, smell, taste or touch.

### Recalling physical activities

To sharpen our senses and become more conscious of what we actually do in certain actions, an instructive exercise is to perform an everyday activity without the objects we would normally use. This is also useful during rehearsal when we may not have props and setting available but actions have to be realistically performed for purposes of timing, thought process, interaction, etc.

For example, clean your teeth without a brush, water and toothpaste. This is not an indicated mime, but as accurate a recreation of the activity as possible. This requires careful observation of what you actually do when cleaning your teeth: what is the weight and shape of the brush, how do you grip it, what is the pressure exerted on your teeth, what is the weight of the toothpaste tube and how hard do you squeeze it to get the required paste on the brush, how long does each action take, etc.? So, you observe weight, space, time, pressure, shape, smell, taste, sound and what you see, and then reproduce this without the objects.

Or you have to pour drinks from a whiskey bottle. Feel the diameter, texture, weight and height of the bottle, the pressure needed to take out the cork top, how much you need to tip the bottle to pour the drinks and how strongly you need to grip it. What is the weight and diameter of the glasses you have to pick up? Note the smell of the whiskey, the sound and sight of it being poured, and so on. Then reproduce the actions without the objects recreating your sensory awareness of them.

## Recalling bodily actions

There are things we do with our own bodies that are rarely made believable onstage because actors don't reproduce a physiological process but instead do a bad imitation of what they see from the outside. For example, yawning, waking up, gagging, staggering with dizziness, starting with surprise.

Usually, when yawning an actor will simply open their jaw and exhale. What actually happens in a yawn is that the brain needs air. We then get that sensation of the upper jaw being prized open and air being sucked into the lungs, followed by that strange low wind-like noise in the ears as the eyes press tight shut and water appears in them as the jaw closes and air is expelled. To get a real, believable yawn we have to recreate that process. So start from lifting that upper jaw and taking in air. The rest will take care of itself. You just have to allow yourself time to do this; don't rush and be worried about the director and cast waiting for you – don't censor yourself. Doing it truthfully will draw the audience in. Doing it crudely will repel them.

Waking up onstage often involves sudden movements and perfunctory stretches with the obligatory token yawn. The first thing is not to pretend to be asleep, but to get into a normal sleeping posture and focus your attention on a particular part of the body, e.g. head or shoulder. Internally focus on an image, something you might like to dream about, such as the sea on a Greek beach or mountains in the Alps. When you need to wake up, address your thought to something in the circumstances about to be entered. Has the postman arrived? Did I miss the alarm? What's the first thing I need to do today? Then let your eyes open. Then the rest of your face and head has to wake up. You change position in bed, then you can start to raise yourself out of bed slowly and heavily. Then maybe there is a genuine yawn, and you believe you've been asleep and are waking up.

If we gag it's because we're feeling nauseous and close to vomiting. What actually happens is we get that sensation of stuff rising from the stomach into the throat. The uvula – the fleshy piece of the soft palate hanging above the throat – contracts, the back of the tongue rises to the soft palate, and you start to gag. So, to recreate this feeling, *imagine* something rising, contract the uvula, let your tongue rise up and you will start to gag genuinely.

If we stagger with dizziness it's because our sense of balance and control are affected by, for example, lack of food or air. Our legs may feel wobbly and weightless and our vision becomes unfocused and blurred. So to reproduce this we can unfocus our eyes and imagine that our legs are lacking firm bones and muscles, like sponge. This will produce a stagger which we then have to deal with by trying to regain focus and steady our movements. Again, we create the symptoms that follow from the basic problem, and that will create a sense of the problem.

When we see an actor start with surprise at the sudden arrival of someone or something done to them, it's often demonstrated with a movement of the shoulders and arms, and depiction of facial alarm. The real impulse for the movement, though, comes from the solar plexus, the nervous system, and the physical movement originates there lifting the rib cage, so that people often place there hand over that area after the first fright as though to comfort it. Try to respond to what's happening as if it's happening for the first time so that a genuine impulse and movement takes place. But whatever happens, the physical movement should be generated from the solar plexus.

There are other examples, of course, like hiccuping, coughing, sneezing, which may be more or less difficult to recreate, but the process is to identify the cause and what actually happens physiologically, to reproduce the symptoms, and then, if necessary, deal with them. What not to do is to give a superficial imitation of poorly observed externals in the form of a stage cliché.

## Recalling physical sensations

This is where we look at sensations created by outside influences like temperature, infections, drink, noise and pressure.

Let's start with heat. Again, the stereotype of acting under the influence of heat is to fan the face with a paper or to wipe away sweat with the back of the hand. Of course, these actions might be completely believable, but that will only be the case if they come from a genuine experience and impulse as opposed to a desire to *indicate* heat. It's that experience combined with imagination that we should take as the starting point.

Recall a time when you experienced, say, intense humid heat. Recreate the situation and imaginatively place yourself back in it. Where were you and why? What were you doing? For example, you might have been on a beach in Thailand, sunbathing on holiday, in summer 2003. Or, you were on a full coach of people and animals on a mountain road in Mexico last year during a research trip.

Next, think of what the specific sensations were as a result of that heat – wet armpits, dry mouth, sweat on the back of your neck, hot aching feet, tiredness? So, don't try to be hot in general. Look at the specific manifestations of heat in you.

Thirdly, how did you deal with the symptoms? Did you put a hanky round your neck, drink a lot of water, shade your eyes with a hat or sunglasses, take off your shoes, sit very still, breathe shallowly? As in the above exercises, we will feel the sensation most when trying to deal with it, rather than waiting for it or trying to force it, as Uta Hagen points out in *A Challenge for the Actor.*

Finally, you should be aware of the physical score in the situation. Do you hear a dog snuffling, see waves and beach huts, smell sweat, taste a fruit drink, feel a rough, uncomfortable seat against your legs?

In this way you create truthful responses to heat because they are based on reality and will prompt your imagination and spontaneity. What you do will inevitably be richer, more varied and interesting because it comes from the imagination and not a cerebral decision to describe heat in a pattern of stock gestures. What you discover in such an exercise can then be transferred to creating humid heat in the situation of a performance, and it will be altered or developed according to the requirements of the specific character and circumstances as created by the writer. Of course, the scene is unlikely to be *about* heat. This will most likely only be an influence on the action, and we don't want to see all the actor's homework displayed if it's not called for. The sense memory has to serve the play, not the other way round.

The same process applies to cold. Recall an experience of, say, icy, bone-chilling cold and place yourself back in it. What were the specific symptoms –

chattering teeth, frozen joints, cracked lips, watering eyes? How did you deal with them – covering the face with a scarf, putting on lip salve, stamping around, drinking something warm? What was the physical score?

A headache is a good one to try because there are so many different types, but invariably you see actors just holding their temples. Many headaches now, because of hours in front of computers and greater stress, may well be at the back of the head or on top, and be accompanied by a stiff neck and sore shoulders, or might be at the front and spread to the eyes. What specific type of headache would your character have? When did you have a similar one or comparable one? What were the pains and other symptoms like? What did you do about them – adjust your posture, massage your neck and lower skull, lie down, take pills?

If you're drunk you don't try to stagger around and slur your speech, you try to stop doing that! So, again, be specific. When were you last inebriated? Imagine yourself back in that state. What were the specific sensations – dizziness, sickness, depression, trouble articulating, sleepiness? How did you deal with them – sit very still holding a table, drape yourself over a toilet bowl, lie face down on a sofa, speak very slowly and clearly?

Flu is a set of sensations we might often experience singly. You may recall a headache like a band of steel, aching joints, stuffed up or runny nose, sore throat and cough, fatigue and shivering, but one or two may predominate. For example, you may walk very slowly and cautiously because everything aches and you don't want to irritate a splitting headache; even coughing or blowing the nose might be too much disturbance to bear.

## Endowment

Whatever happens in performance derives from imagination and action. We give particular qualities to places, people, and relationships. Equally, we need to *endow* objects with physical and psychological qualities so that they become very specific to us as a character. We make them what they are actually not. We *personalise* them. When handling them we release psychological and emotional life that informs an audience more fully about who we are as the character. For example, an old satchel given to you by the stage management team can be endowed with sentimental value by imagining this is the first bag your dead parents gave you for school. I'll handle it with some care and affection, as though I'm in touch with my parents. A blank leather-bound book may become an original seventeenth century first edition of plays by Jean Racine. I'll leaf through its pages with respect, caution and awe. A dulled kitchen knife might become a vicious and sharp murder weapon. I might approach it with reservation and horror, and a dark imagination.

Try handling the following objects according to different qualities with which you endow them:

- A piece of A4 paper is the first love letter you had; a piece of Shakespeare's original *Hamlet*; something to doodle on.
- A feather is Goethe's quill; a souvenir from an African holiday with your ex-partner; the material for an arrow flight.
- A cup of cold water is hot steaming coffee to be smelled, seen, tasted, felt; concentrated sulphuric acid; a priceless white wine from the time of the French Revolution.
- A ring is a memento from a lover; your dead mother's engagement ring; a cheap thing from a stall.
- A piece of cloth is the scarf which strangled Isadora Duncan; a cover for your cats to sit on; a present that might or might not go with your clothes.
- A small rock is a piece of rock from Mars; a stone picked up on a Cornwall beach; something thrown through your window.
- A pen is solid gold; a cheap ball-point; the pen of Nelson Mandela.

Each different endowment requires a different response, which will say something different about your character.

We can also use endowment to prompt quick, spontaneous responses among a group. Everyday objects suddenly become something different and possibly threatening as they are introduced, for example:

- A rolled hanky: a mouse or rat.
- Water: acid.

- A paper ball: a frog.
- A cup of paper scraps: wriggling earthworms.
- A tangle of cotton: a spider.
- The floor: red-hot metal.

Of course, endowment and personalisation don't end here. On a simple practical level things onstage cannot always be as in real life. A hot oven will need to be cold but endowed with heat. Swords will need to be dulled and blunted, but we have to believe they are like razors. Whisky won't be drunk for fear of jeopardising the performance, but we'll believe that apple juice is whisky. Imagination and sense memory can supply belief in the artifice, and as implied in parts of this chapter, can also evoke the emotional life which is the subject of the next chapter.

# Feeling

*Compassion may be called the fundamental of all good art because it alone can tell you what other beings feel and experience*

Michael Chekhov

Stanislavski always emphasised action and he made clear: 'On the stage there cannot be, under any circumstances, action which is directed immediately at the arousing of a feeling for its own sake', and '... forget about your feelings, because they are ... not subject to direct command. Direct all of your attention to the "given circumstances". They are always within reach.' Emotions have to arise out of what's happening in performance and not be manufactured and imposed.

This doesn't minimise the importance of feelings in performance, of course. A performance without feeling would be like a person without feeling. We all have a combination of what Stanislavski called the *inner motive forces*, the main psychological functions: *mind*, *will*, and *feeling*. If you imagine a person without feelings you would see them as less than fully human. As Chekhov points out, their intellectual concepts and will impulses and actions would meet without any harmonising, moderating influence that can keep them within the limits of constructive, creative action. Recent history, of course, is full of political action devoid of empathic human feeling. Chekhov puts the idea that all that's visible and audible in a production, like the words and actions, is the *body*. The ideas are the *spirit*. The atmosphere and individual feelings are the soul or *heart*. If we want to see performances with heart we have to allow and encourage feelings to take place.

## What do we mean by feelings?

First we should be clear what we mean by feelings, passions, or emotions – the terms are often used interchangeably. I think we can be more specific and look at how we usually define them in everyday life.

Normally by a *feeling* we mean an intuition or sense about something – unease or trust; or an attitude towards someone or something – love, respect, indifference.

By a *passion*, we often mean a deep, strong commitment and intensity of feeling for something or someone, e.g. for tennis, painting, a lover.

By an *emotion*, we sometimes refer to experiences that can surge up from our memory and cause us pain or joy, but very often we mean something generated quickly in the moment as a result of a frustrated want, an obstacle not overcome, an unresolved conflict with another person. We want to change our world in some way, but if we can't through rational, logical means then we may attempt to change it *magically* by changing ourselves, e.g. by bursting into tears, fleeing in panic, fainting, a fit of anger. Emotions can represent a different way of escaping a problem – I can't solve a difficult mathematical problem on a piece of paper so I tear it up in frustration and anger, breaking the tension, and irrationally changing the world when I couldn't do it through rational means. I might not have seen a person I love for months. On seeing her arrive at a railway station I cannot encompass her totally and immediately and draw her completely back into my world as I would like, my emotion of joy may produce a symbolic ritual of hugging and hopping and dancing around in an attempt to achieve the rationally impossible. I see a scary face framed in my window in the dead of night. My shock knocks me off guard and I don't rationalise how it could get through the window, how far it is to the door, how it could gain entrance through the locks. Instead, the face merges with the surroundings and adopts a dreamlike power to contact and invade me from where it is, so I freeze to the spot wanting magically to make myself impervious (see J.-P. Sartre, *Sketch for a Theory of the Emotions*, University Paperbacks, 1971).

## The controversy

The controversy over emotion or any kind of feeling has always been: do we feel it or fake it? The Representational approach is for faking it. Representational actors may feel something in one rehearsal, then record what they did and aim to repeat the external form of it. They aim for the 'optimum' performance, a repetition of what they perceive to have worked. It's determined intellectually, formalistically and largely mechanically, and the art is seen as being in the skill with which they create the appearance of reality without recourse to spontaneity and experience. Stanislavski quotes Coquelin, the famous exponent of Representational acting (see the Introduction): 'The actor creates his model in his imagination, and then, just as does the painter, he takes every feature of it and transfers it, not on to canvas, but on himself' (*An Actor Prepares*). The actor remains cold towards acting. He pretends, he doesn't live.

This is very different from Michael Chekhov's visualising of the character, which involves an empathic connection with the character and involvement on every level in its action and world, however grotesque that might be. Stanislavski, no less than Chekhov, didn't believe in total immersion in a character so that the actor is 'lost' in the role, any more than modern teachers such as Uta Hagen or Stella Adler have believed that. Only actors of the Lee Strasberg Method school have followed the path of trying to be the character at all times, but I don't need to commit a murder to kill King Duncan believably in performance. The issue is to find the character in yourself, so it is always rooted in truth, and to find yourself in the character so that you are always exploring the range of your humanity and open to transformation. There is always a level of objectivity in that you are engaging in artistic creation and not actually experiencing everyday reality. That said, the real choice before us is to fake everything, illustrating the action, or to act as *if* what is happening in performance is real, to *make believe*. This argument appeared in the Introduction but it needs to be reiterated because of this problematic issue of feeling. For Stanislavski, as for Chekhov, a production without credible feeling would make a cold dish. The audience's senses may be titillated, their intellects may be challenged, but they won't relate to the production in a fully human way, feeling penetrated, moved and challenged by it. The actual experience of feeling deriving from our own human experience and imagination will give freshness, vibrancy and fullness to the action. 'There can be no true art without living. It begins where feeling comes into its own', Stanislavski insists.

Culturally the British have appeared averse to the open expression of emotion. We're supposed to have this reserve and stiff upper lip. But is this a true reflection of what we are? When talking of this tight, locked-up quality, people are usually referring to the *English*. Do they mean the young Jane Austen-period woman disappointed in love or the Victorian match worker who discovers she's got cancer of the jaw? No, they mean *men*. But do they mean the man who's just been made redundant or the man talking on television about his murdered daughter? No, they mean those *upper-class* men who used to run the country and built the Empire; the public school, Oxbridge-educated chaps who kept their feelings well and truly bottled all the better to go out and conquer for Britain. Of course, even that is a stereotype, but this repression of feeling in the British really relates to the narrow upper stratum of society. What then happens, though, is that the values, morality, and customs of this ruling class filter down from the heights of government and property ownership until they permeate to some degree the whole of society. They are not totally absorbed, we don't all become just like them because our own experience of life is so different, and feelings are more easily wrung out of us because our lives are more likely to be filled with struggle and frustration.

In recent years in the performing arts, the expression of feeling has become much more evident, most likely due to a post-war rejection of that old society led by the aristocracy and landed gentry and the greater influence of organisations based in the working class. The Labour Party has had four periods of government. The trades unions gained in power, at least until Margaret Thatcher attacked them with employment laws. People experienced more of other cultures, had TV, and saw American and European films. Actors like Brando, James Dean and Paul Newman brought a new sensibility to film acting through which men could appear vulnerable, raw, and physical all at the same time. Such film heroes have multiplied in number so the expression of emotion seems completely natural, and many more British actors have opted for variations on the Stanislavski approach, and many more drama courses have incorporated Stanislavski-based work. However, the old self-image, however distorted, of the reserved, cool Brit persists. Actors have often relied on sponsorship from their 'betters' to perform at all, whether in nineteenth century stock companies or in present-day companies financed by Barclay's Bank or the Arts Council. The much-hated but persistent characterisation of actors as 'luvvies' perhaps comes from an unfortunate tendency of certain actors to imitate and identify with mentors from the ruling class. Look at the number of knighthoods and OBEs that are accepted even by allegedly radical actors. Even presidents of Equity, a trade union, used to appear in public looking like old-fashioned stockbrokers and bankers until quite recently. This tradition conflicts with the contemporary consciousness and experience I've outlined and is at least one reason why there is, I believe, a continuing block on creating truthful experience and feeling in performance; and why there is a defective interpretation of the Stanislavski approach and a tendency to adapt it to the British 'temperament' and a representational style of acting. It becomes more an intellectualised approach to preparation and less a means to organic involvement, to release of intuition, inspiration and emotional truth.

## The problem of feeling

If we opt for recreating feelings in performance, then a series of problems and obstacles can arise if, that is, we worry too much about it.

*We won't achieve a truthful feeling if we:*

- think about what emotion we think we should be getting.
- anticipate that it's coming up and when it should happen.
- worry that we won't achieve it.
- try to repeat what we had last time.
- try to produce something for effect and not to serve the play.
- squeeze the emotion out through physical tension so what we see is the agitation of the actor not that of the character.
- disappear into the bell jar of a 'private moment', cutting off from our colleagues and the action, to summon up a vaguely similar experience we might have had in the past, e.g. the character's husband has just died, your fond aunt died five years ago.

In fact, we won't feel believably if we make any conscious effort to get the emotion! It is not subject 'to direct command'.

## Access to feeling

My own experience is that it is not difficult to access emotions. When I work with students and actors, I stop them playing emotional states, manners, the obstacle, and the subtext right at the beginning of rehearsal when it is often their first impulse to do this, and I make them focus on finding truth in simple actions and clear objectives. I ask them to see themselves as the characters, to place themselves imaginatively in the characters' circumstances, to allow those circumstances to work on them rather than push in the circumstances, to react off each other and to pursue what they want against obstacles through a range of actions. When we do this, when we trust in our humanity in believed circumstances, feelings and emotions emerge quite naturally, freshly and credibly. By doing this we are allowing our own experience of life combined with our imagination to kick in. Stanislavski: 'You can borrow clothing, a watch, *things* of all sorts, but you cannot take *feelings* away from another person. My feelings are inalienably mine. You can understand a part, sympathise with the person portrayed, and put yourself in his place, so that you will act as he would. That will arouse feelings in the actor that are *analogous* to those required for the part. But those feelings will belong, not to the person created by the author of the play, but to the actor himself.' So, we always use ourselves but in an infinite variety of permutations of objectives, actions, qualities, circumstances and emotions to *go to* the character.

These different emotions coming through the action will be ones we've experienced before. It's highly unlikely that in performance you'd experience some *new* emotion. We have a memory bank of emotional experience which can be tapped to produce *recurrent* emotions. For example, a humiliating public insult will stick in the gut for a long time and any reminder, like an image of the attacking person or place where it happened, may recreate the painful feeling you had and possibly the physical symptoms of it. The anger you felt at a selfish, insensitive lover will flood back given a small trigger, like hearing a particular word or dialect, and the adrenalin may start to flow. The sense of freedom and joy you had on a walking holiday may be reawakened by a photograph, birdsong, or smell of herb.

Stanislavski looked at how to stimulate our ability to draw on our emotion memory. He simply suggested summoning memories of a wide range of experiences, focusing on the circumstances in which particular emotions arose and, without forcing it, seeing if the emotion stirs to life. For example, imagine an enjoyable party; something that aroused anger; a success or failure; something that prompted envy, shame, curiosity; when you were bored, depressed or terrified; circumstances in which you were grateful, generous, expectant, anxious, and so on (*Stanislavski and the Actor*, Benedetti).

In a role then, our own *past experienced emotions* can emerge. Rehearsals are the place in which particular stimuli can trigger access to these. However, what is triggered may not be *specific* experiences and emotions but something that is more 'archetypal' in Chekhov's thinking, and which Stanislavski refers to as 'one large, condensed, deeper and broader sensation memory of related experience ... It is a kind of synthesis of memory on a large scale ... *Time is a splendid filter for our remembered feelings ... It not only purifies, it also transmutes even painfully realistic memories into poetry.*' I understand this to mean that we have a synthesised body of feelings – for example, of pain, love, anger or joy – and these condensed feelings are often what we tap through opening ourselves to circumstances.

Alternatively, Stanislavski claims we may at first be witnesses of an experienced emotion. The character feels the insult, for example, and we sympathise. But *sympathy* can be transformed into direct experience. The actor identifies so much with the character that they actually feel what the character feels by entering their predicament and wanting to find a resolution. When the actor feels that change happening they start to become the character. Stanislavski was blunt about the unlikelihood of having experienced all the emotions you might be required to create in your working life as an actor. The solution is to get as close to characters as possible through sympathy and also increased *awareness* of the world around us and of its history, art, science, geography, so we can interpret the lives of people from other countries, cultures, and epochs. Where factual knowledge is insufficient for our creative role, then as always, we come back to the importance of *imagination*.

This approach is completely in line with Michael Chekhov's emphasis on *compassion*. On a purely human level, we see many people for whom we feel compassion and imagine ourselves in their shoes, whether it's the homeless, earthquake victims, or children caught up in wars. But he also believed that our creative consciousness is innately compassionate because it observes the characters and seeks to identify: so you suffer for Hamlet and cry with Juliet. Compassion 'severs the bonds of your personal limitations and gives you deep access into the inner life of the character' (*To the Actor*).

Chekhov perceived three different types of consciousness, self, or ego operating in the actor. First, there is the *everyday consciousness*, the 'I' which experiences normal existence: family life, social standing, habits, customary activities. When we work creatively and find intuition and inspiration, a different 'I' takes over: our *creative consciousness*, our real individuality using our everyday self as raw material. He also calls the first the *lower* and the second the *higher* self, and the lower has to exercise control over the higher to make sure that the production plan, its form and content, is carried through and doesn't lurch off the rails through unrestrained or chaotic impulses. To hear some practitioners talk you'd think Chekhov totally rejected Stanislavski, had no interest in form, discipline or detailed work and was only concerned with intuitive moments created without effort, structure or preparation. Nothing could be further from the truth, as must be clear from the basic psycho-physical exercises outlined in Chapter 2. The higher self has the responsibility to draw on the artistic and significant parts of our individuality as opposed to the more narrow, egotistic, inhibited, frustrated aspects we may find in our everyday personality, so that what we create are distilled, truthful, and both specific and universal examples of humanity. The third 'I' is the character *consciousness* created by us and our creative individuality, and whose thoughts we now think, whose feelings we feel, whose desires we will, albeit an imaginary creation inspired by our compassion.

## Creative sources of emotion

In this section I'll summarise some of the elements suggested above, and look at other processes out of which emotion can arise organically.

### Given circumstances

The actors and teachers, Lee Strasberg and Stella Adler, had a lot in common. Both attended the lectures of Richard Boleslavski at the American Laboratory Theatre established in 1924. Boleslavski was a member of the Moscow Art Theatre company touring America at the time and was persuaded to stay, along with Maria Ouspenskaya, to teach the Stanislavski approach. Strasberg and Adler both acted in the left-wing and Stanislavski-based Group Theatre, along with others who would become teachers – Robert Lewis and Sanford Meisner – and the theatre and film director, Elia Kazan. The Actors Studio arose out of this company six years after its closure. They both eventually focused more on teaching than acting, and left an impressive legacy. Both could be witty, sharp and flamboyant (see *A Method to Their Madness – The History of the Actors Studio*, Foster Hirsch, Da Capo Press, 1984).

On the issue, however, of what is variously called affective memory (by the French psychologist, Théodule Ribot (1839–1916)) emotion memory, or emotion recall they diverged acutely and developed a feisty rivalry. I'll call it *emotion recall* since that describes what is actually done, as opposed to *emotion memory*, which is what we all possess and is outlined above. It involves remembering a situation in which you felt something analogous to what your character feels in order to recreate that emotion in performance. As you might have gathered from some of the quotes from *An Actor Prepares* above, Stanislavski did write about emotion memory in this book. The emphasis though is on sharpening up awareness of memories of past emotions so they might more easily be aroused by stimuli in the process of work. In the First Studio and the Opera-Dramatic Studio classes there were also exercises to select and consciously use a particular emotion and put it to the service of the play. Nevertheless, when Stella Adler studied with Stanislavski in Paris in the 1930s his *emphasis* was not on this but on the *circumstances*, and this is evident in the book. Adler conveys this view of what he said at the time: 'All the emotion required of you can be found through your imagination and in the circumstances of the play. You must understand that you can only exist truthfully on stage when you're in the circumstances ... But to remain in your personal past, which made you cry or gave you a past emotion, is false, because you're not now in those circumstances. You cannot stitch together a character from how you felt when your pet rabbit died' (*On the Art of Acting*). This, and Stanislavski's other statements on emotion, are conveniently ignored by those who wish to build a wall between Stanislavski and Chekhov, and identify him with Method.

Sanford Meisner also rejects emotion recall: 'The reason? If you are twenty and work in a delicatessen, the chances are very slim that you can remember that glorious night you had with Sophia Loren. The chances are slight that you know the full pleasure of that glorified sex ... what I am saying is that what you're looking for is not necessarily confined to the reality of your life. It can be in your imagination. If you allow it freedom – with no inhibitions, no proprieties – to imagine what would happen between you and Sophia Loren, your imagination is, in all likelihood, deeper and more persuasive than the real experience'

(*Sanford Meisner on Acting*). In a similar vein here is Mamet again: 'The skill of acting is not the paint-by-numbers ability to amalgamate emotional oases – to string them like pearls into a performance ... [it is] like the skill of sport, which is a physical event,' and also: ' it is the progress of the outward-directed actor, who behaves with no regard to his personal state, but with *all* regard for the responses of his antagonists, which thrills the viewers.' Again, Stanislavski might have written this himself. Where Strasberg encouraged actors to invent a subtext behind the author's words consisting of their *own* emotional memories, Adler says: 'Create the place; reach out to your partner; prepare a past for your character' (quoted in *A Method to Their Madness – The History of the Actors Studio*). Her emphasis, like that of Chekhov in whose work she was very interested, was that actors should embody a writer's words and actions and achieve psychological truth and emotion not through self-analysis and squeezing out their own emotions, but by allowing the imagination to fly. Strasberg's son John broke with the Studio to teach on his own. He says, 'My father's work dealt almost exclusively with the expression of feeling. That's not the same as creating life on the stage. He would tell actors, "Express yourself, forget about the story" ... He said art is for the individual to express his view of life – but art has to have form ... good acting is to be spontaneous within the form of the play, to learn to rely on your knowledge of the play' (*A Method to Their Madness – The History of the Actors Studio*).

A witnessed contrast between the Method approach and that of Russian actors was provided by Harold Clurman in an article called *The Soviet Realism, 1963*: ' The American actor ... often goes through an agony of effort to give his acting emotional substance. In its extreme form this becomes a sweating sincerity ... the Soviet actor takes feeling for granted. It is always present; he does not need to strain himself to achieve it.' He adds that the 'repose' of their acting lies in the 'most basic truth of physical action – of look, movement, and relationship to immediate circumstances' (quoted in *Stanislavski in Focus*).

Of course, the other side of all this is that the Actors Studio helped actors break the mould of the old declamatory, artificial style; it provided an inspiring space in which to experiment and develop inner technique; many will say it enabled actors to develop their *own* 'method', to observe and look at the world and not just play themselves. Many actors have done sessions there and, as is the case with any technique, those who rely on it to provide their identity and talent will be poor or mediocre, merely acting out a perceived style, and those with real ability will transcend the technique, using it to develop their own understanding and fire up their intuition and imagination. A second-rate method actor may take Brando in *On the Waterfront* as his model for all parts, but an actor like Al Pacino will transform for each role and often revel in getting away from the low-key and embrace the big and the bold. Equally, a poor representational actor will emptily state lines and completely fail to convince an audience, and a skilled one will bring out meaning, create a rounded character and the impression of reality.

So, our main focus to prompt involvement in the action and access to feelings should be the given circumstances and what's happened before, and the key elements in this focus are imaginative belief in the circumstances, 'If', doing and being, interacting with other actors, and playing objectives that might be frustrated. I try to get something from you, you stop me, I get angry. You verbally humiliate me, I try to stop you but fail, I start to cry. Committing to the circumstances and the action will spontaneously stimulate our own memories of experience and emotion imprinted on our brains and nervous systems. Our compassion, our desire to experience the character's life, will be aroused. Keeping free of tension and anxiety and trusting in our humanity will usually produce whatever emotion is required.

**Richard Boleslavski 1889–1937**

Born in Poland, he studied at the Moscow Art Theatre and became a director in the First Studio, directing Michael Chekhov in *The Wreck of 'The Good Hope'*. After the First World War he directed films in Poland, and in the early 1920s toured the US with the MAT. He stayed behind to set up the American Laboratory Theatre with Maria Ouspenskaya and taught Stanislavski's process. He later made films in Hollywood and published the first account in English of Stanislavski's ideas: *Acting: the First Six Lessons.*

**Lee Strasberg 1901–82**

Born in what is now the Ukraine, he was a co-founder of the Group Theatre, where he acted, directed productions and supervised acting training, but left in 1935 over disagreements on acting process, mainly challenged by Stella Adler. He joined the Actors Studio in 1949 and taught, among many, Geraldine Page, Marilyn Monroe, Jane Fonda, Dustin Hoffman and Al Pacino. Known as the father of the Method he emphasised the actor's own experiences and identification with a character through emotion recall: he defined Method as 'the procedure by which the actor can use his affective memory to create a reality on stage' (*A Dream of Passion*, Methuen Drama, 1989). He set up the Actors Studio West in Los Angeles and the Lee Strasberg Theatre and Film institute in New York and LA.

**Harold Clurman 1901–80**

Born in New York, he was a theatre director and drama critic. He co-founded the Group Theatre with Cheryl Crawford and Lee Strasberg, about which he wrote *The Fervent Years*, and was the second husband of Stella Adler. He directed many Broadway productions including *Awake and Sing!*, *Desire Under the Elms*, and *Orpheus Descending*.

**The Actors Studio**

Founded after the war in 1947 by Robert Lewis, Elia Kazan, and Cheryl Crawford on New York's West 44th St., it developed Group Theatre techniques with professional actors, directors and playwrights. From 1951, it became associated with Strasberg and Method, and American film is full of actors such as Rod Steiger, Robert De Niro, and Ellen Burstyn who studied there. It mounted a small number of productions including O'Neill's *Strange Interlude* and Chekhov's *Three Sisters*. Since 1994, the Studio has collaborated with universities to offer Masters level training to theatre students.

## Sensation of feeling

One of Michael Chekhov's psycho-physical tools relates directly to stimulation of feeling. If a required feeling is proving elusive through the process of rehearsal, and if we don't want to fake it or force it, then we have to resort to some other creative stimulus. Chekhov suggests creating initially a *sensation* of a particular quality or feeling by simple physical movements that can be achieved easily and through your will. I can easily raise my arm. I can then raise it with a particular quality like caution, impatience, hope. The movement now takes on a psychological quality. I can start to move around the room under the influence of this quality and the sensation will become an actual feeling. Not only this, but many associated feelings will be stimulated by this initial impulse. For example, I sit and read a book with caution. I might also become, as a natural and organic response, excited, nervous, watchful, protective, guilty, fearful – qualities you might not have reached had you intellectually asked yourself, 'How should I act in a cautious way?' The initial physical impulse prompts feelings and then a new physicality responding to the psychological changes. My whole body may have become smaller and closed off, hunched over the book, head and shoulders slowly turning to make sure no doors are opening behind me. You can also make sounds or speak some words that flow from the action, giving the feeling another expression and intensifying it. As we'll see in the next chapter, Chekhov also believed that the wider sensation of atmosphere can affect individual feelings, too.

To really reveal how creatively productive this exercise can be, it's worth looking at contrasting results from using different qualities. I ask actors to move under the influence of a particular quality/feeling, to use the movements and gestures, and also to think the thoughts, associated with it.

Under the influence of generosity.

- Physically, they are very open and embrace and reach out to each other.
- They move through the whole space, intersecting, greeting each other, using the main body of the room, only settling on the sides to form groups.
- They move in a direct, light and sustained, easy manner, gliding along.
- They are also open, friendly, affectionate, supportive, joyful.

Under the influence of suspicion.

- Physically, hands are working in front of the body, arms are crossed, hands come up to the mouth, the body is turned at an angle away from others, closed off.
- They move tentatively through the space but tend towards the walls and become stationary, leaning or sitting.
- They are indirect, heavier and sustained in movement, with the occasional light and quick movement – a wringing or flicking quality.

- Other qualities appearing are caution, anxiety, hostility, self-protection, warning.

Under the influence of aggression.

- Physically, they fold arms tight with fists, chins are out, hands come onto hips.
- They use the whole space, and settle both in the main body of the room and at the sides.
- They are direct and strong, sustained or quick – a thrusting and punching quality.
- They also become provocative, challenging, accusatory, violent, defiant.

All this develops from one simple impulse of creating a *sensation of feeling*, from the imagination and not the intellect, and from intuition arising from their individual and common human experience.

Uta Hagen also recognises the power of verbal and physical action to stir emotions. A bang of the fist on a table can stir anger. Justifying it by wanting to shock and disturb someone will fill the action and stop it being mechanical. A physical action of begging, stroking or clutching someone to gain forgiveness may produce tears. She doesn't, of course, recommend making it a normal practice to predetermine an action to get an emotion but emotion and physical action do feed off each other.

## As if

We can also prompt the emotions through using a *transference* (or *substitution*): I'm having difficulty believing in the situation I'm in as the character and finding a particular emotion, but it's *as if* I'm in a similar situation to one I have been in or one I can imagine. We looked at this in Chapter 3. For example, I have to run from a room in panic believing a bomb is about to explode. I find the action of the script and the stage setting unbelievable and cannot find a sense of real threat and consequent panic. I haven't had to flee anywhere in panic so I don't have that specific emotion to draw on, but I can imagine it's as *if* I'm suddenly faced with a fast-moving bus bearing down on me, or I'm on a mountain facing a sudden avalanche, or even worse, in a ravine in the Rockies facing a flash flood. Think of the circumstances, the threat, and what you actually need to do to escape.

## Emotion recall

I've left this until last for reasons suggested in all the above. Sense memory and recall are about physical sensation. You can imagine and recreate physical symptoms and get a strong sense of the physical cause as a result. Using it produces detail, freshness, and belief. Emotional recall may be triggered by a sensory experience but emotions come from a much wider and more complex range of experience than physical sensation. Your own emotional experience may only be approximately similar to that of the character. Trying to recreate your experience may well cut you off from the action, other actors, and the imaginary circumstances. It could lead to actors getting lost in their own experiences and problems. Stanislavski feared that forcing emotions out of the memory could create inner hysteria. Using separate parts of his system in isolation makes it difficult to grasp the whole process. He emphasised the difference between the *primary* emotions, experienced in life for the first time, and the *recurrent* emotions we experience on stage. If actors continually went through experiences, pain and shock such as we can feel in real life, every time they did a performance, they would become damaged. If we recreate emotions through the imaginary truth of a performance then we find that suffering in performance can give the actor and audience a sense of being uplifted because an unindulged truth about human experience is being communicated through a story and we are wiser for it and feel more connected to our fellow humans. This is what most art does.

So, I would only recommend *emotion recall* as the last resort, and that it only be used as an integral part of a whole process.

Stanislavski suggested that if emotions were not flowing straight into performance, then the actor can:

1. Recall a situation from their past in which they experienced an analogous emotion to that of the character.
2. Improvise an imaginary situation in their present which will prompt that emotion.
3. Rehearse the scene informed by these experiences. In this way the past is

brought into the present but a distance is created between you and your memories.

Benedetti (in *Stanislavski and the Actor*) quotes the following example relating to a character who experiences terror:

1. The past experience was that the actor and a friend were walking through a park at dead of night with shopping. They see someone stealing through the bushes. They get scared and stop. They try to move on tiptoe without attracting attention. Then when they feel they've created distance between themselves and the potential attacker they run until they are clear of the park.
2. The present improvisation involves the actor alone with his sister at home late at night. The bell rings. He asks who is there. No reply. He puts on the security chain and opens the door. There is a tall man with a bunch of keys who says nothing. He bolts the door and pushes furniture against it. They wait. He cautiously opens the door. No one.
3. This experience is applied to Act 2, Scene 2 of Macbeth, where Macbeth has just murdered Duncan and the predominant emotion is terror also. It begins: 'I have done the deed. Didst thou not hear a noise?'

The emphasis here is not on thinking about the emotion itself but on the circumstances and the actions producing the emotion. Strasberg knew his Stanislavski well enough also to stress: 'if you anticipate the result, you choke the emotion'. (*A Method to Their Madness – The History of the Actors Studio*). The tendency of young actors is to think precisely of the emotion to be summoned, to think of a sad or angry occasion and hope that the sadness or anger will erupt or be squeezed out. Uta Hagen recommends looking in detail at the circumstances in which an analogous emotion to the character's was experienced – where was it, what time of year, why were you there and what were you doing, what did you want, what were all the things you were sensing? Somewhere in there will be what she calls a *trigger* or *release object* for the emotion (*Respect for Acting, A Challenge for the Actor*). For example, to feel innocent hope I have to go right back to childhood, and the trigger for me is seeing dew on climber roses in the garden, the sun filtering through, and hearing birds singing on a trellis. Or for happiness, I'm playing on a beach with sand dunes and I can smell wet sand, a paraffin-burner and sandwiches. For seething anger I can go back to an old affair and a phone call, and what always triggers me is the corner of an oatmeal-coloured curtain I was staring at as I talked furiously on the phone. So, the triggers are not necessarily directly connected with the events and emotions being relocated; they can be very indirect.

Examining emotional experiences which you feel unable to deal with is extremely unwise. Directors who try to force actors to go into dangerous areas are control freaks. Acting is not psychotherapy. Directors are not God. Don't put up with it! Only use emotion recall if you must and then with caution. You may find yourself at 7a.m. on a cold wet Wednesday, sitting all alone in front of a camera and student film crew in Leeds being required to cry your eyes out. Where given circumstances, objectives, transferences and physical actions fail, you might try an emotion recall – but prepare beforehand.

## Control

A final word on emotion: it should always be controlled because usually we try to control it in real life. In performance, even if your character is uncontrolled, you still have to hold the reins, you have to communicate an uncontrolled person to an audience, and we do this by keeping our actor's monitor on the alert and not 'losing ourselves' in the performance. Lack of control is embarrassing to watch, whether in real life or in performance. Emotion coming through the action will be most powerful when we only reveal the tip of the iceberg, with a controlled, invisible part supporting it. This is the power in the Maly Theatre's work. Adler emphasises it. The best actors achieve it. If you *play only what you feel* every time you perform a character and keep control, the quality and level of the emotion may well be different every time, but it will be fresh, and to an audience will seem as powerful. If you try to push for the same level every time, it'll be fake. I've experienced this myself. A member of the audience came to see a production I was in twice. He commented that I played an emotional scene on stage alone very differently on the nights he saw it, but the time I contained it more was more powerful. I felt this to be true. In this performance, I felt in the moment, spontaneous, alive and in control and didn't push. On the other occasion, the director had been pushing me to let out more and more emotion and not check it, so I became more self-conscious, and looked for ways to extend moments and find new expressions of the emotion, and lacked control. I won't do that again.

An aspect of this control is finding what are called the *organic moments*: the points where the emotion begins to build and the points where it starts to fade. This may vary marginally in performance, but in rehearsal you find triggers in the text itself, in transitions from one objective to another and in certain actions and words. These help to chart characters' emotional journeys, their *emotion through line*, and keep this in tune with their through line of action, preventing the emotions taking over.

There is also the issue of control once the performance is over. If we have experienced a range of powerful and distressing feelings we may leave the performance exhilarated because it has been part of an artistic experience and for an uplifting purpose. However, if these feelings stay with us we need to wind down somehow so we are not damaged by the experience. This can be done in a variety of ways we can choose for ourselves: physical exercise, yoga, meditation, reading  a good book, a glass of wine in front of the TV, or relaxing with your colleagues in the pub – anything that can create a distance.

# 9 Atmosphere

> *The atmosphere inspires the actor. It unites the audience with the actor as well as the actors with one another*
>
> Michael Chekhov

As stated in the last chapter, Chekhov saw atmosphere and individual feelings as the heart or soul of a production. Every situation we enter has some sort of atmosphere, but how many times have you seen a production in which atmosphere is completely lacking? And doesn't this make for a cold and inadequate experience? If we go into a cathedral it can have an uplifting and awesome atmosphere, or in contrast, a dark and oppressive one. A restaurant may be romantic and intimate or cold and impersonal. A library can exude a focused and studious atmosphere or a hectic and noisy one. Winter can surround us with darkness and isolation, whereas spring may fill us with energy and optimism. Equally, a rainy night and a sunny day. A crowd in a narrow corridor can create a claustrophobic atmosphere. A few people standing in a tree-lined square will create something more calm and relaxed. We walk into a room and say there was an atmosphere you could cut with a knife, atmosphere experienced as something very physical. Or you meet friends and you know something awful has happened to them because you sense an atmosphere of fear. You pick up a harmonious atmosphere or a tense one through peoples' facial expressions and body language. So, atmosphere is something we experience all the time in all situations and it arises not from the subjective individual feelings of one or two people but as a collective, objective feeling, as Chekhov refers to it, and can arise through what people are doing to each other, through spatial relations, light and sound, temperature, and so on. If atmosphere is so prevalent in everyday life then we should surely be concerned with creating it and drawing on it in performance.

## What are its qualities?

As both Chekhov and Stanislavski noted, a performance involves a relationship between the actors and the audience, and where there is a strong atmosphere this will produce the most compelling of performances. Actors will experience a greater *unity* between each other and also with the audience, and the audience will be drawn more into the action and find their *perceptions deepened.* Without an atmosphere present a spectator may understand the action intellectually, but with an atmosphere his or her psychological and emotional understanding is likely to be more heightened. Imagine the verbal, and possibly physical, attack by Angelo on Isabella in Act 2, Scene 4 of *Measure for Measure* without an atmosphere of oppression and intimidation (as I saw it done recently by an acclaimed company in London). All you then have is an intellectually described piece of action but you don't understand the relationship, the full meaning of the action in moral, religious, social and political terms, or in terms of the psychology of the two characters and what it means to their 'souls'. If there is no atmosphere of hysteria or terror at the end of Act 3 of *The Crucible* when the girls 'see' the yellow bird on the ceiling of the courtroom and Proctor is accused of being the devil's man, then you get little psychological, emotional, or historical understanding of this repressive Salem community and of what's at stake for all those accused of witchcraft and for the accusers. Nevertheless, the scene as I've seen it performed is usually demonstrated without deep individual feelings or overall atmosphere. So, we end up with a depiction, a line-reading. Chekhov calls this a *psychologically void space.*

Atmosphere can affect every aspect of our behaviour in performance: our *movements, speech, thoughts and feelings, and relations with others.* It can stir a variety of individual feelings, widening and deepening what the actor may already be feeling. Each time you engage in a performance the atmosphere can arouse new impulses in you, keeping it fresh and alive. Chekhov calls this power and dynamic in the atmosphere its *will*; an objective driving force outside of the actors. It will be created possibly by a number of elements – the actors, the design, music, lighting – but, as in life, you can experience it as something which *fills the air* around you and which you can breathe in and gain inspiration from. For example, an atmosphere of happiness spreading through the space around you will inspire you to expand, open up, release. Conversely, an atmosphere of depression may will you to close up and block things out.

### *Exercises*

Chekhov suggests a number of exercises to sharpen our appreciation of atmosphere, for example:

- Imagine a historical event occurring with different atmospheres. His example is the storming of the Bastille, but it could be the killing of a European peace campaigner or journalist by the Israeli Defence Force or the toppling of Sadam Hussein's statue in the early days of the occupation of Iraq. Imagine the action done in an atmosphere of violent revenge. See how it alters if the atmosphere is one of triumphant exaltation, or alternatively, fearful guilt. See how the body language, verbal expression, individual feelings, interactions of the people involved all change under the different influence.
- Imagine atmospheres without any specific circumstances. In the air around you there is hazy light, smoke, cold, the smell of flowers, jarring music. Then try an atmosphere of panic, tension or harmony. Use imagination not cold analysis, and simply feed off what's spreading through the space around you and others. Open up to the atmosphere and allow your movements and feelings to be affected by it. A peaceful atmosphere will prompt calm movements and a steady inner tempo. An atmosphere of trepidation may prompt quicker, anxious movements and a quicker inner tempo, and so on. Try out different everyday actions such as closing a window or putting on a coat. See what sounds and words come through the different atmospheres. Try speaking a simple sentence such as 'Please close the door' and see how it changes under the different influences. The process here is not about forcing things and intellectually deciding what *should* happen, but to use one's imagination to respond to atmosphere as one does in life.

- Imagine an atmosphere around you until you feel strongly affected by it. Do an action suggested by this atmosphere. For example, in an atmosphere of fear lock the door. Then develop the action further prompted by the atmosphere until you create a short scene.
- Take a section of a script and map out a 'score' of possible atmospheres. An atmosphere may run through a whole scene or there may be several within a scene, often suggested by the dynamic created by peoples' objectives as described earlier.

*Stanislavski created exercises on atmosphere dealing with space, light and sound.* There are no doubt a hundred variations on these, but below are some I've used:

- **Space**: a group communicates to a couple of 'foreigners' how to use the local transport system (how to buy a fare, use a travel card, find connections between different services, etc.) – first, sitting in a circle of which they are a part; second, sitting in chairs facing each other so that you are turned away from the 'foreigners'; and third, lying on the floor relaxing and massaging each others' shoulders. Atmospheres of supportiveness, exclusion, and calm may be created by these different spatial configurations.
- **Light**: the group exchanges stories of weird and ghostly happenings – first, the lights are full on; then they go down to half; then to total darkness; a torch can be used to pick out the face of a speaker. How does the changing intensity of darkness affect the atmosphere? Do people become more intimate and confiding in the half-light? Is it very spooky with the lights off? What is the effect of people being singled out with a torch beam – does the atmosphere become more about power and control?
- **Sound**: the group sit in a room sorting out their personal finances, plans for the week, jobs to be done, or preparing some work. See how the atmosphere changes if a gentle/lively piece of music is playing next door; tomcats are caterwauling and squaring up for a fight in the street outside; builders are drilling and knocking down walls in the building next door; a series of explosions occurs and they appear to be getting closer; there is total silence; people are chatting, laughing and playing music at a party in a house near

by. See how the different noises change the atmosphere from, for example, peaceful to unnerved, fearful to distracted, and affect your ability to focus.

## Conflicting atmospheres

Chekhov elaborates on how atmospheres can also heighten the dramatic action. A conflict between two contrasting atmospheres will result in a change. Both cannot co-exist simultaneously and the stronger will become dominant. He gives the example of a mysterious, tranquil atmosphere in an old deserted castle confronted by an atmosphere of noisy hilarity brought in by a group of lively visitors. Either the group yields to the haunting atmosphere of the castle, or their exuberance overwhelms it. I've experienced another possible result, that one new atmosphere is created but which is a synthesis of the two opposites, so something like an awed playful mirth might result.

Equally, an atmosphere may be in conflict with the *individual feelings* of one or more people, and again, either the subjective feelings or the objective feeling of the atmosphere will predominate. For example, a street accident may have an atmosphere of horror and dread which envelopes a crowd, but two people watching are cold and unmoved or egotistically satisfied at not being a victim. Or into an atmosphere of concern over a robbery a person may bring reassurance and support. Do the odd-ones-out become submerged by the atmosphere or do they gradually change it to something else?

Such conflicts and resolutions will create suspense and dramatic tension for an audience, and convey the story and action more clearly and colourfully.

### *Exercises*

#### Conflicting atmospheres

Give yourselves clear given circumstances for each exercise with objectives and feelings that are in harmony with the chosen atmosphere, and imagine the atmosphere is filling the space around you. Then move and act under this influence.

1. One group has created a relaxed, calm atmosphere after a picnic by a river. People are lying down taking in the sun, meditating, reading or quietly chatting. A second group starts up a game of football and tries to involve the

others, bringing on an atmosphere of raucous boisterousness. See which atmosphere predominates or if some new atmosphere is created.

2. One group is in a churchyard in the dark of night, waiting for the other group which is late. The atmosphere is one of uneasy disquiet. People are huddled together near gravestones and worried about any number of possible real or supernatural occurrences. The other group arrive from the pub well-lubricated and resolve to play with the others, creating a spooky, mischievous atmosphere. See what results.

#### Feelings conflicting with atmosphere

1. You are at a birthday party. It's been on for two hours and is full of noise, talk, music, and movement. The drink is flowing and food is being eaten. People are dancing. The atmosphere is one of infectious pleasure. Into this atmosphere come two friends who are in a totally different mood. One is remote, untalkative, and pained. The other is restless, tearful and desperate to talk to people. Does the atmosphere predominate or do the conflicting individual feelings change it?

2. You are touring with a theatre company that has run out of money. Tonight will be the last performance. You will not get paid because unwisely you are not on an Equity contract. You have little cash and can't pay your rent, and haven't even enough money to get home. You are all sitting in a pub near the theatre in an atmosphere of deep gloom. However, two of the company are not affected. One remains positive, practical, and optimistic, and the other is indifferent, cool and offhand about it all. What will predominate or alter?

#### Text

Try reading a piece of text with one or more colleagues, preferably a group scene. Clarify the circumstances and what you want initially, and then choose a variety of atmospheres to feed off. For example, atmospheres of fear, resentment, fury, frustration or reconciliation. Allow the atmosphere to influence your actions and physical movement, relations to others, individual feelings, and vocal quality. As with the exercises on objectives and responsiveness you will see how flexible you can be with any piece of script as a result of a new imaginative impulse.

# Part 4

## Exploring text and character

# 10 Meeting the play

> *If you penetrate through the external facts of a play and its plot to their inner essence, going from the periphery to the centre, from form to substance, you inevitably enter the inner life of the play*
>
> Stanislavski

We now come on to the actual business of applying our skills, intuition and technique to a script. When actors are cast in a play, it's not uncommon to find they have read the play only once before the obligatory group reading on day one of rehearsals. Preparation may have been limited to highlighting their parts with yellow felt tip pen. Other preparation is not usually done because actors assume the director will work with them individually on how to play the parts. The opposite extreme, of course, is where an actor learns the whole part in advance and knows exactly how they are going to do it regardless of other actors and rehearsal.

Stanislavski's approach was very different and is set down in what we know as *Creating a Role* (Methuen, 1981), written in three parts between 1916 and 1934. Part One, written between 1916 and 1920, examines Stanislavski's own preparation as an actor of the part of Chatski in Griboyedov's comedy, *Woe from Wit*. He divides his work into three parts: *the period of study* – requiring openness, receptivity and enthusiasm; *the period of emotional experience* – deriving from the creation of a provisional through-line of objectives; and *the period of physical embodiment* – the physicalisation of the inner life of the character.

Part Two, written between 1930 and 1933, was an account of Stanislavski's work as a director on *Othello*. In what he called a shift to *'a new and unexpected method'* he starts with a section called *First Acquaintance*, in which he reiterates observations made in section one of Part One. He then goes on to *Creating the Physical Life of the Role* through *improvising the action* of Othello scenes, independent of but informed by the script, and finding appropriate objectives and physical and psychological actions for all the characters including crowd members. Finally, he looks at *analysis and checking work done*, which again includes points made in section one of Part One.

Part Three, written in 1934, examines Gogol's *The Government Inspector* and Appendix B looks at improvisations on *Othello*. Both follow the same plan of working on the action of the play with the company before tackling the actual words of the text. Appendix A offers *A Plan of Work*: this draws together the different elements from all three parts of the book.

There is clearly a different emphasis from Stanislavski between Part One and the rest of the book, but that's all it is, and particularly for we British actors who get so little rehearsal time it becomes an irrelevance when trying to apply Stanislavski's approach. Stanislavski is presenting Part One as an actor preparing for a part, possibly not knowing what the director might be planning, and wanting to be as imaginatively well-prepared as possible. He goes from first impressions and open-minded study to using the 'magic if' to find possible objectives and actions for his character. This opens the door to the emotional life of the character which, of course, develops in rehearsal, and finally, the character takes on a full physical life.

Stanislavski in Part Two is the *director*. Ideally he would prefer every actor to have a full intuitive grasp of the character and to have done detailed preparation work during the initial study period. This is not the case in the scenario presented here, which, as in *An Actor Prepares*, involves Stanislavski as the teacher, Tortsov, with his students. That point aside, every group of actors, however brilliant, needs to be drawn together in some way, and what he now proposes is Creating the Physical Life of the Role, which is usually referred to as the Method of Physical Action mentioned earlier, and should not be confused with the physical embodiment of the character. This process is also described by Vasili Toporkov in his analysis of Stanislavski's last ten years as a director, *Stanislavski in Rehearsal* (trans. by Jean Benedetti, Methuen, 2001). Then follows more in-depth analysis.

The Plan of Action in the Appendix draws together the improvisations of the action, use of 'If', and creating a through-line of action – and all this happens before the first company readthrough!

The different elements of process and their ordering which Stanislavski describes in detail in each part, do not constitute different systems, but alternatives within the same developing approach with the same end in mind: organic involvement to produce a full living character. For us in our current system of theatrical organisation, philosophy, and finance, we have to find ways to condense the approach without losing its value.

For Stanislavski, a year's rehearsal was thought appropriate to accommodate a detailed exploration of a play and allow actors time to fully develop truthful and rounded characters. The Maly Drama Theatre under Lev Dodin, following the principles and inspiration of Stanislavski's approach, also favours long rehearsal periods, extensive time for productions in repertoire, and further development of productions once they've opened. For example, the Maly's production of Dostoievski's *The Devils*, by the time it toured to the Barbican Centre in London, was eight years old. It took three years of preparation and once in the repertoire continued to evolve and renew itself rather than fall into stagnant repetition. The company has created 'a permanent group breathing as one' with a common language, understanding, objective and process. Dodin's emphasis is on creating authenticity through the actors finding the 'living life' of moments, the sensations and feelings behind and through the action. The performance is not a fixed entity but something capable of constant change as a result of the actors being alive and responsive to each other, and finding an appropriate and spontaneous physical expression for inner creative impulses at any point in performance (see *Dodin and the Maly Drama Theatre*, Maria Shevtsova, Routledge, 2004).

This psycho-physical approach will be recognised in what I've outlined in previous chapters, and whatever the reservations of British theatre practitioners and critics towards implementing a full Stanislavski approach a common response to the Maly's actual work is one of huge admiration and superlative praise. Simon Callow, in his Foreword to *Dodin and the Maly Drama Theatre*, relates how he was 'overwhelmed' by his first encounter with the quality of the company. It appeared to be the ideal of a company many of us had always aspired to and had failed to find in Britain: a true ensemble, training, rehearsing, and developing together over a long period and realising the aims of the

Stanislavski approach. Callow compares this to his own experience at the time of working on a project with a woefully inadequate rehearsal period, and an inconsistency of approach among the actors who also lacked a shared view of the work. This, of course, is not the exception in British theatre but the norm. To create the practice of the Maly in the British context we need enlightened and sustained funding policy by the government, which at present is cutting grants in real terms, or by private sponsors, who currently only contribute a very small percentage of companies' total revenues and whose motives are more probably based on increasing their own profits rather than the development of the arts. We need a belief in this type of ensemble organisation – both from funders and practitioners – which pays artistic dividends over a long period and demands great commitment from the actors and other creative staff, who will have to forgo other work and the chance of 'making it'. There is now more interest in the ensemble approach within British theatre but, despite constant pressure from the media unions, secure and expanding theatre funding still looks a long way off. I return to this in Chapter 16.

Despite these obstacles to using Stanislavski's approach and achieving the results we want, there is a great deal of the process that individual actors can absorb – outlined in the previous chapters – and then put into action in relatively short periods of time.

## First impressions

Often when actors pick up the script for the first time there is a desire to 'count the lines', to see how big *my* part is. The next stage is likely to be to whip through the text, possibly not reading scenes *I'm* not actually in and highlighting *my* part with yellow ink. This is more likely to be the case with TV parts but in *Creating a Role* Stanislavski gives examples of actors who 'read' *Othello* but didn't have the whole script or only focused on their characters' lines. 'Imagine', he says, 'that you cut a beautifully drawn figure out of a canvas ... Could you judge or come to know the whole picture from that?' As I emphasised in Chapter 4, Acting with Others, your lines come from the action as a whole and what other people say and do to you. You have to study them as responses to the situation, as something arising organically from what has preceded. This is why I would say *never* highlight parts. To do this separates your character from the script as a whole and discourages not only an organic approach but also communication when reading the text. Because it's a mechanical exercise you can also miss out bits of your part only to discover them later in rehearsal. I've actually encountered this but when I told some student actors not to highlight they were amazed because it's such common practice now. In fact, a Cambridge graduate and no doubt 'good mind' who is now a rising starlet, was quoted in a newspaper interview as saying that she had started to prepare her new part before she went on holiday and had already highlighted all her lines in yellow! To get a true sense of a script we have to *see it as a whole*.

Another early tendency is to judge the play from *prejudices and preconceptions*. You had a bad experience with Shakespeare at school or you've always thought of him as a Tudor propagandist or irrelevant to today so what possible interest can there be in one of his plays? You might have seen productions of a play already and have a view from those that will colour how you read the play. Or things you've read or heard may encourage you to see characters as stereotypes or caricatures. Stanislavski insists that to be creative and free we need to come to a first meeting with a play in an open, *unprejudiced* state of mind, with no preconceptions. We need to do the first readings *objectively*, forming our own opinions from what is actually coming at us from the page. These opinions will be formed by our current state of knowledge, experience, and ability to relate the script to real life, and of course, the more we develop in these areas the deeper and more informed will be our grasp of a text.

To get actors off on the right foot in rehearsal, Stanislavski used to have the play read by one person to the whole company, 'presented simply, clearly, with understanding of its fundamentals, its essence, the main line of its development, and its literary merit' (*Creating a Role*). He would ask actors to relate the contents of the play, to tell the story, to see how much understanding they really had from what they'd read and heard. Lev Dodin and the Maly still follow this practice. When the Northern Stage company worked with Dodin on *Uncle Vanya*, he read the whole play in Russian to them on the first day of rehearsal. He gets his own company to tell the story of the play they are working on: 'they revise each other's points, ask questions, go back to the text and reread different bits, they begin to notice more and can suddenly come up with the detail that will define the course of events' (*Journey Without End*). The American, Robert Lewis, also attests to the value of an objective reading by a director or the author. The whole cast hears the *whole* play; if you're (possibly nervously) reading your own part you may not fully absorb details of the play and other people's parts. Everybody hears the *same* play and starts on the same footing (see *Advice to the Players, Robert Lewis on acting,* Theatre Communications Group, 1980).

Once we see the whole and how each role relates to another and have begun an authentically personal understanding of the script, then we can start to read it *subjectively,* looking specifically at our role and personal connection with it. To really come to terms with a play demands several readings, maybe six, before rehearsals even begin. To get to a strong sense of connection with a play and part we need what Stanislavski describes as *artistic enthusiasm.* Any thought and analysis of the play should not be intellectual and mathematical, which is more the way of the scholar, but should engage the imagination and feeling, and draw us into a deeper grasp of the play and how we relate to it from our own experience. Our enthusiasm will stimulate these creative forces and drive us along to fully engage with the play, to open up its dark corners, to share discoveries with other actors, to agree, argue and get excited, to dream about the play, to absorb it into our everyday consciousness.

Once the play has first been taken in like this we can start initial preparation work on the text.

**Robert Lewis 1909–97**

Born in Brooklyn, he was an actor, director, teacher and author. He was a member of the Group Theatre in the '30s, studied under Michael Chekhov at Dartington Hall, and co-founded the Actors Studio in New York in 1947, teaching Brando, Sydney Lumet and Maureen Stapleton. He directed productions on Broadway including *Brigadoon* and *Teahouse of the August Moon*, and became Chair of Yale Acting and Directing Departments, where he taught Meryl Streep.

## External circumstances

Stanislavski starts this detailed preparation by looking not at possible character feelings or at trying to encapsulate the meanings of the play all in one go but at the circumstances presented by the writer: 'We go from the periphery to the centre, from the external literal form of the play to its spiritual essence' (*Creating a Role*). The first step here is to look at the *facts*.

When we come to break down the action of the text in a later chapter, the facts of the play – details we're given about characters, what they do in the action in each scene, what happens between them to create the main events – can be noted in detail as we work through the text. There are facts we're given, though, right at the start relating to character and situation.

For example, in Lorca's *The House of Bernarda Alba*, he describes it on the title page as 'A drama about the women who live in the villages of Spain'. In the character list we find Bernarda is 60. She has a mother, María Josefa, aged 80. She has five daughters aged from 20 to 39. The first act is in a white room of Bernarda's house. It has thick walls and arched doorways. It is summer. A shadowy silence pervades the room, which is empty. Only the sound of tolling bells is heard. This is already a substantial amount of information. Then the first three pages between the housekeeper of thirty years, Poncia, and the maid yield a plethora of facts that set up the whole play. The tolling bells are from the church where the funeral of Bernarda's husband, Antonio Benavides, is taking place. Priests have come from all the villages around – so it's indicated he was a figure of importance, and we find later that this is the case. His eldest daughter, Magdalena (30), fainted before the end of the first anthem – we're told she's the one who'll miss him most, and later we find out that it's exceptionally hot. The dead man used to have sex with the maid behind his stable door. Angustias, the eldest daughter (39) by Bernarda's first husband, is the only daughter with much inheritance. Bernarda's father is dead, and people no longer come to the house. Poncia deeply resents the way Bernarda has treated her. And so on.

*All such facts should be written down because then you know you've acknowledged and absorbed them.* It's amazing what we can miss or forget when simply reading. These facts are not a dry list, but keys to enable us to enter imaginatively the world of the play, to construct the present and past lives of the characters and how they see their future. They indicate motivation and feeling, relationships and social status, the place and time. As we go through the play we also get a stronger sense of the historic and religious setting and the tensions in Spanish society that gave rise to the Civil War which began shortly after Lorca had written the play.

The facts will give you the *previous circumstances* leading up to the beginning of the play and the *given circumstances* at the start, as you can see from the above. Some authors, like Shakespeare, give very little in the way of information on the setting. Everything is revealed in the action, for example, for Scene 1 of *Othello* all we're given is 'Venice. A street'. By contrast, for Act 1 of *The Crucible*, Arthur Miller gives detailed descriptions of the setting which are then backed up by extensive historical notes. The given circumstances are as follows: Who is in the scene? The Reverend Samuel Parris. Where is he? The small upper bedroom of his daughter, Betty, and he is kneeling by the bed. What time is it? Morning, spring, 1692. Why is he there? Betty is lying on the bed, inert. What is he doing? He is praying and weeping over her. The previous circumstances which emerge through the first act are that Betty, his niece, Abigail, other village girls and his black servant, Tituba, were discovered by Parris dancing and singing in the woods during the night, and one of them was naked. Rumours have spread and talk of witchcraft is in the air. People are crowding into the parlour downstairs to get answers. Understandably, Parris, a reverend and leading figure in the community, is in a panic. The tensions are made more comprehensible by Miller's notes. Salem was established by a community of strict Puritans with a government based on their religion, a theocracy as in present Iran. It was an armed camp threatened by native American tribes to the west, the French to the north, and pressed by the sea on the east. Having been persecuted in England for their views they were quick to persecute their own community members for wrong doing and corruption, and imposed strict discipline on all, particularly the young girls, in order to stamp out dissident behaviour. At the time of the play, there is growing pressure for more individual freedom and the community is in conflict over Parris' religious leadership and various long-standing land disputes. It is a tinderbox ready to ignite. Again, if these circumstances are absorbed imaginatively we go from external facts into the inner life of the play and the characters. We see clearly the rough-hewn wood of Betty's room and the roof raised by the whole community; we feel the reckless atmosphere around a fire in the woods where spells were cast and the girls found some freedom in dancing and singing, entertainments forbidden in the repressive Salem society; we can imagine the desperation of a backwoods cleric trying to hold onto his position and some respect.

Some directors in Russia establish a *primary event* – the event that defines and initiates the story within the previous circumstances, for both the play as a whole and for each individual character, which may be the same or different. This may be something mentioned in the text or something which can be imagined from the facts of the play. For example, the primary event for *The Crucible* is the discovery of the girls dancing in the woods. For John and Elizabeth Proctor, their specific primary event might be the discovery of John's affair with Abigail and her expulsion from the house by Elizabeth seven months earlier. For *Three Sisters* by Anton Chekhov, it could be the end of the year-long mourning period for the sisters' father and the preparation for Irina's name-day celebration for the play as a whole; whereas for Tuzenbakh and Solyony specifically, it could be Tuzenbakh's declaration of love for Irina and Solyony teasing him. Dodin sees the primary event for Chekhov's *Uncle Vanya* as Serebryakov's retirement since it brings him and Yelena back to the estate and changes everybody's lives, destroying hopes and illusions.

The next step is to fully understand and justify why people do what they do; to *appraise the facts* as Stanislavski calls it. To act as a probing detective picking up on clues to discover the truth. For example, in *The Crucible*, why was Abigail in the woods? She wanted to drink blood and make a charm to kill Elizabeth Proctor. Why? She was Elizabeth's maid but was thrown out by her after John Proctor confessed to having sex with Abi. So? She's still in love with him and hasn't talked with him for about seven months and desperately wants him for herself. Why? He awakened her and opened up new possibilities and desires and a discontent with the community. What else drives her? She's all the more desperate because she's an orphan, her parents having been killed by Indians, and she lives with Parris. She's the dominant figure among the girls, their leader, and wants power, influence, and some freedom. Probing the character like this even in the early stages makes a creative, imaginative leap. You start to see yourself as the character in the situation, not observing now but actively being in the centre of the action.

## Research

All the facts and circumstances and their interpretation can be filled out and clarified by research, another activity that can be done by actors before rehearsals begin. The point of it is not to prepare academic theses but to provide more imaginative stimuli that will bring the world of the play to life. Stanislavski does not itemise research as a separate category of study, but it is reflected in all his investigations. His own research for productions was painstaking. He always emphasises the need to understand the whole social situation within which a play is taking place. His notes on *Othello* in *Creating a Role* clearly show substantial knowledge of the nature of the Venetian State, attitudes to race and class, and the competition from the Turks. For Nemirovich-Danchenko's 1903 production of *Julius Caesar*, he went to Rome to gather material, while Stanislavski supervised different departments in Moscow to research the text, customs and social conditions, costumes, props, weapons and music (see *My Life in Art*, Methuen, 2001).

So, our research can cover:

- *The general historical background to the script*: the social, economic, political, and cultural nature of the society portrayed, whether it's nineteenth century Russia for Chekhov, sixteenth and seventeenth century Britain for Shakespeare, or Chile and other Latin American countries in the 1970s for Ariel Dorfman's plays.

- *Subjects specific to the play's action*, e.g. military life during the First World War, factory work for women in the nineteenth century, life on Russian estates in Chekhov's period, medicine in the seventeenth century, or prison life now.

- *Subjects specific to the character you're playing*, e.g. nursing, the law, mining, alcoholism or drugs, agricultural work.

- *Relevant visual material*: paintings, photographs, videos, film. Audio material: music, recorded voices and dialects.

- *Uncovering the literal meaning of everything that is said and done in the script*: use a dictionary, source books, the internet. We can't say any lines with clarity and meaning and fully understand the characters and the action if we don't understand what they mean! For example, in *The House of Bernarda Alba* what is the *rosary* part of a service? We have to investigate Catholic services to know. What is the unit of currency, a *real*? How much was it worth in the 1930s? What is the modern equivalent value? We need to know to get a clearer sense of how wealthy Bernarda is and how important appearances are to her.

- *Visits to places relating to the script (if possible!)*: to experience the environment at first hand and make your own original impressions and records, whether it's of the Fen country or Andalusia.

This sort of research, far from being a chore, is actually an adventure, an exciting journey into a new world you might have known nothing about and which can really trigger that *artistic enthusiasm* and new creative impulses.

## Themes

Once all the above exploratory work has begun and the inner life of the play starts to emerge, the concerns of the writer will become clearer. What are the issues they are tackling and what is their attitude towards them? What are the writer's *themes*? Reading other work by the same writer can clarify this: themes often recur throughout a particular author's work. Many of Ibsen's plays are concerned with the conflict between social conditioning and constraints and the individual's drive for freedom and expression of their essential self. In Shakespeare, the importance of free will and self-knowledge and the conflict between appearance and reality recur as themes. Lorca focuses on how social structure, rules and demands can destroy people's lives. Perceiving such themes in the action of plays will affect the interpretation of character and give strong clues to objectives. Sometimes actors don't look at the author's intentions and choose objectives that are nothing to do with the text and it's main concerns. We have to act in line with what the author is trying to put across, we're part of a team with the writer, which is why, when we finally come together for rehearsal, we should actually discuss the play as a company, its themes and what we think it is essentially saying and continue that exploration during rehearsals.

In over thirty years of working in theatre with many different types of director, I have only been involved in doing this with *one* director. It's often assumed that what the play is about is self-evident, or the director puts their view for the whole director/design concept at the start of rehearsals, or what it's about will be left to discussions during rehearsals, but without the whole company being present. So we can easily become distanced at the outset from the play and the production of which we are a part. The process becomes fragmented. This is a terrible thing, particularly when we consider we're dealing with a work of art and not the manufacture of cars, and especially when we are used to hearing practitioners, particularly directors, talk of theatre as a collaborative process. Without the actors there is *no* theatre and yet we are largely excluded from a true collaboration.

This is a good point to look at the words we use for rehearsal. *Rehearsal*, the British word, means practice and preparation. This, of course, is what we do, however inadequate these things are alone. The French word, *répétition*, and the Russian *repetitiya* are awful because of the connotation that you just learn something, fix it, then repeat it. The best word to me is the German *probe* and the *proba* used by Lev Dodin, which both mean a try, an exploration, because that is what we need to be genuinely creative: to probe, to explore, to discover. Such an approach makes rehearsals what Dodin calls 'a zone of freedom' in which anything is possible and it is the actors' creativity that is the essential element in creating the production as 'a living organism' while working as a team with the director and others (*Dodin and the Maly Drama Theatre*).

The analysis of theme also encompasses things we often take for granted such as the *title* of the play and the *names* of the characters. Why did Ibsen call his play *Hedda Gabler* and not, for example, Hedda Tesman (her married name) or The Manuscript (a key act of the play being Hedda's burning of Eilert Loevborg's new book). The play reveals how out-of-place the aristocratic Hedda is in the home of Tesman and bourgeois society generally. She wants to find some freedom, independence and purpose in her life. She is vulnerable as a woman in male society. This points to the title: Hedda is General Gabler's daughter more than she is Tesman's wife. She is still influenced by that background and her class. She was brought up like a boy, riding and shooting, and she uses her pistols in the play, not least to kill herself. It was Hedda Gabler who held such sway over Eilert Loevborg, an influence she seeks to revive. She is also the protagonist of the play and not an adjunct to Tesman. The themes justify the title and the title elucidates the themes. Why is *The House of Bernarda Alba* not called The Five Sisters or just Bernarda Alba? The play highlights Bernarda's obsession with class, social propriety and status, which are placed above the happiness and fulfilment of the daughters. Material matters are placed above natural desires. Freedom is quashed. Men are kept away. She creates a punitive, cloistered world. So the house has a key role in the play. It is property built by her father, so her family is probably new to relative wealth. The cleanliness of the house is more important than people, and it affords protection and sanctuary from the outside world. It is also primarily a prison in which to keep the daughters locked during their mourning period and away from the attentions of unwanted men. Bernarda is also the head of the house as owner and mother, and since there is a feel of classical Greek tragedy about the play with its violence, deaths, and presence of fatalism, perhaps there is also a nod towards those famous Greek families such as the House of Atreus.

The names of characters may also reveal themes and qualities. This is perhaps most notable in restoration comedies where characters are often given names that describe them: Lord Foppington, a fop; Mr Horner, a man with a restless libido; Mr Pinchwife, who constrains his wife, and so on. Stanislavski notes the significance of names in *Woe from Wit*: for example, Tugoukhov, meaning slow ears, is hard of hearing. In Shakespeare sometimes you find a name that is significant regarding theme. For example, the repressed and hypocritical Angelo in *Measure for Measure* is described as an angel on the outward side, and an angel was also a coin: one of the strongest pieces of imagery in the play is to do with coinage and what is real or counterfeit. In *The House of Bernarda Alba*, the name of Bernarda's mother, María Josefa, has a symbolic importance. Her two names in English are Mary and Joseph and she appears with a lamb and wants to escape to Bethlehem. For me, she represents the antithesis of Bernarda: the aspiration for freedom, innocence, joy, an essential Christian spirit as opposed to the rigid, institutionalised Catholicism of Bernarda and the village.

## The Superobjective or Ruling Idea

From all the different themes we can start to develop an idea of what the writer is essentially getting at, their reason for writing the play in the first place. Stanislavski called this the *Superobjective* of the play, also referred to as the *Ruling Idea* (*Stanislavski on the Art of the Stage*), which has the same meaning but the benefit of being distinguished from the actor's own Superobjective for a character. In the British edition of *An Actor Prepares*, there is some confusion between the two forms of Superobjective, whether it's in the translation or the original text: the two forms seem to become conflated at a certain point in the text and one has to use some discrimination and interpretation. Stanislavski is clear at the start of his chapter on the Superobjective that it is 'the basic purpose of the play'. The *character's* Superobjective is the sum of all smaller objectives linked in a through line of action by which they help to communicate the *play's* Superobjective. It is all the more important that we have discussions in rehearsal so that the company as a whole agree on what the play is saying, that there is a collective understanding and will to pursue it, and that it is not just a director's imposition from on high.

Some actors maintain that writers don't always know what they have written or why so we can't decide on a Ruling Idea for their plays, or plays are about many things and it's simplistic to settle on one. I think writers usually know what they've written, although some may be deliberately enigmatic about it or end up writing something not consciously planned. Nevertheless, once the play is written and out in the public domain to be performed the actors need to know what *they* think the play is about even if the writer is ambivalent. We are not in the business of communicating confusion whether that derives from ignorance or fashion. Of course, there may be ambiguity actually in what the writer is trying to say, in which case the Ruling Idea embodies that uncertainty. Usually though there is a clear idea coming through, whether a writer began writing with it or it took over. Also, what we decide for a Ruling Idea is not a simplification of the ideas in the play but rather a distillation of everything that's there into its essence. That may not leap to mind during the stage of first readings and impressions. It may only formulate later on in rehearsal. Also, whatever our preliminary ideas may be they can always change: nothing is set in stone. Crucially, discussing theme and the Ruling Idea is important for developing an ensemble.

How do we actually formulate a Ruling Idea? It helps to know who the protagonist is because it's often a result of their actions. The protagonist is the character without whom there would not be a play, who moves the action forward and creates the major conflict. Brand, in Ibsen's play of that name, and Hedda Gabler are clearly protagonists. However, Othello, who we may consider as the central character, is not the protagonist. It is Iago who leads everything, so that Othello is actually the antagonist. In *Measure for Measure* it is the Duke who pulls all the strings, moves the plot along and creates the final conflict and dénouement, not Angelo, who is the antagonist. We can look at what the situation is at the start of a play and at how it ends, at what actions lead to what results. So, a Ruling Idea for *Othello* might be: *prejudice and jealous deception bring destruction of order, trust and innocence*. For *Measure for Measure* it could be: *repression and denial of free will must be counterbalanced by mercy and self-knowledge*. For Ibsen's *The Lady from the Sea* it might be: *only through free will can we find our true selves and union with others*.

## Genre and form

Of course, what we cannot escape while gaining our first impressions of a play is the nature of its style or genre, and the form in which it's written, and how this may serve the purpose of the author and the themes of the play. Is it comedy, tragedy, drama, absurdist, melodrama, etc.? Is it in poetry or prose or a mixture? A play like Edward Bond's *Saved* is written with sparse, minimalist dialogue that reflects the alienation of the characters. Lorca uses verse and song to heighten his themes: for example, the washerwomen's song in *Yerma* is a lyrical way of highlighting the joy of fertility and pleasure with a man as opposed to the misery of Yerma's barrenness; the verse form used by Lorca in *Dona Rosita, The Spinster* when Rosita's fiancée comes to say he has to leave her but will return intensifies her sense of loss, desertion and fear for the future. *The House of Bernarda Alba* is usually regarded as Lorca writing more in a social realist style, and while I think this is true there is also the lyricism of the reapers' song in Act 2, and there is symbolism in the references to the stallion and mares and in the character of María and her song. The play reads as a drama but it finishes in tragic manner and there are also darkly comedic moments in it. Samuel Beckett uses a poetic prose that distances his characters from normal everyday life but roots them in the endurance of an absurd and often painful existence and philosophical reflection. Noting the genre and form of a text is not only important to understand how they convey content, but also to be aware of the different demands on you the actor to communicate this in a manner that is appropriate and truthful for each. Being truthful as Clov in Beckett's *Endgame* will be different to the truth of performance as Shakespeare's *Coriolanus* or as Aston in Pinter's *The Caretaker* because the characters and plays present different types of reality in different genres and forms: absurdist in poetic prose, tragedy in verse, comedic drama in prose. You always start with the 'If': 'If I am in these circumstances as this character what do I do?' and the circumstances and language tell you how to be truthful for each particular mode of writing.

# 11 Meeting the character

*Being swept away by the play and by one's part – that is the best way to come close to it, to understand and really know it*

*An actor must adjust himself to the role, not the role to himself*

Stanislavski

Our first impressions of the play as a whole will clearly reveal elements of character: we may have an immediate deep intuitive understanding of the character and all the following explorations will come easily, or we may just get a basic idea of it and find there are blank areas we don't understand yet, so a lot of digging will be necessary.

The Period of Study and Analysis sections in Parts 1 and 2 of *Creating a Role* cover what I've outlined in a briefer manner in Chapter 10. There are other investigations that can be made into character at this point before rehearsals start and which of course will continue throughout rehearsals. Some elements of these are to be found in *An Actor Prepares* and some have been developed by later practitioners following and developing the Stanislavski approach. Exploring them will give a deeper and more wide-ranging grasp of character early on, give us plenty to work off in rehearsal and avoid wasting time and creative energy.

# Four lists

This is a method of acquiring a comprehensive, objective and accurate overview of a character. I'll use *The Crucible* as a source for examples. We write down:

1. **What the author says about the character, that is, the *facts*.**

   For example: *Abigail Williams is Reverend Parris' niece, 17, strikingly beautiful, an orphan, and has an endless capacity for dissembling.*

2. **What the character says about themselves.**

   This, and the material in 3 and 4, is word for word and not a summary, paraphrase, or our opinion of it.

   For example, Abigail says: *My name is good in the village! I will not have it said my name is soiled!*

3. **What the character says about other people, including those not actually in the play.**

   For example, if you're Parris, he says of Abigail and others in the village: *But if you trafficked with spirits in the forest I must know it now, for surely my enemies will, and they will ruin me for it.*

4. **What other people say about the character.**

   For example, if you're Abigail, Proctor says of you: *Abby, I may think of you softly from time to time. But I will cut off my hand before I'll ever reach for you again. Wipe it out of mind. We never touched, Abby.* From Proctor's viewpoint, this is something he is saying about Abi and about himself.

These four lists may demand some extensive writing, particularly if you're playing a large part, and you will need to read the play three or four times. But it is well worth the effort. In giving you an overview of what the writer is *actually* saying about the character, which you are writing down and therefore most likely absorbing, it stops you making wrong assumptions, making possibly whimsical decisions, and missing vital pieces of information: all things that can send you right down the wrong track and waste valuable time. Certain knowledge of the character *can* be discovered early on and enable you to fully use our short rehearsal periods for active and productive creative work, as opposed to having to redirect yourself in week four from false trails travelled in week one.

Doing these lists will give you a wealth of detail about your character and others: for example, social facts like age, birthplace, class, and relationships; psychological elements such as temperament, sexuality, ambitions, and attitudes to life and other people; and physical details. All these will be filled out as rehearsals progress, but will prove invaluable as an early insight.

## The Life Superobjective

As we've seen in the previous chapter, the writer offers themes and from these we can conclude a main theme, Superobjective or Ruling Idea for the play as a whole. This will influence characters' objectives and Superobjectives in the play.

However, it is useful to think of what the characters want in life before the play actually starts; something we can deduce from the play as a whole, and which gives us an imaginative launch into the play, immediately engaging our will and feelings. This Superobjective in life is the *motivating force* of the character up to the starting point of the play. Entering the action with this drive guards against predetermination and anticipation of events and consequences: we play the character without suspicion of what is going to happen, rather than being tempted to present the character at the start as they become later on. For example, Angelo in *Measure for Measure* is not a villain in the first scene of the play. I believe Shakespeare's point is not that he is a seedy and hypocritical civil servant, as he is now usually played, but quite the opposite: that he is a devotee of the Bible and the law attempting to be shiningly pure and rigorous, and has repressed his natural desires and feelings in a misguided attempt to achieve this. It is his repression and lack of self-knowledge that make him susceptible to Isabella's own strict purity and vulnerability, and create confusion, turmoil and a repressive response. What he aspires to before the play starts is very different to his actions towards Isabella.

The Life Superobjective can express comprehensively the essence of the character by defining *a basic desire, the reason for it, and the length they would go to in trying to achieve it.*

So, for example, Angelo's Superobjective in life might be: *I want to attain the highest possible purity in my life, because only then do we truly serve as God's example, and I would go to any length of sacrifice and rigour.*

In *Othello*, Desdemona's might be: *I want to devote my life to the love and support of my Lord, because he's become all the world to me, and I'd go to any length of risk and loyalty.*

Hedda Gabler's could be: *I want to find some way to reach courage and beauty in my life, because I hate being dependent and having no purpose, and I'd go to the length of controlling others and breaking accepted social bounds.*

Neither the Life Superobjective nor the Superobjectives in the play are to be played on every line and action, of course. This results in generalisation and playing a state. They are influences and inform the smaller objectives. We play the specifics while having in our consciousness the wider aspirations.

## Inner motive forces

This is a concept to which Stanislavski has devoted a chapter in *An Actor Prepares*, and which he and Chekhov saw as a key defining aspect of character.

All of us have a combination of three forces, *mind*, *feeling*, and *will*, which move us in our everyday and creative lives, affecting other aspects of the psycho-physical technique.

Mind here means intellect, reason, and imagination. Its centre is the head.

Feeling is all our passion, feeling, emotion, impulsiveness, and intuition. It's centred in the chest, or, more specifically I think, the solar plexus, our breathing and nerve centre.

Will engages you on a given path of action, whether aspirational, mundane or habitual, and whether initially prompted by thought or feeling. Will is centred essentially in the pelvis and thighs, and also engages the arms.

Some practitioners also identify mind, feeling and will in different parts of the mind and will centres: for example, the nose is thought, the eyes are feeling and the chin is will in the mind centre; the fingers and toes are thought, the shoulders and knees are feeling, and the elbows and hips are will in the will/action centre (see *Konstantin Stanislavsky*, Bella Merlin, Routledge, 2003).

Stanislavski says of the three forces, 'They support and incite one another with the result that they always act at the same time and in close relationship. When we call our mind into action by the same token we stir our will and feelings' (*An Actor Prepares*). If we respond to something emotionally first of all, a reasoned concept may form and finally the will is stirred to prompt action. If we are first affected by the thoughts and concepts in our role, this can lead to an opinion on them and the stirring of our feelings and will. If we start with the will through, say, a strong objective, it can stir feelings, and thought may be engaged to further what we are trying to achieve. Stanislavski emphasised the need for balance and harmony between the three forces so that no one would 'crush out' either of the others.

Michael Chekhov took this analysis further by looking at how this balance varied from person to person, believing that few people are *evenly* balanced in their forces. He asserted that we can usually identify a *predominant force* moving a character through the action of a script. Chekhov used this approach in his sessions in Hollywood in the 1940s and '50s, asking actors whether their character was predominantly a thinking, feeling or will character. I know from experience, also, that it's possible for this predominant force to change at different stages of one's own life, and for a character's to change as the action changes. A predominant inner motive force of *mind* would mean you always think, imagine and assess matters before acting. A predominant force of *feeling* might override rational thought. A predominant force of *will* can ride over the opinions and feelings of yourself and others. So, for example, Hamlet is governed mostly by intellect, as is Tesman in *Hedda Gabler*. Hedda, on the other hand, and Richard III are arguably driven by will. Eilert Loevborg, and Ellida, in Ibsen's *The Lady from the Sea*, are moved primarily by their feelings and emotions.

Chekhov elaborates on the nature of the forces. Thinking can be cold and hard, or quick in flashes, or slow and ponderous. Feelings may be intense and passionate, lukewarm and heavy, or light and sunny. Will may be despotic and steely, cold or fiery. Identifying how these forces relate and predominate, and their distinct nature, gives us a strong insight into a character and their mode of operation.

## Qualities

Personality qualities or characteristics come through the character's words and actions, but essentially through the actions. When you get down to it, *we are what we do*. For example, Abigail says to Parris: 'We never conjured spirits,' but later we find out from no less respectable a figure than Mrs Putnam that her daughter, Ruth, went into the forest with Tituba and the girls 'to conjure up the dead'. This makes Abi deceitful and hypocritical. Rebecca Nurse, who is 72 and resented and respected by different factions in Salem, enters Betty's room after she begins a fit of wailing and whimpering. She crosses to Betty and Miller tells us that 'Gentleness exudes from her'. She also commands silence. She simply stands over the girl who becomes quiet to the others' astonishment and relief. So we can say Rebecca is comforting, reassuring, gentle and impressive in her presence. Mrs Putnam, on the other hand, is bitter, haunted and accusatory. This all comes from the words, actions, and commentary of the writer. We have to justify these qualities, however, in the same way as we need to justify other facts. Why do the characters act like this? What has happened to them? What has occurred in particular relationships? What are their hopes, objectives and fears? We need to find the reason and impulse behind everything that is in the text. For example, the script indicates that the Putnams' bitterness and readiness to accuse others of witchcraft comes from competition over land, disagreements over the ministry, and their loss of seven out of eight of their children. We may want to dig deeper imaginatively, though. Mrs Putnam may blame others and witchcraft for her loss but we might imagine that the cause lies in her constitution, or that of her husband, Thomas, or in their parenting. We find from research into the real characters on whom the play is based that the Putnam family were once more prominent in the society than they are in 1692, the year of the play. A John Putnam had 800 acres of land, but it was non-arable and an ironworks failed, and the land was later divided into eleven parts among the numerous sons. Putnams dominated the village committee usually. Thomas' father, Thomas senior, had 500–600 acres and was the wealthiest man in the village, but when he died he left his son fewer than 300 acres and Thomas was opposed by his stepmother and her son. The Putnams were responsible for the prosecution of forty-six 'witches' (*Salem Possessed*, Boyer and Nissenbaum, Harvard University Press, 1974). So, in real life, Thomas had family problems, rejection, and declining land and influence to deal with. How much of this real background you would work into your character and imagined background is up to you, but it has to be justified by the text. For example, nothing in the text indicates that Putnam is anything less than a strong and leading influence in the community or that he owns less land than Proctor or Francis Nurse, but a character awareness and fear of declining influence might be useful in playing him.

When identifying qualities, we should look at the whole range of the character, all the different sides. Look for the *contradictions* – these, as Chekhov points out, are what make us human and not one-dimensional stereotypes, and he was renowned for the sharp contrasts in his performances. So, we may find a character who is generous and short-tempered, kind and violent, energetic and morose. We should try to find at least five major contrasting features. In *Creating a Role*, Stanislavski urges the actor to look for the evil in a good man, the mentally weak spot in an intelligent one, the serious side to a jolly person, and so on.

Also look for the *similarities and differences* to ourselves. We have to start with ourselves otherwise the character will only be a facade. What in the character relates to our own qualities, experiences and relationships and the background which created them? What connects us and makes us identify? How is the character different? This is the important question for actors attempting to transform. Here we need to be honest. We may find that all those qualities like viciousness, maliciousness, selfishness, manipulativeness are ones that we perhaps don't or won't recognise in ourselves at present, but they may have appeared at certain times in our lives, in specific situations with particular people. We are all capable of an infinite variety of actions because we're all human. If you genuinely haven't experienced a particular quality then use your imagination! *If* I am in the circumstances of this character what do I do? If I were to be murderous what circumstances could make me like that and what would I do, how would I be? Find a *point of sympathy* with the character, the main way in which you identify. It could be through one of their qualities, the way they are treated by others, their dilemma, their aspirations, or their own attitude to other people, for example.

There are things to beware in this sort of exploration. When asked what a character is actually *doing* some actors will say that they're sort of feeling angry or sad or give a rundown on what's been happening around them – anything other than being specific and describing their actions. When examining the qualities, which we derive from the action, there is a tendency to just write down, say, four, or, on the other hand, to put down loads, but they're all similar and don't reflect all the contrasting areas of what the character says and does. Generalised value judgements like 'silly', 'strong', 'weak' are to be avoided. Instead we should look at what we mean by these terms, what constitutes strength or silliness. For example, it's much more specific and useful to know that the character is determined, resilient and bold, or over-talkative, confused, and slow-witted. Also avoid inventing qualities which conflict with the text and which may just reflect how you would *like* to see the character. Everything has to be justified by the text and the interpretation of the company and director, but this is not to say the actor can't imaginatively fill out and go beyond what the writer has written, as Chekhov frequently did.

## Attitudes

The attitudes of each character to other characters become much clearer through the four lists. It's worth writing down all the different elements in these attitudes, which are formed by experience, thoughts and feelings, and are demonstrated by what each person says and does to others, so you have a clear sense of your relations to every character with whom you connect.

For example, Elizabeth may love and respect John, her husband, but he was unfaithful with Abigail about seven months before the start of the play, which bred mistrust, resentment and a cold distance on her part, and a suspicion that he is still attached to Abi and she to him. John respects his wife but was drawn to the sexuality of Abi. He feels guilty and wants forgiveness and peace from Elizabeth but resents her for not trusting him still and feels angry and reproachful towards her. Proctor sees Thomas Putnam as a manipulative, grasping, arrogant, power-seeker and does not hesitate to confront and defy him. He treats Parris as a materialistic, self-aggrandising hypocrite, responsible for a large part of the tensions in the community, and whom he holds in contempt.

We bring these attitudes into each entrance. This is not the same as playing a manner: knowing what your attitudes are means you know what your relationships are, what the past is between you and others, and what your objectives and actions are likely to be towards them, and those are what we actually play.

## Impulses and objectives

For Stanislavski, the essential aim of the creative process is to produce the life of the human spirit in performance, to get to the heart of a play, to produce the emotional experience of a role, and he emphasised this particularly because so much of what he saw in the theatre was cold, mechanical, and external.

However, he couldn't stress enough that feeling could not be approached directly or forced. It has to emerge from conscious work, from examining the action and circumstances of a script, from preparation work such as I've outlined above. Once we start to grasp the facts, previous and given circumstances of the action, themes and possible Superobjective of the play, and are beginning to understand and see ourselves as the character in situations and relationships, then we are imaginatively starting to enter the world of the play. We get impulses and inner urges that create action and feelings.

In Part 1 of *Creating a Role*, Stanislavski as actor looks at the character, Chatski, in Griboyedov's *Woe from Wit* and explores what physical and psychological objectives *naturally form themselves* when he imaginatively places himself in the circumstances of the character. In Part 1, he focuses on emotional experience as the stage following preparatory study. In Part 2, it is the physical action that is the prime focus after first impressions and study. However, central to both are action and objectives. In Part 1, though, he looks at the feelings of the character as the inner impulse for the objectives. Chatski has been abroad and is returning to see his childhood friend, Sophie, to whom he was devoted. Stanislavski places himself in the position of a man returning who loves a woman and wants to see her. The objectives that come to mind derive from his own experience and universal experience of people in this situation. He lets them arise consecutively and logically. He wants to get to see his beloved as soon as possible. So, he wants to get through her gates and bypass the welcoming yardman. He wants to get into the house and find out where Sophie is. She appears but is now different and grown-up, so he wants to weigh up how she's changed and to see deep into her soul. He wants to kiss her in a new and appropriate way. Perceiving her coldness and embarrassment he feels wounded and disillusioned and correspondingly wants to escape the situation.

Any text can be approached in a similar way – finding objectives from impulse and imagination, not intellectually, and working out a provisional through line of action that will be tested in rehearsal, and changed or not changed, but which will certainly be useful from the start since you will have ideas about what is behind the lines. It will be of immediate use if you work with a director who, like Stanislavski, breaks the action into units and gets the actors to improvise it using their understanding of what the character wants and might do to achieve it. It is this aspect of the process that we shall look at in the next chapter.

# 12 Discovering the action

> *Real acting begins when there is no character as yet, but an 'I' in the hypothetical circumstances. If that is not the case, you lose contact with yourself, you see the role from the outside, you copy it*
>
> Stanislavski

As I pointed out in the last chapter, in Part 2 of *Creating a Role* Stanislavski focuses on the physical action of *Othello*, which he calls the 'new and unexpected method' of helping the actors to get into the feeling and inner life of their roles by creating the physical life first. The process is what we've come to know as the Method of Physical Action, which is really a method of *psycho-physical action* because it 'is based on the close relationship of inner with outer qualities' (*Creating a Role*).

One always has to bear in mind that Stanislavski was evolving his practice over decades and the terms he uses vary at different times and in different situations and can often appear confusing, which is why I shall attempt to simplify these as we go through this chapter. What is clear, though, is that what Stanislavski wrote in *An Actor Prepares* is consistent with his practice in the Opera-Dramatic Studio sessions and in rehearsals recorded over the last ten years of his life by the actor, Vasili Toporkov. Although he resisted calling his approach a method, implying something rigid and fixed, the aims of it remained constant: the creation of a truthful inner and outer life that reproduces natural human processes and behaviour and serves the writer's play. Central to this approach is the use of objectives and actions. The emphasis we now find is on performing these simply, economically and truthfully *to create the action of a text but without using the words of the text*. 'Perhaps the most difficult thing to do is to execute the simplest physical objectives like a real human being' (*Creating a Role*). We improvise the text at the first stage of rehearsals to uncover the essential action of it, the dynamic between characters, the source which gives rise to the lines so that we avoid the danger of reciting lines mechanically, getting into a speech pattern, and settling too soon on a particular interpretation of them.

Stanislavski, as his alter ego Tortsov in *Creating a Role*, asks two students to play the first scene in *Othello*. Iago and Roderigo enter the street where Brabantio, Desdemona's father, lives. Roderigo is angry that Othello has married Desdemona secretly because he wanted her himself and has paid Iago to help him win her. Iago's plan is to rouse Brabantio, poison him against Othello and set him and his men to confront him. Stanislavski requires them simply to make the entrance and then raise the alarm. This proves difficult because as always in these rehearsals the imaginary students make all sorts of terrible acting mistakes. They 'act' walking, try to entertain, stand facing out to the audience, fail to establish where the house is, falsely bustle and do too much, focus on the audience or themselves as actors, and so on. Tortsov insists that 'every actor must be his own director' and gets them to sort out the geography of the situation. He asks them to use 'If': if I am in front of Brabantio's house (now represented by some rehearsal chairs) and I want to raise the alarm and set him onto Othello what do I do? Then things start to improve. They develop a logical sequence for the score of the action. They enter and check no-one is watching or listening to them. They examine the windows of Brabantio's house for any sign of life. If they see any they must attract attention through simple and realistic methods such as calling up and waving arms. If no-one hears them they throw stones at the windows. If that fails they hammer on the door. During this, the actor playing Iago must also convince Roderigo to play the most active part and keep his own role secret, so a psychological element enters the action. The action as a whole, of course, is meaningless unless it is justified by the actors' understanding of why it is happening, what their larger objectives are, and of the subtext. In Iago's case this is but the first step in trying to destroy Othello. All the objectives and actions he employs will work to that goal, but it will only become clear if the actor plays each simple objective and action truthfully – realistically, logically, organically – as he goes along his through line of action. All the actors need to do at this stage on their entrance is to think of their objectives and the basic actions needed to fulfil them. Words will be invented to express them. Some may actually come from remembered parts of the text, and certainly the lines will be more easily absorbed as a result of having done the action giving rise to them. When rehearsal with the actual text begins, Stanislavski, like successive directors since, observes that the actors 'do not rattle off' their parts but now make full sense of the words and bring them to life in carrying out the objectives.

In Stanislavski's rehearsals for Gogol's *Dead Souls* and Moliere's *Tartuffe*, recorded by Toporkov, there is the same emphasis on physical action and the impulse behind it. He takes the circumstances, looks at the dilemma of the characters, determines their objectives and gets the actors to ask themselves, 'If I am in these circumstances what do I do?'. At one stage Toporkov, who is playing the part of Chichikov in *Dead Souls*, asks Stanislavski, 'But what about his character, his manner. What I do isn't Chichikov' (*Stanislavski in Rehearsal*). Stanislavski responds that we always have to start with ourselves and follow the laws of the creative process, and when he can do the action skilfully and purposefully then he is already near the character. Why? Because if, for example, he wants to make a favourable impression on someone and realistically ingratiates, deceives and flatters them to achieve that he is already being a different person. Other elements like the Superobjective and predominant inner motive force will be influencing the action as well. The full development of the character, with incorporation of an imagined life history, inner images and vocal and physical attributes will grow out of this foundation work as rehearsals progress.

In his study on Gogol's *The Government Inspector* Stanislavski reiterates this basic theme: 'So play every part in your own right in the circumstances given you by the playwright. In this manner you will first of all feel yourself in the part. When that is done it is not difficult to enlarge the whole role in yourself' (*Creating a Role*). So the key points here are: start with yourself in the circumstances of the character, find the impulses behind the action, and play the objectives and actions with sincerity. This will give us a strong and immediate sense of *finding ourselves in the character* and provide the basis for future character development. So we progress from the physical to the spiritual, the conscious to the subconscious, exploring the vital reasons, circumstances, and feelings the actions evoke and which Stanislavski saw as the most important aspect of a performance.

The Method of Physical Action, then, is about the discovery of character and dynamic between characters through exploring the given circumstances and action in the text. The process of putting this into practice was different to long round-the-table discussions Stanislavski had earlier used for analysis of the text, and he called it *analysis through action.* After the actors had done their initial study and made their first acquaintance with the play and their roles, as outlined in Chapters 10 and 11, they would first read a scene in rehearsal, and then discuss briefly the given circumstances, units and possible objectives, facts appearing in the text, and events occurring. Then came the improvisation of the action: without dependence on the words of the text the actors place themselves imaginatively in the circumstances, test how much they understand of the action and their parts, try to find freedom within the agreed structure, and create a genuine dynamic between themselves as the actor/characters, from which emerges a *score of physical actions* that gives the production a basic structure. Initially the impro might be a silent experiment, then use only those words which are necessary, and then move closer to the actual words of the script. The impro would then be assessed in terms of what was achieved and what was missed; whether the objectives and actions played were appropriate for creating the action and perceived intentions of the author.

Eventually the actors need the actual words of the text to express fully their thoughts, actions, and deepest needs, and Stanislavski would provide them through what we know today as the *feeding* process. The director or other actors might stand behind the speaking actors and neutrally but clearly deliver the lines one thought at a time, and the actor uses the language to express what they've come to understand lies behind it. In this way the text is absorbed organically rather than learned mechanically in a particular manner. 'At first they [the words] are alien, strange, remote, and often incomprehensible. But they have to be reborn, made into something vitally necessary, your own, easy, desired – words you would not change, drawn from your own self' (*Creating a Role*). Even if we do not have time for such extensive improvisation, even some degree of it bears fruit.

I want to diverge for a moment and look at a typical critical English viewpoint. Peter Hall, in *Shakespeare's Advice to the Players* (Oberon Books, 2003), insists that with Shakespeare 'First comes the form and second comes the feeling'. Of course, the form, how the content is expressed on the page, is what the actor meets first with *every* writer, and it's only a study of the form *and* the content, the given words and actions, that tells you who the characters are and what they want and can lead you into their inner life and feelings. This is what Stanislavski maintained, although Mr Hall asserts the opposite. He maintains that many English-speaking actors believe 'that if they feel right, they will speak right. If the emotion is there, they trust that Shakespeare's blank verse ... will follow automatically'. I don't believe *many* actors do this, but what is familiarly misleading is that he blames 'a hundred years of Stanislavski and the elaboration of his acting techniques into the American Method' for this alleged approach, indicating that he can't have read closely what Stanislavski actually wrote. As should be clear by now, Stanislavski advocates starting with the text and the action from which you can move to feeling, whereas the Strasberg approach is much more focused on work on emotion memory from the start. The clarity and full expression of any text was of great importance for Stanislavski, and much less so for Strasberg. Hall directed Dustin Hoffman as Shylock in the 1989 production of *The Merchant of Venice* and apparently Hoffman used improvisation 'to get in touch with the character's feeling'. Hall didn't approve but thought it was 'marvellous to watch because the improvisations were very alive. But they weren't Shakespeare'. Well of course they weren't Shakespeare, an improvisation is never the actual words of a writer but they were no doubt inspired by Shakespeare's text and may have helped Hoffman imaginatively bring the text to life. Apparently when he tried to match Hall's 'clues' on approaching the text to an *improvised* speech he lost sleep and concluded 'You can't improvise this shit', which Hall agreed with 'trying to keep the note of triumph out of my voice'. Hall implies that Hoffman was avoiding the actual text, and then acceded to work 'assiduously on the form of the text' having learned the error of his ways but the basic message is that improvisation generally is a waste of time! Clearly Stanislavski's improvisational work on creating the *action* of the play without using the text was, and is, a creative means of exploring the impulses behind the lines and leading actors to the form of the text in a way that discourages mechanical recitation, a fault that is only too familiar in many of our own Shakespeare productions. Detailed work on the form, structure, and precise meaning of the language is then necessary but that doesn't in any way devalue improvisation as a creative tool. As Michel Saint-Denis said in *Training for the Theatre* (Heinmann, 1982), 'Improvisation is the way to liberate and stimulate invention. It is a fundamental way of working that opens up new and unexpected horizons ...'.

## Breaking down the action

When Stanislavski and his actors started working on the action of a text they broke it down into manageable sections, large, medium and small, and he gave these and the objectives within them different names at different stages of his work, for example, in his studio sessions and in his writing. The English translation of his books has alternative terms as well, as I indicated in Chapter 5. I shall opt for more consistent terms that I hope will be clearer, but I'll indicate the alternative terms you might come across as well.

### Episodes and Superobjectives

The larger sections of text are called *episodes* (*bit* in the Russian books and *unit* in the English translation) and should clearly define the main shifts in the plot, action and dynamic between the characters. In the Opera-Dramatic Studio sessions, Stanislavski had his actors study a number of plays. Episodes for Chekhov's *The Cherry Orchard* were conceived as each of the four acts:

1. Ranevskaya and family return home from Paris to her estate in Russia;
2. the last family outing;
3. the cherry orchard is sold to Lopakhin;
4. the family leave their home forever.

For *Hamlet*, he makes the episodes smaller. So, the first few, for example, are:

1. The ghost of Hamlet's father appears on the battlements;
2. Claudius establishes himself as the new king;
3. Hamlet hears of the ghost and agrees to watch that night;
4. Polonius warns Ophelia not to trust Hamlet and Laertes leaves for France (*Stanislavski and the Actor*, Benedetti).

Michael Chekhov, in *To the Actor*, asserts that well-written plays can all be divided into three sections: the plot generates, unfolds and concludes. In *King Lear* these main episodes are Lear's foolishness and tyranny in the division of his kingdom; the onset and development of the destructiveness of Goneril, Regan, and Edmund; and the defeat of these forces and establishment of a new order. Each has a major climax and they mark also the changes and development in Lear, what is sometimes called the *arc of the character.* He begins in error and delusion, enters chaos, suffering and judgment, and ends with an enlightened consciousness. How we all divide a text into episodes will probably vary. This is not an academic rigid exercise but one to help our creativity. The key thing to observe is that they follow the main shifts in the action and dynamic of the play.

Within each episode your character will have numerous objectives and a through line leading to a *Superobjective.* (In the Opera-Dramatic Studio sessions summarised by Benedetti, Stanislavski called this the *Basic Action* or *Creative Task.* Sonia Moore calls it the *Main Action.* In the Russian books it's *Task,* and in the English, *Objective.* For reasons of clarity stated earlier I'll stick with the basic term *Objective* for what I want and *Action* for what I do to achieve it.) You may find you have a Superobjective running through the whole play for your particular character, which would mean the dynamic shifts in the action do not change you fundamentally. Lear clearly is changed dramatically by events of his and others' making. He may have three distinct Superobjectives in the course of the play. To try to attribute one only to him running through the whole play and leading to his state at the end of the play would cause the actor to anticipate the ending and distort the portrayal of Lear at the beginning: to come to some sort of self-knowledge and enlightenment is not what Lear wants at the beginning. On the other hand, in *The House of Bernarda Alba,* Bernarda's possible Life Superobjective to protect the propriety and reputation of her House could be reflected in the play as one Superobjective running all the way through in different ways: *I want to make sure my daughters behave with propriety.* Angustias, the eldest daughter, whom Pepe El Romano has started to court, might also have one Superobjective in the play: *I want to make sure Pepe becomes my husband.* There is no rigid blueprint for working out the episodes and Superobjectives. The pattern will vary for every play and character. The important thing is that we do what will help us best understand and connect with the character. For example, although we can discern one Superobjective for Bernarda, it might help the actor playing her to look at what she actually does to achieve it in each episode and give herself an appropriate objective for each one: in Act 1, to set the girls on their necessary course of mourning following the death of their father; in Act 2, to make them behave with propriety when conflicts are erupting between them; in Act 3, to keep everything calm and harmonious against rumblings of disaster, and finally to put a stop to the uproar created by Adela and Pepe.

## Scenes and given circumstances

Medium-size sections are *scenes*. There are the numbered or named Scenes given us by the writer, of course, but by a scene we usually mean a section of the text in which a clear piece of action takes place between characters on stage together for a period of time. These are marked by significant entrances and exits of characters. So, there may be a number of scenes within a writer's Scene. For example, in *The Crucible*, which we'll look at in some detail soon, we have four acts and no marked Scenes, but in the first three and a half pages there are numerous scenes marked by entrances and exits. So we have short scenes between Parris and Tituba; Parris and Abigail; Parris, Abi and Susanna Walcott; Parris and Abi; and Parris and Mrs Putnam.

For the act as a whole, there are previous and given circumstances, some of which we've already looked at; but for each character coming into each of the scenes there are specific circumstances. Before each entrance the actor has to imagine what's happened before and the circumstances now, as outlined in earlier chapters: Who am I? Where have I been and what happened there? Where am I now? Where might I go to later? Why am I here? What is the time? And what is the first thing I want on entering the situation and my overall objective? Once the scene is over and we leave the circumstances, we need to imagine what happens *between* scenes from what we're given in the text. This constitutes the previous circumstances for our next entrance. In this way, we create a continuing chain of circumstances on and off stage – *the second plan mentioned earlier* – and a stronger sense of the life of the character.

Each scene may be short or long, may involve one character or many, may have one smaller *unit* or several, and the actor may have a number of objectives within it or just one. Again, there is no blueprint. We may find that we have several objectives in a scene but that there is one overall objective linking them like vertebrae in a spine, the through line of the scene. The character's Super-objective in an episode or the whole play performs the same function. Stanislavski drew it like this:

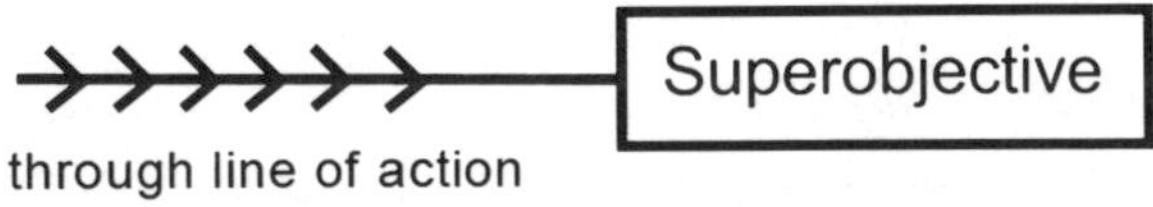

For example, Isabella, in her first scene with Angelo in *Measure for Measure*, Act 2. 2, has an objective running right through the scene marked by her entrance and exit: *I want to persuade Angelo to let my brother, Claudio, live*. Within this are smaller objectives serving that end. We'll look at this in detail later.

## Units and objectives

Here we come to the moment-by-moment business of bringing a text to life. The smallest sections into which we break down the text are *units*. (In the Studio: *events* or *facts*. In the Russian: *bits*. In the English: *units*.) A unit is defined by a clear piece of thought and action, by a specific dynamic between characters. It might be only one word or a line, or it could run for pages. Again, there is no formula. Every page of script may be different. Often actors divide up the text too much, mistaking units for subjects of conversation. For example, two girlfriends discuss boys in general, a particular boy, their clothes, and what they're doing that evening. The reason for the whole conversation is competition over this particular boy. One girl wants to find out the intentions of the other, and the other wants to conceal them. That dynamic creates the unit, not the individual subjects within it.

Once we have decided where the units are we give them titles, and we tend to do this in our own special ways. Some will use a brief heading or a metaphor. So the girlfriends' conversation might be called An Awkward Discussion or Storms Gather. Others may describe the situation a bit more: the friends discuss boys. An example from Stanislavski's study of *The Cherry Orchard* is 'Trofimov, left alone, reveals his love for Anya' (*Stanislavski and the Actor*). I prefer to express the dynamic, the dramatic conflict, what the characters are actually *doing* to each other. So the title could be: A tries to uncover B's true intentions, and B deflects her from the truth. If you read all the unit titles together you should get an accurate grasp of the whole narrative line of the play, *the through line of action*.

We see from the last example that the dynamic of the unit will indicate the *objectives* (*task* in the terminology of the Studio and the Russian text; Sonia Moore uses *action*). Here the objectives are: *I want to uncover B's true intentions*, and *I want to deflect A from the truth*. I explained objectives in Chapter 5. To reiterate briefly, in improvisations we invent lines to pursue the objective, and on text we use primarily our imaginations to uncover what the character wants from the words and actions given us, then we play the objective through the lines to give them full sense, spontaneity and life. The objectives engage our will and prompt feelings and are a key impulse to action. They give an inner structure and avoid conscious thought on *how* lines should be said, allowing for greater freedom of expression. They help us to give the impression we are inventing the lines as we speak them, *creating the living word* (*Creating a Role*). Because we may say them freshly each time, we are improvising on text and finding moment by moment involvement in the action. As Stanislavski says in *Creating a Role*, 'The objective gives a pulse to the living being of a role'. Even if a director does not break the text down into units with a company, we still need to work out our objectives. Of course, this will be the case when working outside theatre in TV, radio and film. All the preparation work on a role is down to you, and the better prepared you are the more confident and flexible you'll be.

As I've said, units may be very short or a page or more. In the longer ones, you may find there is more than one objective. Some practitioners maintain that each unit can only have *one* objective but there is no rigid formula. Even where there is one main objective running through a unit, you may find a closer connection to the text by identifying smaller objectives within it. For example, in *Measure for Measure*, Isabella goes to see her brother, Claudio, after Angelo has proposed she have sex with him in return for Claudio's life. Her overall objective in the first unit is to *resolve him to die for the sake of her chastity*, but the language suggests some changes of tack which are distinct impulses running through a number of lines, so the sub-objectives could be: I want to put him off seeking a way out, to make sure he's willing to die, to make the situation with Angelo clear to him, and then at the end, to resolve him to death. Even in a smaller unit, although there may be a clear main objective you'll often find an objective that shouldn't be ignored if all the action is to be performed fully and clearly and which doesn't constitute a separate unit in itself. For example, the main action in a unit could be an argument between two people but it's triggered by one of them entering and wanting to find out how the other is feeling. Sometimes, actors make all the objectives too short, confusing them with *actions*, the means or tactics to achieve them, and define them as, for example, I want to attack you, I want to shame you, I want to punish you. To have so many tiny thoughts is going to make the process too conscious and hold you back on every line. What we want to aim for is getting an impulse from the objective that will take us through a body of text without having to think consciously, so that our imagination and feelings are evoked and will is engaged until we reach the next objective, which propels us forward again into spontaneous action and interaction, rather like the continuous explosions that drive a car.

The objectives are driven by the *actions*, such as to persuade, shock, and humiliate. Before each action there is a *beat*, a small change of thought and tactic, a new impulse and breath, which gives rise to the action and demands a psycho-physical change in the way the actor communicates vocally and physically. Every new action requires us to come back to our centre as opposed to the common tendency of saying a few lines with different actions in the same way with an inflexible vocal pattern and fixed physicality. In the early stages of study and rehearsal it's important to work slowly on the text to explore the transitions between objectives and how you move organically from one to another. Also, without rushing – another common tendency – to observe all the different beats and allow yourself to have ease and time to fully express the actions. To caress and to warn, to plead and to challenge should have different energies and tempos, and different vocal and physical qualities, but that can only come out of ease and inner stillness. To rush sets you back and you may never recover in our short rehearsal periods. Directors who don't understand the acting process described in this book like to press for early results, and damage the actors and their own productions. They mistake false energy and pushing for giving, and fail to encourage genuine communication between actors.

Amusingly, the term *beats* apparently comes from a misunderstanding. It's a term sometimes applied to smaller units in the States, and it's what American actors thought the actor teachers from the Moscow Art Theatre were saying in their Russian accents when they referred to *bits*. *Bit* is the term Stanislavski used in the Russian text of his books and which is translated as unit in the English versions. Whatever the confusion, as Uta Hagen points out (*Respect for Acting*), *beat* is a good term because it implies 'a pulse as in music'. I, and others, now use the term in connection with actions not the objectives, but it conveys the sense of rhythm, pause, breath, tempo, common to music and important for actors to note on text.

Finally, every objective has obstacles to overcome and there is something at stake, as we saw in the earlier chapter on objectives.

## Text examples

Below are two examples of how we can break down text according to these principles. They are from *The Crucible* and *Measure for Measure*, which I'll print first as they appear in their Penguin texts so you can give them a straight reading, and second in analysed and 'unit-ed' versions. It would obviously help if you know these plays in full.

### **The Crucible** by *Arthur Miller*

#### Act Two

*The common room of Proctor's house, eight days later.*

*At the right is a door opening on the fields outside. A fireplace is at the left, and behind it a stairway leading upstairs. It is the low, dark, and rather long living-room of the time. As the curtain rises, the room is empty. From above,* **ELIZABETH** *is heard softly singing to the children. Presently the door opens and* **JOHN PROCTOR** *enters, carrying his gun. He glances about the room as he comes toward the fireplace, then halts for an instant as he hears her singing. He continues on to the fireplace, leans the gun against the wall as he swings a pot out of the fire and smells it. Then he lifts out the ladle and tastes. He is not quite pleased. He reaches to a cupboard, takes a pinch of salt, and drops it into the pot. As he is tasting again, her footsteps are heard on the stair. He swings the pot into the fireplace and goes to a basin and washes his hands and face.* **ELIZABETH** *enters.*

**ELIZABETH:** What keeps you so late? It's almost dark.
**PROCTOR:** I were planting far out to the forest edge.
**ELIZABETH:** Oh, you're done then.
**PROCTOR:** Aye, the farm is seeded. The boys asleep?
**ELIZABETH:** They will be soon. [*And she goes to the fireplace, proceeds to ladle up stew in a dish*]
**PROCTOR:** Pray now for a fair summer.
**ELIZABETH:** Aye.
**PROCTOR:** Are you well today?
**ELIZABETH:** I am. [*She brings the plate to the table, and, indicating the food*] It is a rabbit.

**PROCTOR:** [*going to the table*] Oh, is it! In Jonathan's trap?

**ELIZABETH:** No, she walked into the house this afternoon; I found her sittin' in the corner like she come to visit.

**PROCTOR:** Oh, that's a good sign walkin' in.

**ELIZABETH:** Pray God. It hurt my heart to strip her, poor rabbit. [*She sits and watches him taste it*]

**PROCTOR:** It's well seasoned.

**ELIZABETH:** [*blushing with pleasure*] I took great care. She's tender?

**PROCTOR:** Aye [*He eats. She watches him*] I think we'll see green fields soon. It's warm as blood beneath the clods.

**ELIZABETH:** That's well.

[*Proctor eats, then looks up*]

**PROCTOR:** If the crop is good I'll buy George Jacob's heifer. How would that please you?

**ELIZABETH:** Aye, it would.

**PROCTOR:** [*with a grin*] I mean to please you, Elizabeth.

**ELIZABETH:** [*it is hard to say*] I know it, John.

[*He gets up, goes to her, kisses her. She receives it. With a certain disappointment, he returns to the table.*]

**PROCTOR:** [*as gently as he can*] Cider?

**ELIZABETH:** [*with a sense of reprimanding herself for having forgot*] Aye! [*She gets up and goes to pour a glass for him. He now arches his back*]

**PROCTOR:** This farm's a continent when you go foot by foot droppin' seeds in it.

**ELIZABETH:** [*coming with the cider*] It must be.

**PROCTOR:** [*drinks a long draught, then, putting the glass down*] You ought to bring some flowers in the house.

**ELIZABETH:** Oh, I forgot! I will tomorrow.

**PROCTOR:** It's winter in here yet. On Sunday let you come with me, and we'll walk the farm together; I never see such a load of flowers on the earth. [*With good feeling he goes and looks up at the sky through the open doorway.*] Lilacs have a purple smell. Lilac is the smell of nightfall, I think. Massachusetts is a beauty in the spring!

**ELIZABETH:** Aye, it is.

[*There is a pause. She is watching him from the table as he stands there absorbing the night. It is as though she would speak but cannot. Instead, now, she takes up his plate and glass and fork and goes with them to the basin. Her back is turned to him. He turns to her and watches her. A sense of their separation rises.*]

**PROCTOR:** I think you're sad again. Are you?

**ELIZABETH:** [*she doesn't want friction, and yet she must*] You come so late I thought you'd gone to Salem this afternoon.

**PROCTOR:** Why? I have no business in Salem.

**ELIZABETH:** You did speak of going, earlier this week.

**PROCTOR:** [*he knows what she means*] I thought better of it since.

**ELIZABETH:** Mary Warren's there today.

**PROCTOR:** Why'd you let her? You heard me forbid her go to Salem anymore!

**ELIZABETH:** I couldn't stop her.

**PROCTOR:** [*holding back a full condemnation of her*] It is a fault, it is a fault, Elizabeth – you're the mistress here, not Mary Warren.

**ELIZABETH:** She frightened all my strength away.

**PROCTOR:** How may that mouse frighten you, Elizabeth? You –

**ELIZABETH:** It is a mouse no more. I forbid her go, and she raises up her chin like the daughter of a prince and says to me, 'I must go to Salem, Goody Proctor; I am an official of the court!'

**PROCTOR:** Court! What court?

**ELIZABETH:** Aye, it is a proper court they have now. They've sent four judges out of Boston, she says, weighty magistrates of the General Court, and at the head sits the Deputy Governor of the Province.

**PROCTOR:** [*astonished*] Why, she's mad.

**ELIZABETH:** I would to God she were. There be fourteen people in jail now, she says.

[**PROCTOR** *simply looks at her, unable to grasp it*]

And they'll be tried, and the court have power to hang them too, she says.

**PROCTOR:** [*scoffing, but without conviction*] Ah, they'd never hang –

**ELIZABETH:** The Deputy Governor promise hangin' if they'll not confess, John. The town's gone wild, I think. She speak of Abigail, and I thought she were a saint, to hear her. Abigail brings the other girls into the court, and where she walks the crowd will part like the sea for Israel. And folks are brought before them, and if they scream and howl and fall to the floor – the person's clapped in the jail for bewitchin' them.

**PROCTOR:** [*wide-eyed*] Oh, it is a black mischief.

**ELIZABETH:** I think you must go to Salem, John.

[*He turns to her*]

I think so. You must tell them it is a fraud.

**PROCTOR:** [*thinking beyond this*] Aye, it is, it is surely.

**ELIZABETH:** Let you go to Ezekiel Cheever – he knows you well. And tell him what she said to you last week in her uncle's house. She said it had naught to do with witchcraft, did she not?

**PROCTOR:** [*in thought*] Aye, she did, she did.

[*Now, a pause*]

**ELIZABETH:** [*quietly, fearing to anger him by prodding*] God forbid you keep that from the court, John. I think they must be told.

**PROCTOR:** [*quietly struggling with his thought*] Aye, they must, they must. It is a wonder they do believe her.

**ELIZABETH:** I would go to Salem now, John – let you go tonight.

**PROCTOR:** I'll think on it.

**ELIZABETH:** [*hurt, and very coldly*] Good, then, let you think on it.

[*She stands and starts to walk out of the room*]

**PROCTOR:** I am only wondering how I may prove what she told me, Elizabeth. If the girl's a saint now, I think it is not easy to prove she's a fraud, and the town gone so silly. She told it to me in a room alone – I have no proof for it.

**ELIZABETH:** You were alone with her?

**PROCTOR:** [*his anger rising*] For a moment, I say. The others come in soon after.

**ELIZABETH:** [*quietly – she has suddenly lost all faith in him*] Do as you wish, then. [*She starts to turn*]

**PROCTOR:** Woman.

[*She turns to him*]

I'll not have your suspicion any more.

**ELIZABETH:** [*a little loftily*] I have no –

**PROCTOR:** I'll not have it!

**ELIZABETH:** Then let you not earn it.

**PROCTOR:** [*with a violent undertone*] You doubt me yet?

**ELIZABETH:** [*with a smile, to keep her dignity*] John, if it were not Abigail that you must go to hurt, would you falter now? I think not.

**PROCTOR:** Now look you –

**ELIZABETH:** I see what I see, John.

**PROCTOR:** [*with solemn warning*] You will not judge me more, Elizabeth. I have good reason to think twice before I charge fraud on Abigail, and I will think on it. Let you look to your own improvement before you go to judge your husband any more. I have forgot Abigail, and –

**ELIZABETH:** And I.

**PROCTOR:** Spare me! You forget nothin' and forgive nothin'. Learn charity, woman. I have gone tiptoe in this house all seven month since she is gone. I have not moved from there to there without I think to please you, and still an everlasting funeral marches round your heart. I cannot speak but I am doubted, every moment judged for lies, as though I come into a court when I come into this house!

**ELIZABETH:** John, you are not open with me. You saw her with a crowd, you said. Now you –

**PROCTOR:** I'll plead my honesty no more, Elizabeth.

**ELIZABETH:** [*now she would justify herself*] John, I am only –

**PROCTOR:** No more! I should have roared you down when first you told me your suspicion. But I wilted, and, like a Christian, I confessed. Confessed! Some dream I had must have taken you for God that day. But you're not, you're not, and let you remember it! Let you look sometimes for the good in me, and judge me not.

**ELIZABETH:** I do not judge you. The magistrate sits in your heart that judges you. I never thought you but a good man, John – [*with a smile*] – only somewhat bewildered.

**PROCTOR:** [*laughing bitterly*] Oh, Elizabeth, your justice would freeze beer!

## Scene analysis

I'll now apply the above concepts to the texts. I have directed and worked on both plays with students and professional actors and should emphasise that what follows below is interpretation. My purpose is not to try to win you to my view of the plays but to set out a process.

**Superobjective/Ruling Idea of *The Crucible*:**
People have to make a sacrifice for their sense of truth to open the way for a free and just society.

| *Protagonist:* | *Antagonist:* |
|---|---|
| Abigail | Proctor |

Her through line of action and his Counteraction drive the play.

Facts from the play and research giving the previous circumstances and given circumstances of the scene:

**The basic facts of the play**
Spring, 1692. Salem Village, Massachusetts, New England.
English Puritan community established in 1626 with a government based on their religion.
Ingrained sense of persecution, resistance, and constraint.
Emphasis on hard work and strict morality with little entertainment.
The young girls in particular suffer under the rigorous discipline.
Land-based economy with serious and violent fights over land ownership.
Salem town, on the coast, is developing a capitalist economy: industry, trade, freer morality, consumer goods.
Village is hemmed in by Native Americans to the west, French to the north, sea to the east.

**The basic previous circumstances**

Eight days ago, local girls were accused of witchcraft with, Tituba, the black servant of Reverend Parris.

One of them, Abigail Williams, niece of Parris, leads accusations of witchery against other people, and old resentments and rivalries are unleashed against people in the community, who become scapegoats.

A court, headed by the Deputy Governor of the Province, has been set up in Salem to try 'witches'. 14 people are in jail. The court has power to hang them.

John Proctor is a mid-30s farmer, confident, feared, respected; but regards himself as a fraud because he had sex with Abigail in his barn. He confessed to Elizabeth, his wife, who dismissed Abi from her service as a maid seven months ago. Mary Warren is now their servant, and has gone into Salem against Proctor's wishes. They live five miles out of the village, and have three boys, one called Jonathan, who is old enough to hunt.

Proctor talked earlier in the week of going to Salem to counter the talk of witchcraft. He told Elizabeth he spoke to Abi in company – but they were actually alone as well and Abi tried to win him back to her, but John resisted.

All of these facts are not known to both characters, however.

**The basic given circumstances**

Elizabeth is upstairs singing to the children, who are in bed. She has prepared rabbit for supper. Proctor has been planting on the farm towards the forest edge. It's nightfall, almost dark. Smell of lilacs in the air. Scene is a low, dark, long living-room in Proctor's house.

**The 5 Ws for the actor playing Elizabeth**

I am Elizabeth Proctor. I am upstairs in my home putting my boys to bed because it's getting dark and I want to speak to John alone. I've cooked a rabbit as something special to please John because I need to confront him about going to Salem to expose Abigail as a liar. I want to sing the boys to sleep.

**The 5 Ws for the actor playing John**

I am John Proctor. I've been working at the forest edge planting the last of the seeds and am approaching my home. It's getting dark and I need some supper. I've been thinking about Elizabeth and the tension between us and I want to do something to ease it.

In the text breakdown I'll mark the end of the Units by a continuous line across the page. The beats and actions are marked by a / where they change within a speech or action. Where there is no slash, a line represents one action. Any commentary on the text will follow it in brackets.

## Act Two

### Unit 1: Elizabeth sings to the boys as John enters and prepares for the evening meal

*Elizabeth's offstage Objective:* I want to settle the boys for sleep
*Obstacle:* They are restless, they want to stay up, I'm nervous about what I need to say to John.
*What's at stake:* Whether I get some calm and privacy with John.

*John's offstage Objective:* I want to get prepared for the meal with Elizabeth.
*Obstacle:* I'm tired from work, anxious about Elizabeth, she may be down soon.
*What's at stake:* Whether I'm prepared for trying to ease her.

---

*The common room of Proctor's house, eight days later.*

*At the right is a door opening on the fields outside. A fireplace is at the left, and behind it a stairway leading upstairs. It is the low, dark, and rather long living-room of the time. As the curtain rises, the room is empty. / From above,* **ELIZABETH** *is heard softly singing to the children. / Presently the door opens / and* **JOHN PROCTOR** *enters, carrying his gun. / He glances about the room as he comes toward the fireplace, / then halts for an instant as he hears her singing. / He continues on to the fireplace, / leans the gun against the wall / as he swings a pot out of the fire and smells it. / Then he lifts out the ladle and tastes. He is not quite pleased. / He reaches to a cupboard, takes a pinch of salt, / and drops it into the pot. / As he is tasting again, her footsteps are heard on the stair. / He swings the pot into the fireplace / and goes to a basin and washes his hands and face.*

(Here we see an excellent example of a series of physical actions that are full of psychological significance. John carries a gun as most of the men would do

– the settlement was originally an armed camp – not just for hunting but for protection from Native Americans and defence in any conflicts over land possession. He knows his own room but glances around on entering – maybe to compare its stark wintriness to the beauty of the spring nature outside, to confirm his desire to soften Elizabeth towards him, to see what she might have prepared. This moment is a good example of how we often enter a space and take it in before we move on; there is a *moment of orientation*. He halts to listen to her singing possibly because it's a rare occurrence these days, and it bodes well for their evening together. He checks the taste of the food maybe because he knows from experience that Elizabeth's cooking is plain and lacks flavour – rather like their life together at the moment. When he hears her approach he moves smartly on to washing because her catching him messing with her meal could set the evening off to a bad start.)

---

**Unit 2: They both try to create a good mood**
In this unit both characters have clear overall objectives but also identifiable smaller objectives to achieve them, marked within the text in bold italics.

*Elizabeth's Objective:* I want to get him in the right mood for talking about Abigail.
*Obstacle:* My resentment over Abi, his silence on the issue, and my anxiety over making things worse between us through a confrontation.

*John's Objective:* I want to break down Elizabeth's coldness and resentment.
*Obstacle:* The strength and persistence of this over seven months, my own guilt, and I haven't been to Salem to expose Abi as agreed.

*What's at stake:* For both of them, through the rest of the scene, it's the future of their marriage, and for Elizabeth, the health of the Salem community as well, so the stakes are high.

---

***E: Find out if he's been to Salem***

**ELIZABETH** *enters*

**ELIZABETH:** What keeps you so late? It's almost dark.

***P: Set a good mood between us***

**PROCTOR:** I were planting far out to the forest edge.

***E: Take in the news***

**ELIZABETH:** Oh,

(Many wouldn't make this one word a separate objective, but Elizabeth is made to change by John's response. Her not-too-strong hope that he'd been to Salem has been dashed, and the information and disappointment has to be dealt with. Also, it's worth illustrating that an objective can be this small.)

***E: Make him content***

you're done then.

**PROCTOR:** Aye, the farm is seeded. / The boys asleep?

**ELIZABETH:** They will be soon. / [*And she goes to the fireplace, proceeds to ladle up stew in a dish*]

**PROCTOR:** Pray now for a fair summer.

**ELIZABETH:** Aye.

**PROCTOR:** Are you well today?

**ELIZABETH:** I am. / [*She brings the plate to the table, and, indicating the food*] It is a rabbit.

**PROCTOR:** [*going to the table*] Oh, is it! / In Jonathan's trap?

**ELIZABETH:** No, she walked into the house this afternoon; I found her sittin' in the corner like she come to visit.

**PROCTOR:** Oh, that's a good sign walkin' in.

**ELIZABETH:** Pray God. / It hurt my heart to strip her, poor rabbit. [*She sits and watches him taste it*]

**PROCTOR:** It's well seasoned.

**ELIZABETH:** [*blushing with pleasure*] I took great care. She's tender?

**PROCTOR:** Aye / [*He eats. / She watches him*] / I think we'll see green fields soon. It's warm as blood beneath the clods.

**ELIZABETH:** That's well.

/ [*Proctor eats,*

***P: Soften her up /***

/ *then looks up.*]

**PROCTOR:** If the crop is good I'll buy George Jacob's heifer. / How would that please you?

***E: Encourage him***

**ELIZABETH:** Aye, it would.

**PROCTOR:** [*with a grin]* I mean to please you, Elizabeth.

**ELIZABETH:** [*it is hard to say]* I know it, John.

/ [*He gets up, goes to her, kisses her. / She receives it.*

(Here is a good example of how an objective is tempered by an obstacle. Elizabeth wants to encourage but her perception of John's conduct with Abigail and his failure to expose her lies makes it very difficult for her to be enthusiastic.)

***P: Make her attend to my needs***

/ *With a certain disappointment, he returns to the table.*]

**PROCTOR:** [*as gently as he can*] Cider?

***E: Make amends***

**ELIZABETH:** [*with a sense of reprimanding herself for having forgot*] Aye! / [*She gets up and goes to pour a glass for him. / He now arches his back.*]

**PROCTOR:** This farm's a continent when you go foot by foot droppin' seeds in it.

**ELIZABETH:** [*coming with the cider*] It must be.

**PROCTOR:** [*drinks a long draught, then, putting the glass down*] / You ought to bring some flowers in the house.

**ELIZABETH:** Oh, I forgot! / I will tomorrow.

**PROCTOR:** It's winter in here yet.

(In this section after the kiss, see how they make each other change tack.)

**P: Open up good feelings in her**

/ On Sunday let you come with me, and we'll walk the farm together; I never see such a load of flowers on the earth. / [*With good feeling he goes and looks up at the sky through the open doorway*] / Lilacs have a purple smell. / Lilac is the smell of nightfall, I think. / Massachusetts is a beauty in the spring!

***E: Reach him***

ELIZABETH: Aye, it is.

[ / *There is a pause. She is watching him from the table as he stands there absorbing the night. It is as though she would speak but cannot.*

(Again, her obstacle is very strong, and this time actually overcomes her objective and changes the dynamic between them.)

---

## Unit 3: Elizabeth confronts Proctor about Salem and he evades her

Here we have a small unit and each character has two possible objectives.

---

***E: Ready myself to confront him (and/or provoke him to respond by my silence)***

***Obstacle: His good mood, defensiveness, my fear of conflict and what he might say***

/ *Instead, now, she takes up his plate and glass and fork and goes with them to the basin. Her back is turned to him.*

***P: Find out what's wrong***

***Obstacle: Guilt over Abi and not having gone to Salem***

/ *He turns to her and watches her. A sense of their separation rises.*]

**PROCTOR:** I think you're sad again. / Are you?

***E: Make him explain why he's not been to Salem***

**ELIZABETH:** [*she doesn't want friction, and yet she must*] You come so late I thought you'd gone to Salem this afternoon.

***P: Justify myself to her***

**PROCTOR:** Why? I have no business in Salem.

**ELIZABETH:** You did speak of going, earlier this week.

**PROCTOR:** [*he knows what she means*] I thought better of it since.

---

## Unit 4: Elizabeth presses John over events in Salem to reveal the truth, and he doubtfully weighs it up

***E: Make him face up to what's happening***

***Obstacle: As before***

**ELIZABETH:** Mary Warren's there today.

***P: Get her to stop this***

***Obstacle: As before, and I still want to break down the tension between us***

**PROCTOR:** Why'd you let her? / You heard me forbid her go to Salem anymore!

**ELIZABETH:** I couldn't stop her.

**PROCTOR:** [*holding back a full condemnation of her*] It is a fault, it is a fault, Elizabeth – you're the mistress here, not Mary Warren.

**ELIZABETH:** She frightened all my strength away.

**PROCTOR:** How may that mouse frighten you, Elizabeth? You –

**ELIZABETH:** It is a mouse no more. / I forbid her go, and she raises up her chin like the daughter of a prince and says to me, 'I must go to Salem, Goody Proctor; I am an official of the court!'

***P: Find out what's going on***

**PROCTOR:** Court! What court?

**ELIZABETH:** Aye, it is a proper court they have now. / They've sent four judges out of Boston, she says, weighty magistrates of the General Court, and at the head sits the Deputy Governor of the Province.

**PROCTOR:** [*astonished*] Why, she's mad.

**ELIZABETH:** I would to God she were. / There be fourteen people in jail now, she says.

[**PROCTOR** *simply looks at her, unable to grasp it*]

And they'll be tried, and the court have power to hang them too, she says.

**PROCTOR:** [*scoffing, but without conviction*] Ah, they'd never hang –

**ELIZABETH:** The Deputy Governor promise hangin' if they'll not confess, John. / The town's gone wild, I think. / She speak of Abigail, and I thought she were a saint, to hear her. / Abigail brings the other girls into the court, and where she walks the crowd will part like the sea for Israel. And folks are brought before them, and if they scream and howl and fall to the floor – the person's clapped in the jail for bewitchin' them.

**PROCTOR:** [*wide-eyed*] Oh, it is a black mischief.

***E: Persuade him to reveal the truth about Abigail***

**ELIZABETH:** I think you must go to Salem, John.

[*He turns to her*]

/ I think so. / You must tell them it is a fraud.

***P: Work out what to do (or make her give me space to think)***
***Obstacle: Elizabeth's pressure and the difficulties of dealing with Abi***
***Stake: Now also thc hcalth of thc community and my own integrity***

**PROCTOR:** [*thinking beyond this*] Aye, it is, / it is surely.

**ELIZABETH:** Let you go to Ezekiel Cheever – he knows you well. / And tell him what she said to you last week in her uncle's house./ She said it had naught to do with witchcraft, did she not?

**PROCTOR:** [*in thought*] Aye, she did, / she did.

[*Now, a pause*]

**ELIZABETH:** [*quietly, fearing to anger him by prodding*] God forbid you keep that from the court, John. / I think they must be told.

**PROCTOR:** [*quietly struggling with his thought*] Aye, they must, / they must. / It is a wonder they do believe her.

(In these last three lines of Proctor, we see how there may be more than one action within a sentence, contrary to the view that there can only ever be one thought and action within one sentence; otherwise the repetition of 'it is', 'she did' and 'they must' is wasted and doesn't reflect his inner turmoil and Elizabeth's pressure on him.)

**ELIZABETH:** I would go to Salem now, John – let you go tonight.
**PROCTOR:** I'll think on it.
**ELIZABETH:** [*hurt, and very coldly*] Good, then, let you think on it. [*She stands and starts to walk out of the room*]
**PROCTOR:** I am only wondering how I may prove what she told me, Elizabeth. / If the girl's a saint now, I think it is not easy to prove she's a fraud, and the town gone so silly. / She told it to me in a room alone – I have no proof for it.

***E: Get to the truth of this***
***Obstacle: Possibility of an even greater rift between us***
**ELIZABETH:** You were alone with her?
**PROCTOR:** [*stubbornly*] For a moment alone, aye
**ELIZABETH:** Why, then, it is not as you told me.
**PROCTOR:** [*his anger rising*] For a moment, I say. / The others come in soon after.

***E: Get away from him and his deceit***
***Obstacle: same***
**ELIZABETH:** [*quietly – she has suddenly lost all faith in him*] Do as you wish, then. [*She starts to turn*]

## Unit 5: Proctor attacks Elizabeth's judgement on him and she justifies herself

In this unit the characters' objectives run through without necessary subdivisions.

*John's Objective:* Stop her judging me
*Obstacle:* Guilt over Abi, and this will increase tension.

*Elizabeth's Objective:* Convince him I'm justified
*Obstacle:* Fear of making things worse between us.
*What's at stake?:* Their relationship, the well-being of the community, his integrity.

---

**PROCTOR:** Woman.
[*She turns to him*]
/ I'll not have your suspicion any more.
**ELIZABETH:** [*a little loftily*] I have no –
**PROCTOR:** I'll not have it!
**ELIZABETH:** Then let you not earn it.
**PROCTOR:** [*with a violent undertone*] You doubt me yet?
**ELIZABETH:** [*with a smile, to keep her dignity*] John, if it were not Abigail that you must go to hurt, would you falter now? / I think not.
**PROCTOR:** Now look you –
**ELIZABETH:** I see what I see, John.
**PROCTOR:** [*with solemn warning*] You will not judge me more, Elizabeth. / I have good reason to think twice before I charge fraud on Abigail, and I will think on it./ Let you look to your own improvement before you go to judge your husband any more. / I have forgot Abigail, and –
**ELIZABETH:** And I.
**PROCTOR:** Spare me! / You forget nothin' and forgive nothin'. / Learn charity, woman. / I have gone tiptoe in this house all seven month since she is gone. / I have not moved from there to there without I think to please you, and still an everlasting funeral marches round your heart. / I cannot speak but I am

doubted, every moment judged for lies, as though I come into a court when I come into this house!

**ELIZABETH:** John, you are not open with me. / You saw her with a crowd, you said. Now you –

**PROCTOR:** I'll plead my honesty no more, Elizabeth.

**ELIZABETH:** [*now she would justify herself*] John, I am only –

**PROCTOR:** No more! / I should have roared you down when first you told me your suspicion. / But I wilted, and, like a Christian, I confessed. / Confessed! / Some dream I had must have taken you for God that day. / But you're not, you're not, and let you remember it! / Let you look sometimes for the good in me, and judge me not.

**ELIZABETH:** I do not judge you. / The magistrate sits in your heart that judges you. / I never thought you but a good man, John – [*with a smile*] – only somewhat bewildered.

**PROCTOR:** [*laughing bitterly*] Oh, Elizabeth, your justice would freeze beer!

From Elizabeth's entrance, this constitutes one scene, and Elizabeth has an objective running through it from the start, the *spine* of the scene, *to get John to go to Salem and reveal the truth that accusations of witchcraft are false*. On the other hand, Proctor's first objective, *to break down Elizabeth's coldness and resentment*, is changed by what she does to him and his subsequent objectives form in response to her actions.

We find extra facts as we go through the scene: for example, the farm is full of flowers, there are lilacs near the door, John drinks cider.

A key theme of the play comes to the fore in the scene: the importance and difficulty of sustaining conscience and integrity.

In each unit, we can identify *key lines* which express the essence of the unit and point to the development of the narrative. For example, in Unit 4, Elizabeth's line: *I think you must go to Salem, John. [He turns to her.] I think so. You must tell them it is a fraud.* And in Unit 5, Elizabeth again: *I do not judge you. The magistrate sits in your heart that judges you.*

I haven't named any actions, and I've emphasised before that these are frequently adaptations to what the other characters are doing to you, and may well change to some degree from performance to performance. Some actions, on the other hand, may be regular and typical for a character, or essential to the action. For example, Proctor *challenges, accuses* and *convinces* at numerous points in the play. Below is an example of how one section of the text *could* run:

### Unit 5: Proctor attacks Elizabeth's judgement on him and she justifies herself

*John's Objective:* Stop her judging me
*Obstacle:* Guilt over Abi, and this will increase tension.

*Elizabeth's Objective:* Convince him I'm justified
*Obstacle:* Fear of making things worse between us.

---

**PROCTOR:** Woman. — ARREST HER
[*She turns to him*]
/ I'll not have your suspicion any more. — WARN
**ELIZABETH:** [*a little loftily*] I have no – — CORRECT
**PROCTOR:** I'll not have it! — ORDER
**ELIZABETH:** Then let you not earn it. — TEACH
**PROCTOR:** [*with a violent undertone*] You doubt me yet? — DARE
**ELIZABETH:** [*with a smile, to keep her dignity*] John, if it were not Abigail that you must go to hurt, would you falter now? — EXPOSE
/ I think not. — CHALLENGE
**PROCTOR:** Now look you – — DISABUSE
**ELIZABETH:** I see what I see, John. — DEFY
**PROCTOR:** [*with solemn warning*] You will not judge me more, Elizabeth. — COMMAND
/ I have good reason to think twice before I charge fraud on Abigail, and I will think on it. — CAUTION
/ Let you look to your own improvement before you go to judge your husband any more. — LECTURE
/ I have forgot Abigail, and – — CONVINCE

| | | |
|---|---|---|
| **ELIZABETH:** | And I. | ASSURE |
| **PROCTOR:** | Spare me! | SCORN |

As you'll note, all these actions are *transitive* verbs, that is, they have a direct object – I arrest *her*, I warn *him* – as opposed to *intransitive* verbs, like to protest or meddle, which don't. In a monologue you can warn or question *yourself*. Transitive verbs keep the actions connected and dynamic, so it's best to use them as much as you can.

In rehearsal, having worked on the text in the above way, we would improvise each unit or a number of units together off the text, using a knowledge of the action and objectives to drive what we invent, as in the earlier examples of Stanislavski at work. In this way we would work through the whole play (and I would take between one and two weeks in a five week rehearsal period) so that we know the action well before coming to use the text directly. By the end of this phase, at least when done extensively and without time pressure (maybe lasting six months in Stanislavski's rehearsals), the actors find the state he calls 'I am', i.e. I have the feeling of being the character in these circumstances. For us in our short rehearsals, we may only reach this state later on in the process.

Stanislavski would then make the transition to using the text. This would take the form of more readings in which the actors clarify the literal sense and the deeper sense of the text; research the social, political, religious, moral, etc. elements to understand the background to the play; go deeper into the given circumstances, justifying actions in detail; and experiment with physical characteristics suggested by their knowledge of the characters. Also, the play would be performed sitting around a table, and the actors would go through it unit by unit, without physical movement, but talking through the thoughts, subtext (the inner monologue of thoughts, and mental images), objectives, and actions of all their characters. They even wrote down in columns the text, subtext and the actions.

In a long rehearsal period, this sort of analytical and written work can be absorbed and will be a reflection of the earlier work on improvised action. In a short period, it can easily become an over-intellectual and cerebral approach which leads actors to think of what they should be thinking and doing while they are performing – the opposite of what Stanislavski wanted – because you spend a disproportionate amount of time sitting and talking, and too little time on organically absorbing and expressing character work, on *active analysis*.

Another Anglicisation of the approach is to spend hours of rehearsal time 'actioning' the text, that is, intellectually working out actions for every line, and possibly saying the action and then the line right through the play, without spontaneous interaction taking place between the actors and without any dynamic between them having been explored. So the actors end up consciously thinking 'what is my action on this line?' before they say the line. Even when done in an accomplished fluent manner the result can lack impulse and spontaneity and appear dry and mechanical. It may produce an intelligent reading of the play and be exactly what the director wants but it's really a process of over-control. Any aspect of process we use must be geared to the actor becoming free, confident and organically involved in the action. Any aspect which inhibits that is unhelpful. Some actors, of course, hate discussion and any form of analysis and just want to follow their 'instinct' – this is the opposite extreme – and what we usually see here is a generalised, mannered performance. We have to steer between these two extremes. A technique, process, system, method, whatever you like to call it, is there to help us through difficulties and to give depth, shape and wholeness to what we do, and as Chekhov quotes in *To the Actor*, 'The technique of any art is sometimes apt to dampen, as it were, the spark of inspiration in a mediocre artist; but the same technique in the hands of a master can fan that spark into an unquenchable flame' (Joseph Jasser).

The final stage of rehearsal was about putting the play on its feet, structuring, getting the tempo and rhythm of performance right, continuing to improvise staging, making sure the action and Ruling Idea/Superobjective were clear; and for the actors to play their own actions and Superobjectives truthfully, develop the *physical embodiment* of their parts – age, appearance, behaviour – and experience their role within the play as a whole. I'll look at the development of the physical life in the next chapter; but below is the second example of text breakdown, this time looking at a Shakespeare piece, to show the relevance of this approach even to classical drama.

## **Measure for Measure** by *Shakespeare*

### Part of Act 2, Scene 2

*Enter* **PROVOST**, *and a* **SERVANT**.

**SERVANT**

He's hearing of a cause; he will come straight;
I'll tell him of you.

**PROVOST** Pray you, do. *Exit* **SERVANT**

I'll know
His pleasure; maybe he'll relent. Alas,
He hath but as offended in a dream.
All sects, all ages smack of this vice, and he
To die for it!

*Enter Angelo*

**ANGELO** Now, what's the matter, provost?

**PROVOST**

Is it your will Claudio shall die tomorrow?

**ANGELO**

Did not I tell thee, yea? Hadst thou not order?
Why dost thou ask again?

**PROVOST** Lest I might be too rash.
Under your good correction, I have seen
When, after execution, judgement hath
Repented o'er his doom.

**ANGELO** Go to; let that be mine.
Do you your office, or give up your place,
And you shall well be spared.

**PROVOST** I crave your honour's pardon.
What shall be done, sir, with the groaning Juliet?
She's very near her hour.

**ANGELO** Dispose of her
To some more fitter place, and that with speed.

*Enter* **SERVANT**

**SERVANT**

Here is the sister of the man condemned

Desires access to you.

**ANGELO** Hath he a sister?

**PROVOST**

Ay, my good lord, a very virtuous maid,
And to be shortly of a sisterhood,
If not already.

**ANGELO**

Well, let her be admitted. *Exit* **SERVANT**
See you the fornicatress be removed;
Let her have needful, but not lavish, means.
There shall be order for't.

*Enter* **LUCIO** *and* **ISABELLA**

**PROVOST** God save your honour.

**ANGELO**

Stay a little while. (*To* **ISABELLA**) Y'are welcome. What's your will?

**ISABELLA**

I am a woeful suitor to your honour,
Please but your honour hear me.

**ANGELO** Well, what's your suit?

**ISABELLA**

There is a vice that most I do abhor,
And most desire should meet the blow of justice,
For which I would not plead, but that I must,
For which I must not plead, but that I am
At war 'twixt will and will not.

**ANGELO** Well: the matter?

**ISABELLA**

I have a brother is condemned to die.
I do beseech you, let it be his fault,
And not my brother.

**PROVOST** (*aside*) Heaven give thee moving graces.

**ANGELO**

Condemn the fault, and not the actor of it?
Why, every fault's condemned ere it be done.
Mine were the very cipher of a function,

To fine the faults whose fine stands in record,
And let go by the actor.

**ISABELLA** O just, but severe law!
I had a brother then; heaven keep your honour.

**LUCIO** (*aside to* **ISABELLA**)
Give't not o'er so. To him again, entreat him,
Kneel down before him, hang upon his gown;
You are too cold. If you should need a pin,
You could not with more tame a tongue desire it.
To him, I say.

**ISABELLA**
Must he needs die?

**ANGELO** Maiden, no remedy.

**ISABELLA**
Yes, I do think that you might pardon him,
And neither heaven nor man grieve at the mercy.

**ANGELO**
I will not do't

**ISABELLA** But can you if you would?

**ANGELO**
Look what I will not, that I cannot do.

**ISABELLA**
But might you do't, and do the world no wrong,
If so your heart were touched with that remorse
As mine is to him?

**ANGELO**
He's sentenced; 'tis too late.

**LUCIO** (*aside to* **ISABELLA**) You are too cold.

**ISABELLA**
Too late? Why, no. I that do speak a word
May call it back again. Well, believe this,
No ceremony that to great ones longs,
Not the king's crown, nor the deputed sword,
The marshal's truncheon, nor the judge's robe,
Become them with one half so good a grace

As mercy does.
If he had been as you, and you as he,
You would have slipped like him; but he, like you
Would not have been so stern.

**ANGELO** Pray you, be gone.

**ISABELLA**

I would to heaven I had your potency,
And you were Isabel; should it then be thus?
No, I would tell what 'twere to be a judge,
And what a prisoner.

**LUCIO** (*aside to* **ISABELLA**)

Ay, touch him; there's the vein.

**ANGELO**

Your brother is a forfeit of the law,
And you but waste your words.

**ISABELLA** Alas, alas;

Why, all the souls that were were forfeit once,
And He that might the vantage best have took
Found out the remedy. How would you be,
If He, which is the top of judgement, should
But judge you as you are? O think on that,
And mercy then will breathe within your lips,
Like a man new made.

**ANGELO** Be you content, fair maid,

It is the law, not I, condemns your brother;
Were he my kinsman, brother, or my son,
It should be thus with him. He must die tomorrow.

## Scene analysis

**Superobjective/Ruling Idea of *Measure for Measure*:**

Repression and denial of free will must be counterbalanced by mercy and self-knowledge.

*Protagonist:* The Duke *Antagonist:* Angelo

They provide the main Action and Counteraction in the play.

Facts from the play giving the previous circumstances and given circumstances of the scene:

**The basic facts of the play**

Set in Vienna.

The Duke has decided to go away, leaving power in the hands of Angelo as his Deputy. Escalus will assist him.

The Duke is at war with the King of Hungary, and he and other dukes are suing for peace.

There have been plague, poverty and hangings.

Over the last fourteen years the Duke has let the laws slip leaving vice and licence, which he wants Angelo to eradicate.

**The basic previous circumstances**

Before the scene, Angelo has started to wield power with strict rigour.

All brothels in the suburbs are to be destroyed.

He is making a moral example of a young nobleman, Claudio, by sentencing him to be executed for getting Juliet, to whom he is betrothed, pregnant.

Claudio's sister, Isabella, is to become a novice nun this day, and Lucio, a dissolute friend of Claudio, urges her to go to Angelo to plead for her brother's life.

**The basic given circumstances**

We are in the Duke's palace. In a room used by Angelo as his office and to receive people. He is at present 'hearing of a cause' elsewhere. The Provost has come to speak with him. The time is not given so we can make it whatever we imagine, e.g. Monday 4p.m., 5th March, 1603. The Provost runs the prison and is subject to Angelo's orders. Claudio is to be executed by tomorrow morning. Isabella is on the way to see Angelo.

**The 5 Ws for the actor playing Angelo**

I'm Angelo. I've been listening to the case of a bawd called Pompey, and have just been informed by my servant that the Provost wishes to speak with me. I'm going to my office to attend to that. It's 4p.m., Monday. I want to find out his business.

**The 5 Ws for the actor playing the Provost**

I am ... (whatever name I imagine for this character). In one of the counsel rooms Angelo has ordered me to execute Claudio by tomorrow morning. I have left the palace and headed for the prison and then stopped to consider the injustice of this command. I've returned to the palace to try to change Lord Angelo's mind. It's 4p.m. I want to win mercy for Claudio.

**The 5Ws for the actor playing Isabella**

I'm Isabella, Claudio's sister. His friend, Lucio, met me at the convent and informed me of Claudio's plight. I explained my situation to the Mother and have come here to the palace to plead with Angelo. It's 4p.m. I want to persuade him to let Claudio live.

**The 5Ws for the actor playing Lucio**

I'm Lucio. I heard of my friend Claudio's sentence from Mistress Overdone and met him in the street on the way to prison. He urged me to appeal to his sister, Isabella, for help, which I have done and am now at the Duke's palace where I have met her again. I thought it best to come and support and advise her in a meeting with Lord Angelo. It's 4p.m. I want to spur her on to win mercy for Claudio.

**The 5Ws for the actor playing the Servant**

Stanislavski went into detail even with actors playing unnamed crowd members. For example, in his work on *Othello*, Brabantio's servants knew exactly their backgrounds, their relationship to him, their response to the alarm raised against Othello and their specific tasks in organising the move to confront him.

So, the Servant must be a specific character with a name, have a specific relationship to Angelo, with specific given circumstances before each scene. For example: I am Darius, the personal assistant to Lord Angelo. I attend him in all counselling sessions, such as this last one with the bawd, Pompey. I have been informed by another servant that the Provost has come back and wishes to speak to my Master and I am now back at Angelo's office to see what he wants. It's 4p.m., Monday 5th.

In the breakdown of the text, Units, Objectives and Actions will be set out as before.

## Part of
## Act 2, Scene 2

### Unit 1: The Servant informs the Provost he'll summon Angelo

This unit is a small scene in itself.

---

*Enter* **PROVOST**, *and a* **SERVANT**.

***S: Reassure him***
***Obstacle: Angelo is busy***
***Stake: My job or reputation? The Provost is an important man***

**SERVANT**

He's hearing of a cause; / he will come straight;
I'll tell him of you.

***P: Get him to bring him***
***Obstacle: Angelo is busy. I've recently seen him***
***His clarity on the issue. My far lower status***
***Stake: Claudio's life***
***The establishment of justice in the State***

**PROVOST** Pray you, do. *Exit* **SERVANT**

---

### Unit 2: The Provost justifies his defence of Claudio

This monologue is also a small scene.

---

***P: Strengthen my resolve***
***Obstacle: Fear of Angelo. The law. Self-doubt***
***Stake: Claudio's life***

I'll know
His pleasure; maybe he'll relent. / Alas,
He hath but as offended in a dream.
/ All sects, all ages smack of this vice, and he
To die for it!

## Unit 3: The Provost questions the order and Angelo threatens him

Units 3 and 4 constitute another short scene.

---

***A: Find out his business***
***Obstacle: I have a lot of other important affairs***
***Stake: Whether I get on with them or not***

*Enter* **ANGELO**

**ANGELO** Now, what's the matter, provost?

***P: Persuade him to let Claudio live***
***Obstacle: Angelo's inflexible strictness***
***Stake: As before***

**PROVOST**

Is it your will Claudio shall die tomorrow?

***A: Press him to accept the judgement***
***Obstacle: My understanding of his humanity***
***Stake: The integrity of the law. My authority***

**ANGELO**

Did not I tell thee, yea? / Hadst thou not order?
/Why dost thou ask again?

**PROVOST** Lest I might be too rash.
/ Under your good correction, I have seen
When, after execution, judgement hath
Repented o'er his doom.

**ANGELO** Go to;/ let that be mine.
/ Do you your office, or give up your place,
And you shall well be spared.

**PROVOST** I crave your honour's pardon.

---

## Unit 4: They determine what to do with Juliet

***P: Get help for Juliet***
***Obstacle: I've already failed to move Angelo's lack of compassion***
***Stake: Juliet's health and well-being***
***My own standing and influence***

What shall be done, sir, with the groaning Juliet?
She's very near her hour.

***A: Have it properly sorted***
***Obstacle: Provost's lack of clarity***
***Stake: My humanity and integrity***

**ANGELO** Dispose of her
To some more fitter place, and that with speed.

---

## Unit 5: Isabella is announced and Angelo agrees to see her

Another short scene.

---

***S: Make him aware the sister is here***
***Obstacle: He's busy with the Provost***
***Stake: The future of her brother possibly***

*Enter* **SERVANT**

**SERVANT**
Here is the sister of the man condemned
Desires access to you.

***A: Determine what to do***
***Obstacle: He, like me, may not know her***
***Stake: My dignity, I don't want to be deceived***

**ANGELO** Hath he a sister?

***P: Persuade him to see her***
***Obstacle: Angelo's single-mindedness***
***Stake: Claudio's life***

**PROVOST**

Ay, my good lord, a very virtuous maid,
And to be shortly of a sisterhood,
If not already.

**ANGELO**

Well, let her be admitted. *Exit* **SERVANT**

---

## Unit 6: Angelo orders what should be done with Juliet

Another, even shorter, scene.

---

***A: Have him deal correctly with Juliet***
***Obstacle: The Provost's leniency and equivocation***
***Stake: The law. My authority***

See you the fornicatress be removed;
/ Let her have needful, but not lavish, means.
/ There shall be order for't.

---

## Unit 7: Isabella and Lucio enter and Angelo makes the Provost stay

*Enter* **LUCIO** *and* **ISABELLA**

***P: Take my leave***
***Obstacle: I'd like to see what happens***
***Stake: As before***

**PROVOST** God save your honour.

***A: Make him stay and learn***
***Obstacle: His own affairs***
***Stake: As before***

**ANGELO**

Stay a little while.

(Angelo perceives a leniency in the Provost that can compromise the law. He wants him to stay so he can learn from his handling of a possible plea from Claudio's sister. Also, there is a probable dramatic irony in the Provost's 'God save your *honour*', repeated in Isabella's 'heaven keep your *honour*': *honour* having the double meaning of *your lordship* and *integrity*. Later on in the scene, not printed here, Angelo becomes overwhelmed and bemused by her and, as a result, in their next meeting makes his corrupt proposition to save Claudio in return for sex.

The entrance of Isabella changes the dynamic between Angelo and the Provost, even though the dialogue between her and Angelo has not begun – so this justifies a separate unit.)

---

**Unit 8: Isabella makes an uncertain appeal for Claudio's life and Angelo rejects it unequivocally**

Units 8 and 9 are part of a scene that runs for six pages. In this part of the scene, all four characters have overall objectives, *spines*, running through it and, in the case of Isabella and Angelo, smaller objectives to accomplish them.

*Isabella's Objective:* I want to persuade Angelo to let Claudio live.
*Obstacle:* The decision's made. Angelo's reputation, clarity and strictness. My own uncertainty.
*Stake:* Claudio's life. My honour in appealing against the law.

*Angelo's Objective:* Make her accept I have no choice but to implement the law.
*Obstacle:* Her innocence, persistence, and strong impression on me.
*Stake:* The law. Society's well-being. My integrity and authority.

*Lucio's Objective:* Spur Isabella on to save Claudio.
*Obstacle:* Her timidity, youth, innocence. Angelo's coldness.
*Stake:* My friend's life.

*Provost's Objective:* Win Heaven to support her.
*Obstacle:* Angelo's inflexibility. Her inexperience. My own inadequacy.
*Stake:* A life. Justice.

---

***A: Find out her cause***

(*To* **ISABELLA**) Y'are welcome. / What's your will?

***I: Disarm his defences (by proving my equal morality)***

**ISABELLA**

I am a woeful suitor to your honour,
Please but your honour hear me.

**ANGELO** Well, what's your suit?

**ISABELLA**

There is a vice that most I do abhor,
And most desire should meet the blow of justice,
For which I would not plead, but that I must,
For which I must not plead, but that I am
At war 'twixt will and will not.

**ANGELO** Well: the matter?

**ISABELLA**

I have a brother is condemned to die.
/ I do beseech you, let it be his fault,
And not my brother. (*i.e. condemn his fault, not him*)

**PROVOST** (*aside*) Heaven give thee moving graces.

***A: Convince her that's nonsense***

**ANGELO**

Condemn the fault, and not the actor of it?
/ Why, every fault's condemned ere it be done.
/ Mine were the very cipher of a function,
To fine the faults whose fine stands in record,
And let go by the actor.

(i.e. to punish the crimes whose penalty has been established in Law, but not the criminal himself.)

***I: Make him see I have to be resigned***

**ISABELLA** O just, but severe law!
I had a brother then; heaven keep your honour.

## Unit 9: Lucio persuades Isabella to try again but Angelo is unrelenting

**LUCIO** (*aside to* **ISABELLA**)

Give't not o'er so. / To him again, entreat him,
Kneel down before him, hang upon his gown;
/ You are too cold. If you should need a pin,
You could not with more tame a tongue desire it.
/ To him, I say.

***I: Convince him mercy would do no harm***

**ISABELLA**

Must he needs die?

***A: Make her clear it's definitive***

**ANGELO** Maiden, no remedy.

**ISABELLA**

Yes, I do think that you might pardon him,
And neither heaven nor man grieve at the mercy.

**ANGELO**

I will not do't

**ISABELLA** But can you if you would?

**ANGELO**

Look what I will not, that I cannot do.

**ISABELLA**

But might you do't, and do the world no wrong,
If so your heart were touched with that remorse
As mine is to him? (i.e. compassion)

**ANGELO**

He's sentenced; / 'tis too late.

**LUCIO** (*aside to* **ISABELLA**) You are too cold.

**ISABELLA**

Too late? / Why, no. I that do speak a word
May call it back again. / Well, believe this,
No ceremony that to great ones longs, (i.e. belongs)

Not the king's crown, nor the deputed sword,
The marshal's truncheon, nor the judge's robe,
Become them with one half so good a grace
As mercy does. /
If he had been as you, and you as he,
You would have slipped like him; but he, like you
Would not have been so stern.

**ANGELO** Pray you, be gone.

(In the scene we have to identify the points at which Angelo starts to be affected by Isabella. In Angelo's last two lines here we see a change of tack in response to her direct appeal to mercy : ''tis too late' offers a justification other than that of the law, implying he might have considered her words had she come earlier *before* sentencing; then he tries simply to get rid of her. The actions are possibly to *soften* her and *dismiss* her, different to earlier actions of *assuring* and *rejecting*.)

***I: Convince him mercy is a virtue***

**ISABELLA**

I would to heaven I had your potency,
And you were Isabel; should it then be thus?
/ No, I would tell what 'twere to be a judge,
And what a prisoner.

**LUCIO** (*aside to* **ISABELLA**)

Ay, touch him; there's the vein.

***A: Make her comprehend it's the law which condemns***

**ANGELO**

Your brother is a forfeit of the law,
And you but waste your words.

**ISABELLA** Alas, alas;

Why, all the souls that were were forfeit once,
And He that might the vantage best have took
Found out the remedy. / How would you be,
If He, which is the top of judgement, should
But judge you as you are? / O think on that,

And mercy then will breathe within your lips,
Like a man new made.

**ANGELO** Be you content, fair maid,
It is the law, not I, condemns your brother;
Were he my kinsman, brother, or my son,
It should be thus with him. / He must die tomorrow.

In this piece of the text we discover a new fact: Juliet is near to giving birth and is currently in the prison.
The central theme of repression versus mercy is evident here.
Examples of key lines would be:
Provost, in Unit 1 – *All sects, all ages smack of this vice; and he / To die for't!*
Isabella, in Unit 9 – *How would you be, / If He, which is the top of judgement, should / But judge you as you are?*

---

Below is an example of what some actions might be:

### Unit 3: The Provost questions the order and Angelo threatens him

***A: Find out his business***
***Obstacle: I have a lot of other important affairs***
***Stake: Whether I get on with them or not***
*Enter* **ANGELO**
**ANGELO** Now, what's the matter, provost? QUERY

***P: Persuade him to let Claudio live***
***Obstacle: Angelo's inflexible strictness***
***Stake: Claudio's life***

**PROVOST**
Is it your will Claudio shall die tomorrow? SEARCH

***A: Press him to accept the judgement***
***Obstacle: My understanding of his humanity***

***Stake: The integrity of the law. My authority***

**ANGELO**

Did not I tell thee, yea? REMIND Hadst thou not order? CHARGE
Why dost thou ask again? WARN

**PROVOST** Lest I might be too rash. EASE
Under your good correction, I have seen
When, after execution, judgement hath
Repented o'er his doom. ENLIGHTEN

**ANGELO** Go to; CURTAIL let that be mine. CORRECT
Do you your office, or give up your place,
And you shall well be spared. THREATEN

**PROVOST** I crave your honour's pardon. APPEASE

A last word on this sort of breakdown into units and objectives: always write them into the *script*. Some actors write them into an exercise book which they then have to consult separately. This is practical organic work and not an academic exercise, so have your through line where you can access it easily. Also, it is the objectives that we act, and the obstacles and what's at stake inform how we do it, so we need to concentrate primarily on what we want.

# 13 Creating the physical life of the role

> *Without an external form neither your inner characterisation nor the spirit of your image will reach the public*
>
> Stanislavski

Once the work on the inner life of the character, the text and the action are under way, then the physical embodiment of the character will start to develop – assuming, of course, that the actor's body is responsive to imaginative impulse. Stanislavski saw the development of the physical life as a response to the inner life and psychological and physical action, and not as the thing with which we start. The representational actor will most likely start with some aspect of physicality – for example, a posture, manner or vocal characteristic – and then work through to the inner life, or not, depending on the actor.

## Physical expression

The process of physicalisation is a gradual one. In The Period of Physical Embodiment section in the first part of *Creating a Role*, Stanislavski, while sitting in a cab on the way to rehearsal, wants to start to 'transform myself physically into Chatski, while still being first and foremost myself'. He begins with 'If'. If I am in a cab, not on the way to the theatre, but on the way to see the woman I love, what do I do? He finds his feet and body become filled with energy, impatience and excitement. He greets people in the street in a manner that is not his normal one, but more in tune with his imagination. A particular gesture arises spontaneously from a simple action such as this greeting, or scolding or warning. It may happen again truthfully only by recreating the circumstances and impulse out of which it came, and may then become a regular aspect of your character. To rush into physical characterisation invites stereotyping and cliché: a crudely described generalisation of, for example, politeness, superciliousness or shyness. Avoiding haste, allowing a physical expression to emerge organically from impulse and action, will allow that expression to be individual, richer, and specific.

What starts in the actor's imagination will find truthful expression initially through the eyes, which reveal our thoughts and feelings, our immediate responses to internal and external happenings. Whether in theatre or on screen, if we start with the eyes we are sure of a basis in truth. From them, expression moves into the face, and then if a more overt and defined form of expression is demanded by circumstances, we are prompted to use words and our whole body, while trying to ensure that our voices and bodies are easy and flexible and give an exact and subtle expression of our feelings and objectives. (See the Silent Reaction exercise in Chapter 4.) The physicalisation of a role only really develops in the final stages of rehearsal because then the imaginative life of the part is strong enough to stimulate and control the voice and body, and tension and cliché are less likely to appear. Stanislavski emphasised a rigorous training in gymnastics, acrobatics and dance to make the body expressive, but also plasticity of motion: the inner flow of energy and line of movement. This and the basic Chekhov exercises on control of the body and sensitivity to creative impulse were examined in Chapter 2.

Acting on inner impulse is one aspect of physical expression. We also develop imaginative images of our characters as we progress through rehearsal. We start to see the appearance – height, build, colouring, posture, distinctive and hereditary features – walk, mannerisms, and clothes of the character; hear its voice; sense its smell. These aspects may come from ourselves, our memories of people we've met, fiction, observation of strangers in various physical conditions, and social and professional situations, or research from photos, film, and art. Whatever we draw on, our images must be based on recognisable human experience so that they are believable, detailed and justified by the text and our understanding of the rest of the character. Crutches and prosthetic noses might not be a good idea. Nor is 'rubber stamp' acting: for example, playing a stereotype or caricature, always trying to present oneself in a flattering light, or using the same bag of mannerisms and tricks for every part however different.

We can also watch the character live aspects of their life and incorporate the images we see into performance. This is a Michael Chekhov technique mentioned in Seeing the Character in Chapter 6, and like Stanislavski, he urges a gradual, unrushed approach. As indicated before, the physical elements incorporated will have a reciprocal effect on the psychology. We all know the effects of dressing up as a different person such as a judge, gangster, or nurse. Our experience of the external aspects of these types of character will prompt a certain quality, tempo, and manner of thinking, speaking and movement, but it's important in this process not to lose connection with yourself or the creation of a specific character. 'Learn to love your role in yourself', Stanislavski says in *Building a Character*, rather than yourself in the role. A fully physicalised characterisation both hides the 'actor-individual' and allows us to bare ourselves as well. The character should be derived from our own nature but we also observe it as a creation.

## Voice and speech

Contrary to the conventional wisdom on Stanislavski, he was a stickler on the importance of clear, structured speech and a well-produced, resonant voice, and would have been horrified by the association of inarticulate mumbling and dismissal of language with his approach. He said, 'Of what use will all the subtleties of emotion be if they are expressed in poor speech? A first-class musician should never play on an instrument out of tune'. The voice and speech, as well as the body, should be trained and subtle instruments for communicating all the character's thoughts, objectives, and feelings, and be ready for each demand made upon them. If you're having to think about overcoming deficiencies while you're working it will detract from the main creative demands of the play. You become self-conscious and unable to allow your intuition to work freely. The work on voice and speech has to be constant, so that correct speech and vocal production becomes a habit in everyday life. Stanislavski insisted that speech is music. A text is like a symphony, and only *an unbroken line of sound* produced with virtuosity will bring it to life. Individual sounds outside of any sense of structure and design will not do this.

First of all a text must be understood, and all the analysis we looked at in the last chapters will ensure that. We can understand the play's through line by examining units, objectives, and actions. In order to communicate them to an audience, Stanislavski highlights the importance of the following elements.

## Diction

Actors have to shape sounds to be intelligible, and articulate not only phrases and words but also each syllable and letter. To miss any of these elements would be like dropping notes in a piece of music, or missing out letters in a book in a way that damages an appreciation of the whole. Poor diction will make the audience struggle to understand, take their attention away from an appreciation of the important creative aspects of a production, and break the all-important contact with the actors. Stanislavski also indicates the different qualities of vowels and consonants, likening vowels to a river full of emotional and spiritual content and consonants to the banks which keep them contained. This is very like Rudolph Steiner's identification of emotion with vowels and the will with consonants. Often vowels are spoken in a truncated, tightened way that doesn't allow for emotions to be communicated through the language. Equally, consonants are often blurred and softened, or barked out.

Sometimes, poor diction is a result of the actors' confusion over what they are saying. They and the director haven't made clear the meaning of the language, the objectives behind it and the actions to pursue them. It's an acting problem. If the clarity of meaning *is* there but speech is not clear then you have a speech problem, and work on the articulators of lips, tongue, and teeth is necessary to produce ease, flow, clarity and expressiveness. In the instance where a character is *written* with poor diction, possibly for comic effect, it's important that the actor still makes clear what is meant to be clear and doesn't worsen the articulation further.

## Voice production

Stanislavski emphasises good *tone* to engage an audience; *range* to express language with flexibility using low, high and middle registers; and *power* to ensure the voice is heard at the back of the theatre. Affecting all of these elements is *placement*. He focused on singing as the means to develop a good speaking voice, and on the recommendation of singers he opted for a placement in the 'mask', the front of the face, so that sound is produced on the hard palate to produce a ring and clarity, as opposed to muffled sounds produced on the soft palate at the back of the mouth. This is still what is taught by voice teachers today. However, although we have singing tuition in the acting schools, we have specialist voice teachers for the speaking voice. Uta Hagen, in *A Challenge for the Actor*, recommends *only* singing training for the voice as a defence against vocal exercises that can cause self-conscious listening to oneself. If voice training is fully integrated into acting courses favouring the organic approach then the dangers of self-listening are minimised because the voice is there to serve the acting. Of course, if voice and movement are seen as all-important, and acting technique and methodology are not taught then we can see actors observing themselves instead of using their physical instruments to serve the character and play. Both singing and speech tuition emphasise good alignment and breath support, but also important is the *onset of sound*, how the breath acts on the vocal folds. With singing, pitch range is given in the notes on the page. With speaking, we improvise our pitch range and intonation (see below). Often when working on breath support, student actors in particular may concentrate on this so much that their expression becomes monotonous. Speech work focuses on keeping the voice centred – grounded, easy and controlled – and can work with the organic approach to free up the actor's range and flexibility in a way that singing alone may not.

Stanislavski doesn't dwell on the importance of breathing, breath support and body alignment. Without good alignment there will be areas of tension which will damage breath support, and without good support and inspiration of the breath you'll damage your creative inspiration. This is not a book that sets out to include detailed recommendations on movement and voice training – I'll leave that to specialists in the field – but I shall come back to the essentials required of a voice in performance.

## Intonation

This means the variation and accenting of the voice according to what we're saying, why and to whom. In real life, we listen and respond and speak because we want to hear something and communicate something back, and our voices usually reflect this. In performance, if this need isn't cultivated and made strong in ways we've looked at in earlier chapters speech becomes mechanical and actors, through error, incompetence or laziness, speak in a monotone, emptily reciting lines. Some actors, on the other hand, consciously render lines in a perverse way to follow a particular fashion or to show off an ability in vocal pyrotechnics. For example, at least one leading actor is renowned for manipulating lines in a manner that is certainly unexpected but also obliterates their sense. At the National Theatre last night I heard an actor technically run sentences together and then break them in the middle making nonsense of the thought process behind them. Another actor, playing a part full of subtext, complexity and long speeches gave a delivery with an unchanging speech pattern and low energy.

For Stanislavski, the way to overcome these aberrations was to make everything mean more, to raise the stakes, to reproduce what we do in life. A key element in this is the *subtext*: all those circumstances, images, thoughts, objectives and feelings that give rise to what we say and do in a role, and without which the audience might as well read the play for themselves because there would be no point in presenting it in performance. The vocal aspect of communicating the text and subtext should be completely responsive to all these inner impulses. When we speak it has to be for the person playing with us, and not to impress the audience with the beauty of our voices or the cleverness of our delivery. Equally, to really connect with that person we need to *speak to the eye* rather than the ear, to convey all those images associated with the words we have inside our heads so that they receive them. In Chapter 6, Visualising the Action, I talked about the inner film we run when relating events. This gives the words life: talking of a person and where she lives and her relations with her mother will not have the smack of truth unless you construct an imaginary history of these people and know what they look like. You see them in your mind's eye and then speak the words about them, trying to communicate them to the other person. So when we *speak* we run images first, when we *hear* we see what is spoken. Conveying our thoughts and images is *verbal action* aimed at effecting a change in the other person.

## Punctuation and pauses

A fundamental assistance to intonation given by the author is punctuation, which clarifies how the sentences are phrased and structured, and therefore indicates where breath is taken and whether the voice rises or falls. Look at this

Iago speech from Act 1, Scene 3 of *Othello*, which I used in Chapter 4:

Thus do I ever make my fool my purse;
For I mine own gained knowledge should profane
If I would time expend with such snipe
But for my sport and profit. I hate the Moor,
And it is thought abroad that 'twixt my sheets
H'as done my office. I know not if 't be true,
But I, for mere suspicion in that kind,
Will do, as if for surety. He holds me well;
The better shall my purpose work on him.
Cassio's a proper man. Let me see now:
To get his place, and to plume up my will
In double knavery ... how? how? ... let's see.
After some time, to abuse Othello's ears
That he is too familiar with his wife.
He hath a person and a smooth dispose
To be suspected – framed to make women false.
The Moor is of a free and open nature
That thinks men honest that but seem to be so;
And will as tenderly be led by th'nose
As asses are.
I have't! It is engendered! Hell and night
Must bring this monstrous birth to the world's light.

I've chosen a Shakespeare piece because a lot of modern writing minimises punctuation marks and this piece offers a good variety of them. Of course, I recognise that Shakespeare may not have used punctuation and different editors may use slightly different punctuation. The actor, however, can use the punctuation in the chosen edition to reveal the structure of thought and rhythm.

First, we should note where there is no punctuation at the end of a line, where there is an *enjambment*: a linking of one line to another. This occurs, for example, at the end of lines 2 and 3. Some would advocate a slight pause at the end of such a line (as, in fact, does Stanislavski in one of his text examples), but it seems old-fashioned today and also breaks the flow of the sense.

The *comma* is used to separate words and phrases and indicates that a thought is not yet complete, usually prompting a rising inflexion in the voice: as in lines 6–8.

The *semicolon* is used between clauses with associated ideas, which are too short to be made into separate sentences; and again, the vocal inflexion indicates an incomplete thought: as in lines 8–9.

The *colon* is used before a clause that explains or enlarges on the one before: see lines 10–11.

*Dots* are used to indicate thought, or that thoughts are trailing off: as in line 12.

The *dash* is used to mark the beginning and end of an interruption in a sentence, or to indicate an afterthought or emphasis, as in line 16; and may also be used to indicate a thought trailing off at the end of a line or a line interrupted by another speaker.

These punctuation marks demand that the listener pays attention and listens to what follows.

The *full stop* ends a sentence and indicates a thought is complete, prompting a downward inflexion of the voice usually.

The *question mark* also ends a thought but invites an answer and prompts an upward inflexion, as in line 12.

The *exclamation mark* ends a thought in an emphatic manner indicating enthusiasm, anger, insistence, hurt or surprise, and calls for sympathy, obedience or approval, as in line 21.

Simply observing the structure of the lines given by the punctuation will clearly affect our intonation patterns.

Punctuation also indicates *pauses*, by which Stanislavski did not mean long pauses such as we might create between chunks of tense dialogue, but slight breaks which are *logical* according to the punctuation, pauses for *breath*, or *psychological* pauses. Pauses group words together in *measures* of speech, and divide measures from each other. *Logical* pauses in the speech are marked by the commas in lines 6–7: 'I know not if't be true, But I, for mere suspicion in that kind, Will do, as if for surety'. They break the line into different elements: an uncertainty, an indication of his intent, the justification for it, his commitment to action, and the quality of it. According to the text analysis we looked at in Chapter 12, this line arises from a new *beat*, a clear thought with an *action*, which could be to spur himself on. The articulation of each measure within the thought helps the actor to keep in each moment of the thought and express it to the full, rather than rushing through it and losing the sense. A *pause for breath* could be taken at the end of line 1, where there is a semicolon, and then after the full stop in line 4. Then, after: 'I hate the Moor', and after the full stop in line 6, and so on. So we see that a logical pause is formal, following the punctuation, and a breathing pause is determined by the punctuation and the need to flow the lines and not break up the sense. A *psychological pause* is determined by an actor's inner life and Stanislavski calls it an *eloquent silence* – but it has to be used judiciously. It should enhance a logical pause where there is a stop and where – as in Shakespeare and other verse drama – the demands of the metre and necessary tempo-rhythm allow. Possible such pauses could be after 'let's see.' at the end of line 12, where Iago is formulating his course of action; and after 'As asses are' in line 20. This is a broken line and indicates thought for at least the remaining three feet of the pentameter line.

Chekhov elaborates on this sort of pause in *Lessons for the Professional Actor*. A pause is never just a gap – 'it is always the result of what has just happened, or it is the preparation for a coming event'. It might even be both a continuation of something and a turning point of preparation for a new action.

When actors produce intonation which fully expresses meaning, an audience receives not only clarity but also the emotional content. Even where we don't speak their language this can be the case: we can sense what is happening by the nature of their actions and emotions conveyed through vocal and physical expressiveness.

## Accentuation

One of the characteristics of a monotonous expression is the stressing of words equally, either by evening out a delivery in a low-key manner so *nothing* is accentuated or by hitting *every* word emphatically. Sometimes the wrong individual words in a sentence are stressed. Actors may be following a habitual or fashionable pattern of speaking, or the voice is not responding to creative impulse, or, as is very often the case, the meaning hasn't been properly grasped. The accent should 'single out the key word in a phrase or measure' (*Building a*

*Character*) so that the essence of the subtext is highlighted, reflecting, for example, affection, dislike, sarcasm, or distrust. Often, less is more – fewer stresses will most clearly convey meaning.

Another common mistake is to try to calculate the stress as a mental puzzle, accenting each word in turn to see what 'sounds' right, whereas the stress will come naturally if we understand the literal meaning of the lines, what we want by saying them and our relationship to the person we're addressing. The stresses will then come from what we want the other person to understand, what is in our mind and heart and will, and not from us listening to ourselves speaking. So again, we need to *speak to the eye*. For example: *I want you to go out of my room* could have the following accents, and meanings, and qualities:

***I*** want you to go out of my room. Other people may not, but I'm pleading with you.
I want you to ***go*** out of my room! Angrily, to get rid of you.
I want you to go out of my ***room***. Persuasively, to make you look for something elsewhere.

Once the key stresses have been found, there will be other varying degrees of strong and light accentuation, major and minor stresses, that give movement and life to a phrase. Just as words will be stressed, so particular phrases or sentences may be accented above others to bring out their relative importance through inflection, pauses, tempo and rhythm.

In the Iago speech, possible key words are italicised and accented phrases and sentences are underlined:

*Thus* do I ever make my *fool* my *purse*;
For I mine own gained *knowledge* should *profane*
If I would *time* expend with such *snipe*
But for my *sport* and *profit*. <u>I *hate* the *Moor*,</u>
And it is thought *abroad* that 'twixt my *sheets*
H'as done my *office*. I know not if't be *true*,
But *I*, for mere *suspicion* in that kind,
Will *do*, as if for *surety*. He holds me *well*;
The *better* shall my *purpose* work on him.
*Cassio's* a *proper* man. Let me *see* now:

To *get* his *place*, and to *plume* up my *will*
In *double knavery* ... how? *how?* ... let's *see*.
After some time, to *abuse* Othello's *ears*
That he is too *familiar* with his *wife*.
He hath a *person* and a smooth *dispose*
To be *suspected* – framed to make women *false*.
The *Moor* is of a *free* and *open* nature
That thinks men *honest* that but *seem* to be so;
And will as tenderly be *led* by th'*nose*
As *asses* are.
I *have't!* It is *engendered*! *Hell* and *night*
Must *bring* this *monstrous birth* to the *world's light*.

'I hate the Moor' in line 6 might be accented by a slow, steady tempo-rhythm. Lines 13–14 could be highlighted by the psychological pause I suggested earlier after 'let's see' at the end of line 12, and by a different vocal range. The last two lines are marked by a prior pause and a possibly quicker tempo. Note, too, how the stresses on key words increase in the last rhyming couplet, which rounds off the speech with defiant resolution.

This speech is in the *iambic pentameter* form or metre common to Shakespearean and Jacobean drama: an *iamb* is a foot of an unstressed and stressed syllable: – / (de-*dum*); *pentameter* is a line of five feet and ten syllables. This is frequently irregular, though, as we see in this passage. Particularly with blank verse like this we can see how tonal variation in accent works. Below, I've put *my* suggestions in bold for the five beats that must be in each line, however irregular – others may do it differently – and left the key words in italics.

**Af**ter **some** time, to *a**buse*** O**thell**o's ***ears***
That **he** is **too** *fa**mil**iar* **with** his ***wife***.
He **hath** a ***per**son* **and** a **smooth** *dis**pose***
To **be** *sus**pect**ed* – **framed** to make **wom**en ***false***.
The ***Moor*** is **of** a ***free*** and ***op**en* **nat**ure
That **thinks** men ***hon**est* **that** but ***seem*** to **be** so;
And **will** as **ten**der**ly** be ***led*** by th'***nose***
As ***ass**es* **are**.

I ***have't!*** It **is** *en**gen**dered!* ***Hell*** and ***night***
Must ***bring*** this ***monst**rous* ***birth*** to the ***world's light***.

These are just examples of how stress conveys meaning, but again I should emphasise that accentuation must come, not from a dry intellectual calculation, but from imagination, objectives, and a feel for sense and rhythm.

## Tempo-rhythm

Stanislavski stressed tempo and rhythm as elements which give physical and verbal action a distinctive quality and have a strong effect on the emotions. I'll look at this psycho-physical aspect in more detail in the following section. Regarding voice, they are another element determining our intonation patterns.

*Tempo* is the speed of our movement, speech, or music.

*Rhythm* is the pattern of the length and stress of beats of movement, sound and stillness in a particular measure or bar. For example, a waltz has three beats to the bar with a stress on the first beat. Iago's speech has five beats to each line and usually the rhythm is formed by the iambic – /. But we find in Shakespeare four other classical Greek verse rhythms that vary the dominant iambic pattern or metre for the sake of the sense of the line:

| | | |
|---|---|---|
| trochee | / - | **dum**-de |
| anapaest | -- / | de-de-**dum** |
| dactyl | / -- | **dum**-de-de |
| spondee | / / | **dum-dum** |

We can see some examples in the passage above. To reinforce the earlier point, the rhythm will come from the sense and the basic metre and not from mechanical recitation. Stanislavski: 'Rhythm does not consist in stressing iambs and anapaests ... There is nothing more vulgar than a made, sweetish, quasi-poetical voice in lyric poems, which rises and falls like waves during a dead calm' (*My Life in Art*).The tempo in the speech appears to be a steady, medium one, but it might speed up to discordant effect in the last couplet, as suggested above.

In prose, the tempo-rhythm is more flexible. We could speak one phrase of short words in a quick, staccato tempo-rhythm as though we were producing quavers or semi-quavers in a piece of music. The next phrase could consist of longer, slower sounds like half-notes. There might be a pause dividing the two. For example:

*Get out quick while you can! ... I love you so much I can't bear to see you harmed.*

Of course, this is determined by the demands of the text and subtext and not by a desire for external effect, but it's another consideration that enables us to convey the richness of language and the range of emotions we find from comedy to tragedy. Stanislavski's justification is that, 'Art requires order, discipline, precision and finish' (*Building a Character*), and tempo-rhythm, together with the through line and subtext, runs through all movement, speech and emotional experience. It needs to change, however subtly, according to the action. If we decide on one constant tempo-rhythm for sustained passages we'll produce a boring monotony. Some actors and directors fear pauses, particularly in verse, and want to whip things along to a mathematical rhythm because they have created, in Stanislavski's expressive phrase, a *vacuum of subtext*. Of course, the other extreme is to exaggerate attention to the subtext and make numerous and extended pauses that break up the sense of verse and prose. The balanced approach is to achieve a union of the inner tempo-rhythm of the subtext and the external tempo-rhythm of the text so that pauses are organic and not indulged and emotions flow through the lines: an emotion may prompt a particular tempo-rhythm and a tempo-rhythm will stimulate the emotion.

## Accent and dialect

Stanislavski doesn't talk about accents, but we are frequently required to learn them, whether British or foreign, and possibly with a dialect, a specific form of speech and language associated with a particular area, e.g. a Newcastle accent may have a coal miner dialect. Obviously, it helps to have a good 'ear', an ability to hear and reproduce different sounds and rhythms, but most of the time, we need to put in some work on making an accent sound authentic.

A number of factors influence accents, e.g. geography, history, culture, climate, class, occupation, gender and education. We need to be aware of our own accent and how it differs from the one we are working on, plus a variety of other elements. What is the tune, rhythm, energy, and pace? How is it stressed and how loud is it? How is the sound actually formed through the vowels and consonants?

Where is the accent placed in the mouth? What shapes do the tongue and lips make when making the sounds? How does it affect the rest of the body?

We have to do our research on all these elements, do breakdowns of the accent – preferably through phonetics – get hold of recordings of authentic voices, and listen to them regularly. CDs can be bought in theatre bookshops, some are included with dialect books, and you can listen to recordings at the National Sound Archive at the British Museum. We will have different approaches to mastering an accent according to our abilities. Some may get on top of an accent before rehearsals begin and be able to use it on text from the start without falling into the main danger of accent work: just doing the accent and obliterating the sense of the lines. Others may need a more gradual approach and the help of a dialect coach. Whatever your pace of working, the accent should first be mastered *off* the text, by reading newspapers, novels, or other plays in the accent. Only when you're confident and fluent in the accent should you try it out on the text you're working on, so that it becomes an organic part of the character.

## Vocal aims

As a result of vocal training we should aim to have developed a well-produced, resonant and clearly-articulated voice, the essential elements of which are:

- Good alignment with spinal and rib flexibility.
- Expressive pitch range.
- A centred impulse for breath and abdominal support for breath and sound.
- Developed use of areas of resonance (e.g. head, chest, pelvis).
- Open and free vocal folds.
- Clear placement of the voice and onset of sound.
- Power to fill a performance space.
- Expressive intonation (e.g. through use of pitch range, tempo-rhythm and stress).
- Muscular, clear articulation.
- Developed ear for accent and dialect.
- Connection to the audience (through connection of breath to thought and thought to language).

# Psycho-physical tools

The whole approach of Stanislavski and Michael Chekhov is a psycho-physical one: one that elicits a physical effect from a psychological impulse and a psychological effect from a physical one. This is the case whether we are focusing on objectives, atmosphere, or sense memory. When we come to look specifically at the physical embodiment of our characters there are some useful techniques in addition to those I described at the beginning of the chapter.

## Tempo-rhythm in movement

As we saw above, tempo-rhythm can help us give fuller expression to language. A particular inner impulse, like an emotion, can prompt a particular tempo-rhythm. Stanislavski also observed that a tempo-rhythm can stimulate the inner life and feelings and arouse in the actor 'a true sense of living his part'. He even goes so far as to say that the words and thoughts in a text arouse our mind, our will is affected by the objectives, and our 'feelings are directly worked on by tempo-rhythm'.

He demonstrated this by using metronome beats and clapping. A repeated clap on the first of four even beats produced a feeling of boredom and monotony in his students. Changing the crochets (quarter notes) to quavers (eighth notes) and stressing the first of each pair of quavers, livened things up: *One* and *two* and *three* and *four* and ... When he increased the time of the metronome to produce sixteenth and thirty-second notes, and got the students to clap on each note with a stress on the first note of each quarter of the bar they became sweaty, pained and disturbed. So, their mood altered from soporific to overexcited as a result of the change in tempo-rhythm. They then clapped out the tempo-rhythm of a storm at sea, quacking ducks and throbbing toothaches, grief and ecstasy.

A more direct application to performance was revealed when he looked at specific circumstances. He asks a student to beat out the tempo-rhythm of someone embarking on a train journey: queuing for a ticket, sorting out hand luggage, looking over the news stand, getting a meal, settling in to the train, reading a paper, losing and finding an item of luggage. The numerous objectives are executed in a leisurely manner because there is plenty of time before the train leaves. Then the same actions are performed with only five minutes to go and then with no time to spare at all, so the tempo-rhythm becomes increasingly full of agitation and haste. The tempo-rhythm cannot be recreated in an organic way unless the circumstances and images giving rise to the objectives and emotions are recalled. The imagined circumstances create the tempo-rhythm and the tempo-rhythm can then stimulate the thoughts, images and emotions. This is the psycho-physical interrelationship.

In this last exercise the tempo-rhythm is not likely to be simply physical. An inner one is also created. For example, when the traveller is rushing to find his lost luggage the external and internal tempo-rhythm may be fast and jerky, but when he is sitting reading a paper the external may be slower and steadier while the internal may still be racing. Even when the actor is sitting quietly in performance there is still action happening inside and that action will have a specific tempo and rhythm according to the intensity of the state of mind and emotions, the speed of thought and imagination, of taking things in through the senses, of impulses from images. If the actor intuitively creates the actions, interaction and atmosphere that serve the writer's intentions, the right tempo-rhythm is likely to emerge. If this doesn't happen then we have to experiment with tempo-rhythm. There is no single means for getting the tempo-rhythm right if actors' individual and collective sense of pace is out of synch with the play. It is the sum total of elements in a performance that will create the tempo-rhythms and actors need to develop a strong sense of the whole and the tempo-rhythms required by it and then be able to reproduce these in every performance like a good musician.

The great actors Stanislavski observed had a developed sense of this but would also stand in the wings well before their entrances and take in the tempo and rhythm already established on the stage, and so become more able to strike the right note having entered the action. Of course, the converse of this is that if the tempo and rhythm are wrong onstage you can enter and try to rectify them, providing a new burst of energy or slowing down an inappropriate rush. Knowing the level of *performance energy* required is important in judging tempo and rhythm – and imagining the radiating golden ball of energy in your solar plexus is a good means for creating this and bringing it onstage (see the basic Michael Chekhov exercise in Chapter 2). Sometimes directors say 'Act quicker', or 'Act slower'; without elaboration this can be a glib direction. However, there is often some validity in the instruction. If a piece of dialogue is written in short sentences which indicate an urgent need to come to a decision and the actors are placing pauses before every line, then speeding up the tempo can create tighter interaction, stronger and clearer objectives and actions, and more intense feelings as a result. Equally, if actors rush a tender scene in which two people are exploring their love for each other then the objectives will not be played correctly and genuine feeling will not be allowed to happen.

Where the inner and outer tempo-rhythms are different – for example, a quick inner and slow outer, a slow inner and quick outer – we set up an *internal conflict* which can heighten the actor's experience of the part and the dramatic content of the action. It's not always the case that we have slow or fast inner *and* outer tempo-rhythms. For example, a person may sit motionless but absorbed in powerful emotions that are being concealed. The inner tempo is fast and the outer slow. Every now and then the person may get up and pace with a quick tempo and staccato rhythm like the inner ones: Hedda Gabler or Hamlet perhaps. A woman being led to execution at a slow measured pace may have a seething quick inner tempo, full of anxious thoughts, feelings and memories. In addition she may be reciting a prayer in a different tempo-rhythm and her hands might be wringing in a fourth one: Joan of Arc or Lorca's Mariana Pineda, for example. A slow-witted person may have a slow inner tempo but a quick, fidgety, jerky outer tempo-rhythm. The inner and outer tempo-rhythms would be the same if, for example, you are calmly reading a book; or if you are very late for an important appointment and are rushing to find your way through a maze of streets. Different styles of play clearly have different recurring tempo-rhythms: a Feydeau farce like *A Flea in Her Ear* has some frenetic inner and outer ones; Chekhov and Ibsen plays often have characters who are controlled and still outwardly, while inwardly in turmoil. The more complex and contradictory the human situation in a play the more likely are there to be two or more tempo-rhythms in the characters.

Within a performance there will not be one fixed set of tempo-rhythms for each character all the way through. They must change according to each change in circumstances. Equally, each character in a set of circumstances may well have different tempo-rhythms to each other. Everyone, for example, will not be overcome by blind panic if a hurricane strikes, or show total lethargy in a heat wave. All the actors' tempo-rhythms combined will create a particular integrated tempo-rhythm and atmosphere, whether anxious or carefree, formal or anarchic. If this is sustained throughout the whole performance, however, it will get very monotonous, so each scene may well demand a different collective tempo-rhythm according to the circumstances and different objectives and emotions of all the characters. This is something which can only be achieved by the director and actors working as a team.

## Laban's efforts

The analysis of movement by Rudolph Laban, the Hungarian dance theorist, complements any consideration of tempo-rhythm and other aspects of physicalisation, and provided it is used in acting in an imaginative and not a cerebral way can be a useful prompt to creativity and inspiration. He used three basic categories to define movement: *space, weight,* and *time*. We move through space in a direct or flexible, indirect way. Our weight is strong, heavy, and forceful, or light, delicate and buoyant. Our timing is quick, sudden, broken, or sustained and steady. All movement contains some combination of these elements to produce what Laban termed *efforts*.

There are eight actions, which I've placed below in pairs of opposites and with their combination of elements:

| ACTION | SPACE | WEIGHT | TIME |
|---|---|---|---|
| *Pressing* | Direct | Heavy | Sustained |
| *Flicking* | Flexible/Indirect | Light | Sudden |
| *Punching or Thrusting* | Direct | Heavy | Sudden |
| *Floating* | Flexible/Indirect | Light | Sustained |
| *Slashing* | Flexible/Indirect | Heavy | Sudden |
| *Gliding* | Direct | Light | Sustained |
| *Wringing* | Flexible/Indirect | Heavy | Sustained |
| *Dabbing* | Direct | Light | Sudden |

So, when we talk of a character having a quick and jerky tempo-rhythm they could be using the efforts of *flicking* or *slashing*: indirect, light/heavy, sudden. If we have a strong and steady tempo-rhythm we might be *pressing* or *wringing*: direct/indirect, heavy, sustained. If we are explosive and fast we could be *punching* or *slashing*: direct/indirect, heavy, sudden. If our tempo-rhythm is slow and calm we might be *floating* or *gliding*: indirect/direct, light, sustained. This analysis also relates to the next section on Michael Chekhov's work on gesture.

Laban elaborates on these efforts through the concept of *flow*. An action is *bound* if it meets resistance and is controlled. It is *free* if it meets little resistance. The actions of pressing and wringing clearly have a *bound* flow. Gliding also has a bound flow, although to a lesser degree, because of some resistance from, say, ice or air. The actions of flicking and slashing have a *free* flow. Punching or thrusting, dabbing and floating can be performed with a bound *or* free flow. To get a grasp of these efforts try performing them in the sequence of opposite pairs above and use your whole body – hands, arms, legs, feet, shoulders, head, bottom – to create the action of pressing, floating, wringing, etc.

Although Laban devised these categories to define movement and dance, we can use them as actors to define the physicality of our characters in a more detailed and precise way. So, having developed the action and inner life of the character we can ask what its predominant effort actions might be, and what the quality of its outer *and* inner movement is. A busy person with many interests might be a dabber, but they might be uncertain and flexible over life's priorities and floating inside. A controlled, determined person with an inner turmoil might be pressing externally and wringing inside. An easy-going person who usually takes life as it comes but has occasional bouts of violence and anger might be a glider and a puncher. Someone who is very indirect and abrupt and rejects people with differing degrees of strength or lightness may be a slasher and a flicker. Different efforts might also help to reveal a subtext of feelings contrary to what is being said: tell someone to 'Go away' using a punching action on the words when you really want them to stay and are wringing inside; say 'I love you' in an easy gliding manner when inside you really want to flick the person away; say 'That's fine, fine' as a float when inside you'd prefer to slash a problem aside. Try improvising or reading scenes under the influence of one particular effort and then look at different combinations of effort that might express the scene more fully.

This outline of Laban's analysis above is rudimentary, but I include it to point out that there are strands of theory and practice not connected with Stanislavski that are useful and complementary. If you are interested in finding out more about Laban, there are numerous books by and about him, there is a Laban Centre in London, and acting schools like East 15 and Drama Centre have classes in Laban technique.

## Psychological gesture

This is one of the best-known of Michael Chekhov's techniques. We've looked at his ideas on atmosphere – the objective feeling – and on the stimulation of individual feelings. The *Psychological Gesture* (PG) is a key to engaging our *will*. In *To the Actor*, Chekhov devotes two-thirds of the chapter, How to Approach the Part, to Stanislavski's ideas on objectives and Superobjectives and describes units and objectives as 'perhaps his most brilliant inventions, and when properly understood and correctly used can lead the actor immediately to the very core of the play and the part': an insight effectively deleted from the practice of some Chekhov 'experts'. Objectives engage the will and the feelings, provided they are strongly imagined and experienced. Physical actions and gestures will arise organically from their execution if the body is responsive to creative impulse. Also, a physical action and gesture can arouse and strengthen the will.

The PG is a means of physicalising the psychological essence of the whole character with its basic desire or Superobjective at its core. Chekhov got the idea for it from experience. Stanislavski and Vakhtangov, as his directors when playing Khlestakov in *The Government Inspector* and Erik XIV in Strindberg's play of that name, made vivid gestures to demonstrate to him the whole psychology of the characters. He said from that point he grasped what they were. The PG stirs and directs the will in a particular direction. It is a full-body gesture. It is non-naturalistic and expressive – everyday gestures being too limited and weak to stir the will in the same way. It is an active gesture not a pose – like the basic exercises in Chapter 2, (growing bigger, smaller, etc.) it has a clear starting point, an execution, and a finishing point. Crucially it is an imaginative means for grasping a sense of the whole character, which avoids 'vague floundering and arid reasoning' (*On the Technique of Acting*).

The *kind* of gesture will awaken a specific desire.
The *strength* of it stirs the will.
The *quality* evokes particular feelings.

Here are two examples. Imagine a character who wants to gain absolute power because they see it as their right and will go to any lengths to achieve it, who has a very strong will, and callous, ruthless feelings. An appropriate gesture might start with the legs apart and hands at the side. The right arm swings back and then thrusts up to the sky with fingers stretched and grasping as the right leg thrusts forward and the left arm swings across the chest and then slashes down to the left of the body as if suppressing opposition. Hold and radiate the gesture for a few moments, as in Chapter 3. Do it several times, and you will be filled with the sense of a strong will and a desire to gain power, and the qualities of the gesture will evoke feelings of ruthlessness.

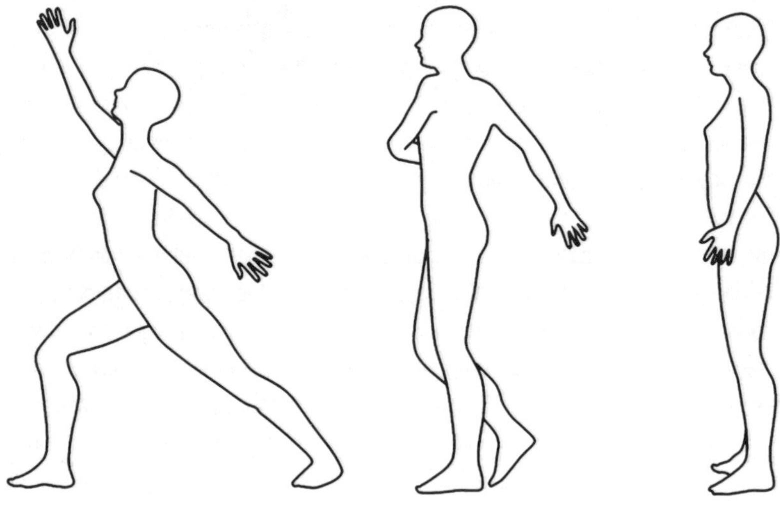

In contrast, let's take a character who wants to find love because they are alone and lost, but the will is weak and their feelings are ones of suffering and fear. The starting position could be feet together and on an angle with the body slightly leaning back and the hands cupped over the stomach. The left hand moves gently forward, palm up, searching and appealing, as the left foot makes a small step forward and the right hand raises to protect the chest area. Radiate the gesture, do it several times, and you can experience a yearning desire, fearful feelings and a hesitant will.

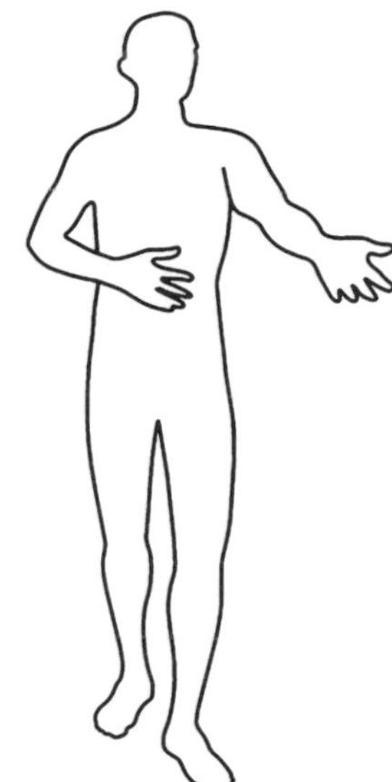

All PGs, however different, should be:

**Strong** – this means strong in conception and execution, as opposed to forceful; not all characters are like the first example, some are like the second. You can embody gentle, weak or lazy qualities in the PG but it must be executed in a way that stirs us: the actor's gesture must not be weak and lazy even if the character is. Also, the gesture must be performed with *ease*, without muscular tension.

**Simple** – in the sense of condensing a complex character into its essential core. The gesture is one flowing sustained movement – not a series of demonstrations of different aspects of the character, or a depiction of a typical movement or activity you've discovered in rehearsal. If you are using two or three stages in the gesture, condense them to one unified continuous movement. Although it needs to be simple in this respect, it can nevertheless embody a quality that Chekhov believes makes us human, as referred to before: contradiction. Just as every objective has an obstacle to overcome, so every will-based gesture can include a resistance. In the first example, as the character grasps upwards for power, they also suppress opposition with a slashing gesture. In the Laban terms we've just examined, they thrust and slash. In the second gesture, the character reaches out tentatively while they also protect their centre. In Laban terms, they might be floating and wringing.

**Clear in form** – as with the basic exercises in Chapter 2, all PGs should have clarity and cleanness of execution with no imprecision. The action, just like actions in performance, should begin, be executed, and finish with conviction and a sense of form and entirety. Any vagueness will weaken the effect of the gesture on your inner life.

**Definite in tempo** – as we've seen in the section on tempo-rhythm, each character will have different ones. We can sense the different tempos in the two examples. The first is a gesture executed with force and violence and a quick driven tempo. The second suffering and yearning gesture is uncertainly slow. However, if you changed the tempos of these two gestures it would alter the whole sense of the character. A slow tempo with the first would make the character more intellectually calculating and deliberate so the nature of the will and qualities is altered. A quick tempo with the second would make the character slightly manic, even threatening and provocative, with a stronger thrusting will.

To arrive at the PG which captures the essence of the character we have to experiment, monitor the effect of it, try different things until we are genuinely satisfied that it makes us feel we have the character. We can try creating a PG early on in rehearsal, using our basic intuitive grasp of the character as a guide. The first question to ask as a stimulus to this creative imaginative work is 'What is the main desire of the character?' This is worth stressing, because the PG is essentially working on the will. I've attended classes where it was presented as a depiction of emotional states. This is not to say that gesture work cannot be about this. Augusto Boal, the Brazilian practitioner best-known for his *Theatre of the Oppressed*, uses expression of personal, social and political relationships through physical tableaux, and explores emotional states in a play through physical gesture. You can use gestures to express anything in fact. I was once required by a director to physicalise a character's attitude to his environment. All such work can aid the process of achieving organic acting, and I personally find it a useful addition to the Stanislavski/Chekhov process.

The PG, though, is very specifically concerned with grasping the essential character through its will and desires. Once you have a sense of what the character basically wants you can start with hand and arm gestures that express, for example, dominating, acquisitive, loving desires. The hands thrust down to the ground, or reach and gather imagined wealth, or open and lift to reach the object of love, in the same way as we've already looked at physicalising individual actions. You can then progress to engaging all the other body parts: head, trunk, legs and feet, so that the whole body is employed in expressing the character's qualities, and their particular mix of intellect, will and emotion. The starting position could be a neutral one, but I opt for one that reflects where the character is coming from, as in the two examples above. So, someone who feels inferior and rejected but wants to find fame and fortune might start from a crouched wrapped-over position (as in the 'growing smaller' basic exercise) and then unwrap and stretch out and up into a fully opened one.

Having made these first attempts at the PG we can keep returning to it during rehearsal as we get to know and experience more of our character, and refine it. Speak your Superobjective before and while doing the PG. Are they an accurate expression of each other? If not, one of them needs modifying. Informed by the PG, you may find your objective isn't clear and specific enough. If the PG needs adapting, small adjustments can produce significant effects. Chekhov gives examples: bending one knee might suggest surrender; the head tilted back can produce qualities of pain and pleading; the palms turned outwards suggest self-defence, and so on. A different tempo might be called for. We can also add a vocal expression for the PG. As we do the gesture, we make a sound that fits it and expresses the character's essential qualities, for example, a fully voiced roar of triumph, a reedy note of yearning, a sustained sigh of relief. This refining is designed to increase the sensitivity and responsiveness of our body, psychology and speech so they become fully integrated. Ultimately, you alone know if you've got the right PG, because you know if it serves your creation of a character. Chekhov saw the PG as the spine or scaffolding of a part, and as such it should not be shown to an audience; but as an archetypal gesture, one that is a model for other similar gestures, it may inspire what gestures and vocal qualities you develop as the character through rehearsal and performance. When we get to performance, we can use the PG beforehand as part of our imaginative preparation. Doing it a few times gets a sense of the whole character into our body, will and emotions.

To practice working on the PG, we can take characters from novels, history, or real people we know or see in the street. Imagine their lives and main desires and then intuitively find the gesture for them. Do a PG for a character from a play that interests you and then rehearse a speech or scene under the influence of it.

Apart from using the PG to grasp the character as a whole, Chekhov also applied it to find a score of physical gestures to express the content and development of whole scenes, and changing atmospheres, which all the actors concerned would work on. In terms of work on a role, the PG can be applied to a speech, sentences or individual moments. As an example, he looks at Horatio's speech to the Ghost in Act 1, Scene 1 of *Hamlet*:

> I'll cross it, though it blast me.
> *Stay, illusion!*
> If thou hast any sound, or use of voice,
> *Speak to me:*
> If there be any good thing to be done,
> That may to thee do ease, and grace to me,
> *Speak to me:*
> If thou art privy to thy country's fate,
> Which happily foreknowing may avoid,
> *O! speak;*
> Or if thou hast uphoarded in thy life
> Extorted treasure in the womb of earth,
> For which, they say, you spirits oft walk in death,
> *Speak of it: stay and speak! Stop it, Marcellus.*

First, we create a PG for the speech on the basis of Horatio's objective: to fix the unknown being and make it speak its secrets, with a quality of commanding excitement. Chekhov suggests this could be a violent thrust forward on the right leg with the right arm striving forward and up, and the left extended behind and facing the ground. The gesture is executed several times so that the objective and quality are fully absorbed into the whole body. Then you speak the lines with the gesture, and finally without the gesture but so that it affects how you say them. Next he looks at how this PG may vary if applied to each of the italicised commands, as above. Horatio starts addressing the Ghost firmly but with a sense of respect and awe. The Ghost doesn't answer though and starts to leave. Horatio grows impatient and bewildered, and ends up with an offensive irritability. The gesture Chekhov creates for this quality with the same objective involves the right arm pointed to the ground with the right leg extended and the left leg bent with the left arm circled up. So, he creates a polarity between the two gestures. He then looks at the commands in the middle part of the speech for which there should be variant PGs which form transitions from the first to the last. Finally, PGs can be found for the lines in between each command. In each case, the PG is executed, then done with the line, and finally the line is said without the gesture but expressing it through the words.

Chekhov emphasised two other elements which affect the performance of the PG: *imaginary space and time*. Imagine that the space in which you are performing is open and endless or narrow and confined. Imagine the time in which you do it is a long period or a short period. Each will have a clear effect on how the PG is executed. As an example, do the growing bigger, opening out gesture from Chapter 2. First, do it as if in endless space with an infinite amount of time, then try it in a confined space with very little time. Next, start in a fully opened position and then contract into the growing smaller, closing gesture from Chapter 2, and do it as if in a confined space but with a lot of time, and then in an open space with little time. Experiment with other combinations. Imagine characters with different predominant qualities such as curiosity, shyness or arrogance and place them in a simple situation like choosing a book to read or looking at goods in a shop. Then create a sense of expanded or contracted time and space around them, for example, the arrogant person may expand the space and time, whereas the curious person may expand the space but contract time.

Chekhov perceptively sees our emotions as having different scales: joy, love and excitement exist in a large space for a short period of time, whereas sorrow, grief, and longing are more confined and last longer. Experimenting in this way gives our work a 'fantastic' element – something heightened beyond the everyday and naturalistic – which can make the actor an 'actor-magician' rather than an 'actor-reporter'.

As should be clear by now, the point of the PG is to stir a particular desire, engage the will, stimulate the feelings and get the character into the whole body.

## Imaginary centre

We all experience ourselves in a different way. There is usually one place where we feel we 'live' inside our bodies, our particular character centre. For example, a very brainy scholar will most likely exist in the head; a strong, driven person in the lower body or thighs; an emotional, sensitive person in the chest. These three examples relate to the inner motive forces of mind, will and feeling, mentioned earlier. The centres can be placed anywhere, though. When we adopt a different centre to our own for a character we are creating what Chekhov calls an *Imaginary Centre*. If we open ourselves imaginatively and respond physically with ease to the influence of new centres then they will affect us both psychologically and physically, and we will experience our identity and activity as coming from a different place.

First of all we locate the Imaginary Centre. We can then play with it and give it size, softness or hardness, stillness or movement. We can also give it texture, colour and temperature; there are really no limits to this because there are no limits to our imagination. If I place a light, white centre in the top of my head I get a feeling of egotism and arrogance. If I place a fuzzy smoky black cloud of a centre in the back of my head I feel vague, dreamy and melancholic. If I place a shiny black smooth still cold hard ball-bearing in the middle of my forehead I get a sense of an unfeeling, single-minded, ruthless person. A light small hard centre in the tip of my nose could make me inquisitive or supercilious. A revolving warm golden ball of energy in my solar plexus gives me the ideal centre of confidence and energy (see Chapter 2). A large soft centre in my pelvis makes me feel languorous and sexy. Two firm rods in my thighs give me a sense of weight, power and earthiness. The centre can also be outside the body. A bright light circling round and above my head makes me feel unstable and out of control. Every different centre should have a different effect not only on how we feel but also on our physicality. Subtle changes should be occurring with each new imaginative influence so that we are not moving as we normally do. Perhaps our posture straightens, our pace lengthens or quickens, our hands clasp and arms fold, our knees bend more, our pelvis swings forward, and our head angle alters. So, the Imaginary Centre is a way of changing ourselves through the creative imagination, as opposed to consciously deciding on some manner for effect or simply staying as we are in everyday life. As Chekhov says: 'How would you evaluate a painter who is unable to create anything but self-portraits?' (*To the Actor*).

To get a sense of these centres before working on a character centre try walking around as yourself and locate your own centre. Then experiment with placing different types of centre in various areas of your body and note how you feel and change physically, monitoring the differences to how you normally are. Once you've found a possible centre for your character, move under its influence. Try out all the usual types of movement we do in a day: walk quickly and slowly, run, sit, lie down, get up. Then handle objects under its influence: put on a coat, unpack a bag, open a window, close a door, carry a chair across the room, drink from a bottle. Only focus on this specific stimulus, not the whole character, and it is *you* with a different centre initially. You must start with yourself, keep your actions truthful and not lapse into caricature and clowning. When you feel the centre is genuinely transforming you, choose a typical activity the character might do and execute it with the centre: washing dishes, grooming a horse, brushing your hair, writing a letter, painting a wall, etc. This should be a task you can tackle and finish – sitting thinking or lying in the sun doesn't count! While doing the actions express sounds, words and sentences suggested by the centre.

Sometimes actors think a character has more than one centre, for example, the head and womb, or the eyes and chest. This may be so, but only work on one at a time. You may find that the different centres actually appear not simultaneously but at different points of the action. For example, a character who is idealistic and visionary could be centred in the eyes, but at some points there may be deep suffering and the centre may be in the solar plexus, and at another point the will takes over and they drive forward from a centre in the pelvis. How much the centre changes is for you and the director to judge, as is the degree to which the sensation of it is displayed. It may appear very strongly or very subtly depending on the style of play and nature of the character.

## Imaginary body

Chekhov looks at this concept first and the Imaginary Centre afterwards. I find that the Centre literally provides a centre for a new body and gives the actor a firm basis for developing physicalisation further, and helps to avoid the temptation of putting on a whole new body like a wig. In arriving at an *Imaginary Body* we need to imagine what sort of body fits essential aspects of the character: its main qualities, Superobjective, balance of intellect, emotion and will. It could be fat or thin, tall or short, muscled or flabby. Imagine that *in the space of your body* there exists this other different body which you have just brought to mind. It's as if it's grown out of your own flesh and bones.

You can do some preparatory exercises to get a feel for the process before working on your character. Lift your arm and note its weight, shape and the ease with which it moves. Then do the same with a leg. Walk around with an awareness of your height, weight, build, posture, your centre and the space you fill. Now imagine that in the space of your arm is a long, spindly and angular arm and lift it. Imagine your leg is the same and lift and lower that. Now imagine that in the space of your whole body is that of a tall, spindly, angular one. Adapt your body to that image as much as you can – by lengthening the spine, for example – and start to move under its influence. Locate where this body's Imaginary Centre is. As we did with the centre, walk, run, sit, lie. Experiment with objects. Place yourself in a crowded shop or try running for a bus. You'll find that the new body also affects your psychology, will and feelings far more than would any piece of clothing.

Chekhov suggests a lazy, sluggish and awkward character, who might have a full, plump, short body with drooping shoulders, thick neck, and listlessly hanging arms. You may look nothing like this, any more than you resembled the tall, spindly character. To apply padding or prosthetics would simply create an external effect. So again, we should start imaginatively. Begin by imagining and moving the arms and legs. Then imagine that in the space of your whole body is this short, plump, heavy one. Your own will have to transform into it by shortening the spine, allowing your stomach to sag, your knees to bend, and a double chin to appear, while always remaining free from tension as the actor. A supple, easy body is again essential here! Once the body is imaginatively created in this way, then external clothing and padding will appear credible. Move under the influence of this body and see where its Centre may be. As before, walk, run, sit, lie down, get up. Handle objects and perform tasks. Then choose an activity this lazy, sluggish person might typically do: make a cup of tea, fill in a lottery card, take shoes off, for example. All the time, focus only on this particular influence rather than trying to play the whole character. It may be big, bold and even grotesque, but it has to come out of you in a truthful way. Allow sounds, words and sentences to appear.

To experiment further, take three qualities – for example, energetic, humorous and shallow, or grumpy, lonely and intellectual – and imagine the body which fits them, then work on it as above.

From this work may emerge what Chekhov calls *peculiar features of characterisation*: a typical movement, manner of speech, a way of laughing, of walking or holding the hands. For example, a self-conscious person might straighten his cuffs or pick fluff off his jacket while in conversation. A controlling person might arrange things on the table in front of him. A misanthropic one may push away things within her reach. A nervous person may clear her throat. An impatient one may click his fingers. These will emerge organically from playful invention around the Imaginary Centre and Body and the development of the character's whole psychology.

## Sensation of feeling

We looked at this in Chapter 8 on Feeling, but it's worth looking at it again from the point of view of physicalisation. We create a sensation of a particular quality or feeling by making simple physical movements associated with it. For example, I move under the influence of a quality of fear, creating the gestures and thoughts associated with it, and as a result, reach a genuine feeling of fear, other feelings associated with it – and also a physicality arising from it. This was evident from the examples I gave in this earlier chapter of working under the influence of generosity, suspicion and aggression, which all produced very different physicalities, sense of space, and relationship to others.

Here's another example, of actors working under the influence of fear for a production of *The House of Bernarda Alba*:

- Physically, the arms hang loose by the sides but the chests recede.
- They keep to the walls and often crouch, keeping a distance and making no contact.
- They move in an indirect, heavy, sustained way or sometimes directly, strongly and suddenly. The tempo is either slow or very quick and darting: in Laban terms, they wring and punch.
- Other qualities appearing are watchfulness, isolation, and suspicion.

What struck me about this, was the avoidance of stock gestures you might immediately associate with fear, and the occurrence of the unpredictable. They didn't hold their hands and arms in front of their faces or protectively wrap the arms around themselves, for example. Instead, the arms hung loose in a sort of transfixed paralysis. For me, this produced a more rich and credible physicalisation of fear than could be created intellectually from the outside. Through the imaginative impulse of creating a sensation of a particular quality or feeling they freed their intuition arising from common human experience.

We can also do the exercises from the earlier sections. Under the influence of fear try the various everyday types of movement, work with objects, and execute a task while adding sounds, words and maybe an internal monologue, again integrating imagination, physicality and voice.

# 14 Refining the role

> *Art is search, not final form*
>
> Yevgeny Vakhtangov

> *The process of creating a performance is not like laying bricks but more like giving birth: all the elements have to work organically*
>
> Lev Dodin

In the work on the role so far we have placed ourselves in the circumstances of the character, found interaction with our fellow actors, played our objectives within the action, and started to develop the sensory, emotional and physical life of the character. We have arrived at that state of 'I am' where we feel a unity between ourselves and the character and believe in what is happening in the action. This is where our creative intuition and subconscious take over. We've used conscious exploration of physical and psychological action to reach the subconscious and the spirit of the role. Within the structure of the play and production we now find a spontaneity, invention and freedom so that we act truthfully according to nature as though in real life. The preparation is done and the way is clear for inspiration to occur.

## The search is all

To get to this position is not just a question of doing all the right things in a set order. Acting is a creative process and developments might happen unexpectedly if we remain constantly open and sensitised. A genuine feeling might occur in the first rehearsal. An atmosphere might only be achieved in performance. Some aspect of physicality could emerge organically in the early stages. As Michael Chekhov points out, you can approach different parts in different ways: for example, seeing and hearing the character in your imagination, sensing atmosphere or working under the influence of the main qualities of the character, trying out a Psychological Gesture or Imaginary Centre, or getting to grips with the through line of action. We may well be focused on some elements simultaneously. We have, of course, to start with the circumstances and action we're given, but beyond that there is no set formula other than a willingness to keep searching for truthful involvement in a role from before rehearsal to the end of the run of performances. The search is of key importance because we are not likely to achieve fully what we are aiming for. It is unlikely that any performance we ever do will hit all the marks leaving us unreservedly contented. There will always be some element that wasn't quite right: something that could have been played more or less strongly, an interchange that lacked the total spark of spontaneity, some emotion not experienced freshly and fully, a line that got lost, an objective that lacked commitment, an action that was poorly defined. We never achieve one hundred per cent belief in what we do because performance is not reality and we, the audience and our fellow actors are not machines. Everything is unpredictable: the thing which makes performance alive also makes it variable in quality. How nice to have everything perfect, but it would be short-lived. The pursuit of an ever higher standard, on the other hand, is an unending source of both frustration and fulfilment. We have to aspire to develop each time we rehearse and perform and not get trapped in a particular way of doing the character. The questions to ask continue to be: If I'm in the circumstances of the character what do I want? Why? What do I do to achieve it? What obstacles are in my way? What is at stake? What are my relations to others? These give you how you will act and provide a continuous prompt to exploration.

## Solving problems

The later stages of rehearsal are the time to look critically at your performance and do one of your jobs as a professional actor: solve problems. These may be as wide-ranging as there are different elements in the acting process, but assuming you have a rounded and believable character the problems are likely to be ones just requiring adjustment. They are common and not to be agonised over. Just deal with them.

### Imprecision

You are still unclear about what a line means or why you're saying it or what to do with it. Weigh up the different possibilities imaginatively – if I were in these circumstances what might I mean and want? Find the different interpretations which fit the character's Superobjective, qualities, relationships, etc. Don't vacillate and not commit – play one meaning and action in turn with full conviction and see how it feels. Experiment. Or, see and listen to the character speaking in your mind's eye – your imagination may reveal all.

### Gaps

You don't know what you're doing at a point where you have no dialogue so you go blank; there is a gap in your through line. Make sure you have a silent objective such as I want to make sense of what this person is saying, to calm myself, to work out my next move, to sort out my papers. Work it out according to what you've just been pursuing and what follows. *Really* listening and reacting to your partner will inform this. What is a logical, justified missing link? Again, try out alternatives and see what your character tells you in your imagination. What we should create is an unbroken flow of impulses, of thoughts, feelings, images and sensations. Any gap in this will break your belief and that of the audience.

### Tension

This will arise if we're not confident and easy about what we're doing – if an objective doesn't really engage me, if I'm not connecting with my partner, if responses feel acted and false. The effect of tension in the mind will be to create tension in the body; we become vocally and physically tight, our focus suffers, we become increasingly self-conscious, lose more belief and then get more tense, and so on. We can always focus on easing the physical tension, but if we're tense in the head the problem won't go away. The only solution is clarity! Make sure the basics are in place: create a strong objective, clarify why you are pursuing it with this particular person, and listen and react at all times, keeping an inner monologue of responses going, but only react in proportion to what the other is actually doing to you. Or, if appropriate, focus on a point of attention or a small circle of concentration so you lose self-consciousness.

**Pushing**

This is when we try too hard. When I was in the first years at my primary school we were told to 'work hard' and I thought this meant pressing down hard with my pencil as I wrote and writing very quickly – my writing never recovered! Pushing comes from a similar mental instruction to oneself rather than an organic drive in you as the character: 'I've really got to keep focused and in the moment and pursue my objective strongly!'. Of course, if this sort of thought is in your head, your head isn't in the character. While we need commitment, earnestness and conviction we also need ease and never to lose our centred stillness. Rather than pushing through the circumstances allow the circumstances to work on you, entering you like a breath that literally inspires you to act. Pushing will break communication with others, being at ease will keep you responsive

**Wrong tempo-rhythm**

We may feel we've got the right objectives, good interaction and all the other elements of a scene but it just feels wrong. Maybe the tempo is too slow or fast, or the rhythm is jerky and should be more even and sustained, there are too many pauses or overlapping of lines. If the problem appears to lie here then re-examine the atmosphere and quality of the scene – is it fearful and romantic, or exuberant and hectic? Focus on creating the circumstances with the right atmosphere and note how the tempo and rhythm change. Blocks may also have appeared in the dialogue resulting from consciously deciding how it should go. Try to ease these out by looking at the scene afresh, listening and reacting, pursuing what you want and allowing it to take a new shape naturally.

**Blocked feeling**

We're not accessing the feelings and emotions required by the script. As is evident from the problems above, the solutions do not involve a 'quick fix' or trick but applying the basic elements of our process: doing and being in circumstances, interacting and playing objectives. If we do this, the emotion will appear because we are human. If there is a block then it's probably because we are anticipating the emotion and what form it should take, worrying about not producing it, trying to reproduce what we had last time, aiming for a particular effect, or dropping out of the action to squeeze it out or conjure it up through a personal memory. Essentially, we are not doing what *will* create the emotion: keeping focused on the object of your attention and the action.

### Personal defects

I'm not referring to picking your nose onstage so much as abuse of what Stanislavski calls *stage charm* and which today we call charisma. Some actors have this quality without necessarily having good voices, attractive features, or much ability, but the possession of it makes them attractive to an audience. A problem arises where this gift is not used to enhance the character being played but to display the ego of the actor through self-admiration and exhibitionism. I'll never forget a conversation I once had with an older actor about acting process. He insisted that the Stanislavski approach ended up with indulgence, and then told me that his motive for being an actor was simply exhibitionism! There is one quite well-known English actor who has charisma and clear ability in certain roles but who diminishes his integrity and talent by taking every opportunity to face out to the audience in a pouting pose. There is nothing in his head other than an instruction to the audience to 'look at me'!

The reverse of this is the actor who is not attractive to an audience and who displays personal mannerisms. Such blocks to communicating a character different to oneself can only be eradicated by becoming more self-aware, analysing performances, particularly ones you can see on screen, and making attempts to change; and also by emphasising the attractive elements in one's makeup and performance ability such as warmth, clarity and honesty.

### Not letting go

Sometimes actors hang on to the preparation work too long and over-control what they're doing, because they don't trust that the preparation has sunk in and will enable them simply to 'be'. They feel safer keeping inside a protective cocoon but it holds back creative development. This makes the performance mechanical and dry. There has to come a point where you do what Edith Evans described as 'pop': you release conscious control, make an imaginative leap and let the character take over, just as a good pianist will not be thinking of the notes or a good dancer of the steps when they perform.

## Perspective

Attending to problems like these is all part of developing *perspective* in a role. By this Stanislavski means a harmonious interrelationship between all the parts of a role, and the key elements in assuring this are the Superobjective and through line of action. These give the overview, the framework for everything and the goal. Each simple action, sentence, gesture, feeling, tempo-rhythm or thought will have a perspective within the context of a single unit, a scene, an episode and then the whole play and production. As we approach the end of rehearsal we need to check that all the elements we've created are integrated, that there is nothing superfluous, that what we are doing is geared to the character's Superobjective and to telling the story clearly and fulfilling the play's Superobjective. It's only when we've reached the end of rehearsal and worked in detail on the whole play that we can make such judgements. We have a sense of the whole picture not just parts of it.

When a perspective on the whole is lacking we see actors playing the end of the play at the beginning, for example, playing Lear as 'tragic' because the play ends in tragedy, or Ibsen's Brand as weak because his point of weakness is revealed at the end. One of the most prominent aspects of strong writing is that characters change through the story, and this change is revealed if we go through each unit and scene playing the action clearly. Our Superobjectives in life, in the main episodes or in the play as a whole, like the obstacles we have to overcome and what is at stake in the action, imaginatively influence how we act out all the smaller objectives. They give us the 'arc' of the character – Michael Chekhov's sense of form and entirety I outlined back in Chapter 2. Stanislavski stresses that unless we understand Hamlet's deep disturbance at what the Ghost tells him then we won't understand his subsequent doubts, efforts to make sense of life, and his confusing conduct with Ophelia and others. Unless we see his consternation at his mother's early behaviour in the court, his later confrontation with her won't make sense. Hamlet has no sense of perspective in that he doesn't know the future, but the actor playing him does know his future and can artistically structure his performance accordingly, finding all the elements which organically lead up to the conclusion. Of course, when in performance we have to live through each moment as it unfolds and *not* think ahead, trusting that all our preparation will see us through without having to think about it. The readiness is all! Equally, the emotion through line has to be ordered. If we play a part in which there is great passion, such as Othello, this is unlikely to appear at the beginning. It will gradually build as the action develops, so we see the tip of the iceberg only emerging at the start. The emotion has to grow *through* the action and not be imposed or over-released so that a peak is hit too soon.

Stanislavski observed the finest actors of his day structure a performance with this sense of perspective, drawing you into a performance, then gradually unfolding the character piece by piece until a mosaic of qualities, emotions and intentions is composed. He called this ability to round off a role and give it light, shade and colour so that it is vividly brought to life, *finish*, and saw it as one of the highest qualities in an actor.

What we need to achieve also is the balance between performance and reality. We believe in ourselves as the character while in performance but know in our actor's consciousness that this is a performance. We may cry and laugh freely and truthfully but our artistic consciousness sees us doing it. If a role has been given structure and detail an actor will have what Chekhov calls a kind of blueprint, which will enable him to perform *correctly* even if he doesn't feel inspired. He will see the perspective on the whole role and be able to move from one part to another without losing focus and confidence, and that assurance may well reignite the creative spark.

## Control

While we may have to experience extremes of emotion in performance like jealousy, hate, or obsessive love or perform extreme actions such as murders, rapes or daredevil feats, it's important that we retain a sense of restraint and control, that we never completely lose ourselves in the action. First, because that would be dangerous to other actors and ourselves, and secondly, because we need to communicate what we do and feel to an audience. If we are totally overcome by grief or euphoria the emotion will very likely obscure what we have to say, as often happens in real life. While keeping the depth of feeling, we have to exercise enough control to make ourselves understood. While acting with intent and conviction we mustn't actually hurt or murder our colleagues. It is the sincerity of the intention we see in the eyes and through the quality of physical action that is important. It's the dying of the spirit, rather than gruesome butchery, that fascinates us in a death scene. Seeing the light simply and quietly extinguish from Kevin Spacy's eyes in *LA Confidential* is worth a thousand fashionably gruesome deaths in Tarantino-style bloodfests because it affects us deeply as opposed to offering sensory titillation and fake daring.

Another area of performance prone to excess is gesture and mannerism. First, we need to exclude our own everyday mannerisms and typical gestures so that we as the character can emerge. Secondly, mannerisms should not be endlessly repeated to indicate a character, producing caricature, but used with economy and subtlety. Gestures should be an organic response to an action, whether psychological or physical, and should therefore be clear and distinct and not involuntary expressions of the *actor's* vagueness or tension (see Chapter 2). Anything that doesn't conform to Chekhov's four artistic qualities of ease, form, entirety and beauty will inevitably be undefined and inexpressive and the character will be blurred. Even simple actions like running across the stage or grabbing hold of someone need economy and control. They often lack it because an actor will *indicate* wild running instead of really running towards an object with a purpose; for example, I'm running towards my lover to escape with her, so that my movement becomes imbued with that objective. Instead of cleanly and purposefully taking hold of someone to stop them leaving we sometimes see flailing arms indicating an upset emotional state, which is not only unclear but dangerous. Control is about applying elements of performance we've looked at earlier: ease, form, entirety, economy, centredness, which will produce a clear purposeful action with a beginning and an end.

## Improvisation

We looked at improvising the action of the text in Chapter 12, and this work may be continued if the text is still not being brought to life in late rehearsal in order to break blocked patterns and stimulate spontaneity and interaction. Improvisation is common in drama schools in the form of class exercises on objectives or atmospheres, for example, or just as a stimulus for the imagination and inventiveness. In rehearsal we can also use improvisation to explore character and circumstances off the text in order to inform and elucidate the text and bring greater belief to what we do with it. Some directors and actors talk darkly of improv and how popular it is with modern actors and how pointless ('God, why can't we just stick to the text!'), but I honestly can't remember doing this sort of improvisation with more than one director in over thirty-five years, and far from being pointless it was very useful. Once when I was required to do a piece of quiet, improvised dialogue upstage with another actor in a Shakespeare production, I started to discuss with the actor what we might in fact be talking about given where we were, what had just happened, and so on. An older actor in the company immediately intervened aggressively to stop what he clearly saw as unwonted interference with another actor and as completely unnecessary. And we were all actors in what was claiming to be an international ensemble company! This again reflects the myth of how deeply Stanislavski has entered the culture of British theatre.

Character improvisations can be about anything outside the action of the text, so we build up a fuller imaginative picture of the character's life off stage, screen or microphone in the period before the play actually starts or between scenes: creating an actual experience of events and relationships in what the Moscow Art Theatre knew as the *second plan*, which I've referred to before. We can imagine all these aspects and create visual images for ourselves and weave them into a life history of the character, but to create an improvised event between you and other actors playing the other parts is of a more tangible and exploratory nature. We may look at how two people met, their first argument, how they broke up; or a group scene in a pub in which events reported in the text took place; the first time a sensitive issue was addressed; the stages in a friendship which have led to breakdown; an agreement on which a marriage was based – situations which are indicated in the text but whose full content is left to our imagination and which we must fully envisage if we are to bring the text to life.

An improvisation with others can reveal unexpected feelings and attitudes, unanticipated by our own imagination in isolation. Other impros might inform what has been said and done immediately before an entrance or before a scene that starts in the middle of a piece of action so that the actors are better able to bring the previous circumstances on with them. These impros need to be structured to be effective. We create the given circumstances for each situation: exactly when the action is happening, what comes before and after this event, where it's happening, why, and what the initial objectives of the characters are. We then commit to the situation and see what happens to find out what will be useful when acting the text.

We can also investigate the social and political aspects of a situation. Of special interest here is Augusto Boal's use of improvisation and the creation of tableau images to explore power relations and how actors visualise their characters' view of, for example, the present and future. (See *Theatre of the Oppressed* and *Games for Actors and Non-Actors* (Routledge, 1992), in which he outlines his own study and use of Stanislavski's approach at the Arena Theatre in Sao Paulo in Brazil.) We can examine as a group the status relationships between characters to clarify who is high, low and middle status according to the objective social system in a particular place and period; and then look at how the characters see their status subjectively.

## Life history

I mentioned the character's life history earlier. Basic ideas about background that come to us early in rehearsal can be amplified in the later stages when we are more imaginatively engaged. We write this history in the way we might write down our own, in the first person as the character. We record from the script, and imagine on the basis of it, all the events, possessions, relationships, places and actions from early life to the present which make the character what it is. Believing in this autobiography helps us to *bring on the whole character* when we make our first appearance. This story will be assisted by the impros we do in imaginary circumstances as well.

Essential points which I would include in a life history – I know there are hundreds of others! – are:

### Social

Family background – what your parents, brothers, sisters, etc. are like and what your relationship is with them.
Class – original and present class status.
Marital status – or other intimate relations.
Occupation – what it entails, suitability, income, etc.
Education – what, where, beneficial or not.
Religion – what, and how serious.
Politics – what, and how committed.
Nationality – where born, and current nationality.

Position in the community – clubs, societies, official roles.
Hobbies.
Sports.

**Psychological**
Ambition.
Attitude to life – militant, resigned, optimistic, defeatist, etc.
Disappointments and joys.
Complexes – obsessions, phobias, manias.
Introvert, extrovert, ambivert (a mixture).
Temperament – angry, balanced, neurotic, fiery, placid, etc.
Sex – amount, orientation, pleasurable or not.
Intelligence.
Skills.

**Physical**
Age.
Weight.
Build.
Height.
Complexion.
Hair colour and style.
Posture.
Appearance – neat, scruffy, fashionable, eccentric, etc.
Hereditary features.

## Points of concentration

Once we are getting into runs of the play, our imaginative understanding of the circumstances can be made richer by working under the influence of *points of concentration*. This involves focusing during a run on a specific aspect of the subject matter and themes of the play, e.g. war, poverty, love. For *Measure for Measure*, we could choose the outer form of things, God, or the law. For *The House of Bernarda Alba*: village life, freedom, propriety, death, or sex. For *The Crucible*: God and the Devil, land, justice, or the truth. Each point of concentration will bring a new emphasis to certain parts of the text and a different colour into our performance. Each new focus adds a new layer in our appreciation and realisation of the text. This influence is applied not by consciously thinking of a subject all the way through a performance but in a more subliminal way. We consider the point of concentration before the performance starts; what does this subject mean to our character, how important is it? We then take that awareness into a run of the play and allow our performance to be affected.

We can do a similar thing by experimenting with different atmospheres. A scene may benefit by an atmosphere of anxiety as opposed to one of resentment, or one of wonderment rather than cynicism. With any imaginative influence like these, the structure of the play and production with its through line of objectives remains but its quality and feeling can change.

## Challenges in rehearsal and performance

### Time

A rehearsal process may or may not have been enjoyable, creative, free or structured. Whatever the situation, we have to be prepared, compensate for any difficulties – not liking the director, other cast members not liking you, actors getting sacked, breaches of contract, etc. etc. – and, while doing what the director asks, follow one's own creative process to achieve the best possible result. A major block to producing a truthful organic performance is lack of time and, as I've emphasised before, this places the onus on the actor to prepare very well. Early on in my career I worked for a summer in weekly rep. I'd left a drama school where I studied the Stanislavski process and was now faced with doing eight plays in eight weeks. The week of each rehearsal and production was totally taken up with rehearsal, performance and learning an act a night after the performance, so there was no time for preparation. The only solution was to do it all before I even arrived at the theatre. So, I worked out basic character studies and my through lines for each of the eight plays so that what I was doing and why was clear to me and I could focus in rehearsal on trying to find an imaginative involvement. Results of course were variable, but preparation stopped me getting into bad, mechanical habits. Most television productions won't involve rehearsal other than 'on camera', although there might be a read-through. In the average soap, you will arrive on set, go through the lines with the director or first assistant, rehearse with sound and camera and then go straight into takes, probably not more than two or three. While being fully prepared, we also need to be fully flexible so we can respond to demands to do a scene very differently to how we imagined it would be. The stronger the preparation in terms of what we're doing and why, the more confident we'll be when it comes to changing the how.

## Read-through

If there's a read-through for a TV play with no rehearsal period, then the director – or more accurately, the producer/s – will want to see as near to the full performance as possible. Where there is a rehearsal period, as in theatre, it seems ridiculous to make all your choices for the first reading. What's the point of rehearsal if not to allow for some creative development? It's best to read as yourself in the imaginary circumstances, to draw out the literal sense of the lines, look at what lies behind them in terms of objectives and subtext, and communicate with the other actors. That's enough to ask of anyone at this stage. I once played Edmund in a production of King Lear with Anthony Quayle as Lear and on the first day of rehearsal everybody in the cast gathered into a huge circle for the read-through. Anthony Quayle and another actor of equally vast experience urged the director to make two smaller circles so the actors could communicate quietly and not declaim at each other across a wide circumference. They knew that the reading would be pointless without that closer intimacy for human contact. Of course, there are directors who favour the recitation approach from an early stage, and it shows in performance.

Some practitioners believe actors shouldn't need rehearsal at all. During a project I did for John Arden and Margaretta D'Arcy they said that actors should be like musicians and be able simply to pick up a piece and perform it. Of course, actors *can* do this in exactly the way musicians do it. We can pick up a script and read it making total sense of it, as a musician can read a piece of music and play it by sight. What they ignored is that to get to *performance* level, musicians, just like us, have a period of rehearsal with someone to direct them.

## First night

The first challenge after rehearsal is, of course, the first night. Up to this point we've only performed for the director, a stage manager and some technicians and wardrobe people focusing on their specialist areas and looking distinctly impassive, and to an actor's eye, unimpressed. Now we have a full audience, including the press, family, friends, enemies, agents, other actors and managements, hopefully chattering and literally buzzing with expectation, all of whom could affect whether you ever work again. Understandably nerves run high. Trips to the toilet multiply, an irritating and unaccountable dryness appears in the throat, you may even be sick or be overcome with a heady excitement. Whatever your first night symptoms it is not easy to just focus on the task in hand. Nerves are good when they heighten our focus, increase our energy, and when they derive from wanting to do our best. However, they're destructive if we focus mainly on the audience, keep assessing how we're doing, slow down and get quiet, race ahead and overproject, or tighten up with shaking hands and knees. We all have a particular manifestation of nerves. The only way I know to keep them under control and of service to our creativity is to put the importance of this particular audience out of mind, try to treat it like any other performance, focus on the action onstage, your fellow actors, and your inner through line. As with every other performance, make sure you get into the theatre well before the half hour call so there is time for preparation. Do your physical and vocal warm-up before the performance. Get dressed and made up without rush. Do your imaginative preparation work – whatever you need to get you into the world of the play and the character. Prepare in the wings – go through your 5 Ws and enter the action thinking only of your first objective. Once the performance is under way and nerves have been controlled you should be alright, but if they return and your attention is disrupted you have to restore it by refocusing on your particular objects of attention and aiming to change the circumstances through your objectives. This will reconnect you with the action.

## Second night

This, of course, is the night which is supposed to be completely flat and on which everything goes wrong. There is nothing inevitable about this, and the supposition is as much superstition as anything, but it can turn out to be a self-fulfilling prophecy. If it runs true to myth it's because the first night generated great excitement, adrenalin, and hopefully, feelings of success and confidence. Anything after that could easily be a let-down, and there might be a tendency to rest on your laurels and allow your customary attention to detail and preparation slip a bit. If you're aware of this you can do something about it. Get the energy back up after the morning's lie-in and possible hangover. Exercise: run, go to the gym, yoga, etc. Re-adjust and focus on the evening's performance. Make sure you get in early, do your vocal and physical preparation, and everything else as per the first night and every other night. Give especial attention to technical details like props: do you have your personal props, are others set correctly? However good the stage management team, something might at some time go wrong, and it may well be on the second night; but *always* check technical details as a matter of course. Finally, while having regenerated energy, find a sense of real ease and stillness before entering the wings for your first entrance, and then play the action in the circumstances as for any other performance.

## The run

Once the play is on, or you're settled into a long-running TV series, there may be a tendency to go onto automatic pilot. You may not be feeling as lively, fit, well, optimistic, interested, etc. as you did at the start of the run. If you allow yourself to run out of steam you'll get mechanical and bore the audience. You are there and being paid to produce a performance worthy of being seen every time. How would it be if a surgeon just couldn't be bothered to give a heart operation full commitment, or if a ballet dancer didn't find the energy required for a lift? This is your job and you have to come to each performance as if you are doing it for *the first time*, giving maximum energy and commitment every time. However apathetic, tired, or bored you may feel, taking that approach will invigorate you and guarantee you'll feel good at the end of the performance. If you allow your mood to get the better of you, you'll feel so much the worse at the end and you'll be on a downward spiral.

There may be a tendency to under-act, to play a low-key naturalism with low energy and quiet speech; or to over-act, to feel you're not doing enough and allow more confidence to produce less control. Both are mistakes. There is only one level of acting worth achieving: living truthfully in imaginary circumstances and according to the specific reality in the script, whether it's Shakespeare reality, Edward Bond reality, or Feydeau reality.

You should see the run of a play or series as an opportunity to develop the performance: to deepen the experience of the circumstances and the emotions, find a wider range of actions to play within the objectives, to allow the inner structure of the objectives to give you more freedom to produce spontaneous and fresh delivery of the lines, to find greater ease and responsiveness, explore particular qualities of the character more fully, or themes and atmospheres in the play through different points of concentration. It was the challenge of the run of a production and his tendency to go stale and mechanical that initially prompted Stanislavski to re-examine acting process and study the great actors.

Another pitfall is to try to liven things up by game-playing with your fellow actors. For example, playing tricks like coming on from a different entrance, putting rude messages or erotic pictures where they will see them in performance, making them 'corpse', upstaging, introducing a particular word like 'bottom' into every scene, and so on. Hilarious, of course, for you. Unfortunately it undermines the quality of the performance and if you think the audience doesn't pick something up you're deluded. Of course, in a comedy something unpredictable may happen and the actors break up and the audience may love it, but only because it was unavoidable. If it's engineered it's deadly. We shouldn't be solemn about our work but we should be serious, and respect for the audience and the integrity of the work has to be paramount.

### Last night

I've always found this more difficult than the first or second nights. It can fall very flat. Again, knowing why this happens can be the best form of prevention. You may become over conscious that this is the very last time you'll play this part and your words start to echo in your ears, you observe what you're doing, and always seem a couple of beats behind the action. The solution, of course, is the same as for the other difficulties: you must focus on the objects of your attention – a person, a particular task, on trying to change the circumstances, on keeping the focus on each moment of the action and not on yourself or the audience.

## The myth of acting styles

### Different media

'Stanislavski is OK for film and TV because they demand that type of naturalistic acting.' How many times have we heard that sort of comment. In theatre we *don't* have to be real? Did Stanislavski have a television? People start with the accurate observation that theatre involves performing in spaces larger than those we live in and communicating to possibly large numbers of people in the audience, whereas working on screen or in radio is very intimate and done for a camera and microphone. Therefore, so the conclusion goes, there are different styles or techniques of acting required for each medium. Wrong. Acting is about doing, creating characters out of ourselves and our imagination, and communicating these and a story to an audience. This is what we do in *all* media and the creative process of doing this doesn't change.

Of course, there are differences in the work situation, in what is demanded of us, in how much of ourselves we can fully use in a performance, and there are specific tools of the trade we have to learn in each medium. In theatre, we have to use all our creative attributes including our bodies. In radio, our bodies are invisible and everything has to be communicated through our voices (although the ease, suppleness, and alignment of our bodies will affect our voices). In radio, also, we hold the script, turning the pages without rustle, and don't actually do many of the things being indicated or relate to other actors as we do on stage or screen. Much more has to be seen in the mind's eye. For film and TV we have less freedom of movement than on stage. We have to hit marks and find the camera. We don't have a rehearsal period to get us up to performance level. We have to do our own preparation and arrive on set at performance level, and do the same lines over again in quick succession while trying to keep fresh, flexible and alive.

Apart from these different elements of technique, there are different levels of projection of the character required, and therefore of the voice and body. We usually speak more quietly for the screen and radio than in the theatre. Much of the focus on screen will be on the face and eyes and small body movement. This doesn't mean that we don't need or can't use a flexible voice and body. It is a myth perpetrated by some TV directors and actors that we can only be believable by whispering with a hoarse rasp at the back of the throat and using a flat monotone. Look at the good vocal support and tone used by, say, Christopher Lee and Julia Roberts – rather more impressive than that of some leading theatre divas. Also, screen work is not limited to tight close-ups. We do see medium and long shots, farcical or action sequences, in which physical and vocal action may be on a much larger scale. Also, look at how actors like Daniel

Auteuil, Marlon Brando, Al Pacino, Daniel Day-Lewis or Meryl Streep have transformed physically in some of their best roles on screen. Some practitioners, misunderstanding Stanislavski as applied to the screen, say 'You can't change on film, you have to do nothing'. What we see if that is applied is nothing: dead eyes and lack of inner life. In good screen acting – as in good stage acting – the actor doesn't push and do too much but absorbs the circumstances, plays the action, and develops a rich inner life which is seen initially through the eyes. Beyond that, we can be big and bold if we're believable! 'The simple must have a great deal of content. Bare of content it is as useless as a nutshell without meat'. (*My Life in Art.*)

Those responsible for employing actors like to categorise us. We're compressed and squeezed into convenient little casting boxes called 'theatre actor', 'radio actor', or 'TV actor', definitions which assume a limitation on our part rather than on the imagination of the employers. Actually, we are 'actors', possibly with different preferences and more skill in one area than another, but we are not different types of species when we work in different media. To say actors need a completely different technique and style when working in different media is like saying a violinist needs a different technique to play Bach or Bartok, when they actually apply their same knowledge, skill and inspiration to each different form. It's not like changing from a violinist into a trombonist!

## Different drama styles

Another myth is that different drama styles or genres require different acting styles and even different types of actor. So we have further categorisation and limitation: the 'comedy actor', the 'classical actor', the 'dramatic actor'. Then, of course, we're broken down into types for 'casting purposes': the 'professional' type, the 'villain' type, the 'tart' type, a blonde one or a brown one, white or black, etc. etc.

Often, when we come to do a Restoration play or a Brecht play the director starts with a sense of the 'style' and we're encouraged to act in an effete and affected manner or do alienation acting. This misses the point. The plays are first of all *about* something. What they're about, whether sexual mores in the 1660s or the revolutionary proletariat; the issues the writer wants to convey, whether slight or heavy, entertaining or educative; the type of characters portrayed, whether shallow or complex; and the effect on an audience, all really determine the style; but through use and abuse the plays come to be seen as fitting into 'a style', as defined by critics and drama theorists, not by writers and actors, and which Stanislavski calls 'false traditions' (*My Life in Art*). This becomes an ossified formula adopted by directors that determines how plays are tackled and expected to be seen by audiences.

The actor should go for the reality within each genre. Beckett and Ionesco write about human beings, albeit in extreme and metaphorical situations. Shakespeare writes about contradictory human beings who speak in blank verse. Brecht writes about human beings in extreme social and political situations who break into song and address the audience. No writer tells us we have to represent their characters as one-dimensional, cardboard cyphers. We have to discover the real people in these different forms of artifice. If we do our normal job as actors well then the 'style' will come through. If we play 'style' then we'll lose the real style, falling into mannerism and obliterating the content.

Different types of writing do demand that we make adjustments. Michael Chekhov focuses on the four most evident and diverse of forms: tragedy, comedy, drama, and clowning, and offers an approach to each. In tragedy we face extremes of mental and physical experience and the normal boundaries of our consciousness are shattered. Our whole being may be shaken as though we are in the presence of something more powerful and bigger than us which acts on us and works through us: God, fate, supernatural forces, the power of nature, overwhelming circumstances, for example. So, Lear and Hamlet have a tragic experience whereas Hedda Gabler has a dramatic one. We can imagine this *superhuman* presence following alongside, behind or above us as an influence on our actions. It can help us to avoid inflating ourselves and playing 'tragic', and to remain true without lapsing into an everyday naturalness that loses the tragic dimension. These presences are like the Ghost in *Hamlet*, the three witches in *Macbeth*, or the Furies in the *Oresteia*, but if not specified by the author, can be created by the actor.

In a drama, on the other hand, our consciousness is purely human as in everyday life. The same applies to comedy – we act truthfully within these confines. Chekhov warns against 'playing for laughs' because this breaks any sense of truth and ease. It creates pushing and crudeness and the result will be less funny, not more. We've all witnessed those desperate actors who put their own egos before the integrity of a scene and their colleagues' work, and draw attention to themselves by upstaging or bits of business and cheap gags. Apart from ease, comedies usually require lightness, energy, and a quick tempo, though not one sustained uniformly all the way through so that we're battered and ultimately repelled by it. Anything rushed will seem paradoxically slow to an audience. Also, we can find a predominant quality in the character that is the source of what makes them amusing, for example, bravado in Falstaff or conceit in Malvolio, but which must always be played with inner truth and without commenting on the character for effect.

Finally, in clowning and, I would add, some farce, we enter a world of chaotic, uncontrollable events in which we are influenced by a *subhuman* presence of a mischievous nature, causing us to experience embarrassing and unexpected occurrences and swings of emotion, from joy to tears, and panic to laughter. We have to have a childlike ability to believe in these unlikely things we're seeing, doing and feeling for the audience to find it funny.

Each of these different forms are not hermetically sealed off from each other and will be more interesting and affecting for that. For example, there is comedy in *King Lear* through the Fool and in *Hedda Gabler* through Tesman's dry fussiness. There are often poignant and uncomfortable moments in comedies, as during the tricks played on Malvolio. To find drama and pathos in comedy and comedic moments in drama and tragedy heightens our appreciation of the predominant aspects of each form because we are faced with contradiction. Equally, playing tragedy and farce will extend our ability to imagine ourselves in the more likely circumstances of drama.

# Part 5

## Beyond the role

# Acting ethics

*Love art in yourself not yourself in art*

Stanislavski

Actors are not respected like opera singers, ballet dancers, musicians, painters or photographers. Whereas all these are assumed to have skill and dedication, the actor is more likely to be seen as a bit of an exhibitionist, an egotist with a dubious lifestyle. We often don't do ourselves many favours. Actors can present their occupation as just a bit of a laugh, not to be taken too seriously, while taking themselves very seriously. In British law we're still linked with 'rogues and vagabonds'. Our training isn't anywhere near as rigorous as in Russia and some other East European countries. Once the main training is complete, further classes, regular exercises and continuing attempts at development are definitely not the norm as they are for practitioners in other artforms. When in work, actors do not usually do physical, vocal, and imaginative preparation for their performance, and such exercise is often viewed with disdain. Anything with a methodology and discipline is alright for those abroad or for those in other artistic fields but not for we British actor laddies. Of course, there are exceptions to this view and self-view of acting, for example, in certain theatre companies which have forged a consistent style and use a regular pool of actors, but this is the norm I've experienced in over thirty-five years of wide-ranging work.

This book is concerned with how to break this mould. Essentially, I think actors should respect their artform as much as any other. We should acknowledge that we have a useful role in the world in recreating and elucidating human experience. We should not be apologetic about our work but, on the contrary, trumpet the fact that we benefit society both economically and spiritually. The Arts Council's 'Economic impact study of UK theatre', April 2004, points out that a state investment of around £121 million yields £2.6 *billion*. In 1994, during the appalling conflict in former Yugoslavia, Katja Doric, an actor and teacher from Saravejo, maintained that the power and importance of theatre had really made itself felt; people flocked into theatres desperate for civilised values, and experienced it not just as 'the cream on top of the cake. It is real bread. It is essential for life.'

If we are serious about our work but not overly serious about ourselves then a particular ethics of work becomes obvious.

## Dedication

If we are committed actors, we are *essentially* actors. We don't do a job simply to make some money and then go home and have the enjoyable and fulfilling part of life there or in leisure pursuits or other commitments. Acting is the core of our life, not necessarily the only important thing in it, but the central part. Our prime concern is to serve the play, production and audience, and to devote our energies and skills to that end. We need a discipline and order to give this shape. Dreams of 'success', which all actors have in some form, can be shattered on a daily basis and the need for acknowledgement can distort what we are, our relationships and our ability. A passion for the work itself and for learning more is the best antidote to this, and to the anxieties, jealousies, and petty conflicts to which we're all prone and which can lead us away from a creative focus. 'Never come into the theatre with mud on your feet', says Stanislavski (*Building a Character*).

## Discipline

**Always be punctual and ready**. Sometimes lateness is unavoidable – train cancellations, tube breakdowns, car accidents, etc. Where it is avoidable it is totally disrespectful to the director and other actors not to be on time. Rehearsals, filming or recording will be held up. Time, and sometimes money, are wasted – unforgivable in an industry where there is often little money and little time. Being late gets you and everyone else off to a bad start. *Be ready* for rehearsal, which means arriving at a comfortable time before it starts so you can settle down after the journey, get your script, pencil, notes, etc. together, and prepare yourself for what you will be doing. If you need tea, coffee, cigarettes, and chats before any work can even be considered organise them so there is time to spare. If you are doing improvisation work make sure you have whatever objects and clothes you might need to create the circumstances. If you've been required to prepare some work for rehearsal or to learn lines make sure it's done. Half-hearted work holds everyone back because we're all working together. For every performance, you need to prepare so that you are never in a rush, under-energised, or unfocused.

## Self-motivation

**Take the initiative**. We should not be dependent on a director. The only dependence we should have is on the circumstances to tell us where we are and who we're with, which guides us to what we're doing, why, and what's in our way. Directors can help us and need to co-ordinate a production, but they can't act for us. We have to take the initiative and motivate ourselves to explore all the avenues which will stimulate our creativity, so we do our preparation work and research regardless of whether the director is requiring it or not. Actors who show little independence and initiative take up a disproportionate amount of a director's time and then the time of the whole company. We all have to deal with someone else's laziness, unimaginativeness, self-obsession and problems. Rehearsals are not only held up through excessive attention going to the weak point but other people can't progress in the actual communication process of acting with this person. It is the actor's job to have ideas about the text and what the character is doing. Equally, if a problem arises for us in rehearsal we need to go home and consider it and work on it so that it may be resolved in the next rehearsal. Rehearsals are where we bring our own preparation and then explore with others, rather than a classroom in which we wait to be told what to do. That also means we should allow our imaginations to work to feed our role outside the rehearsal room and outside home, in fact, anywhere. There isn't a point where the serious actor decides tools go down and work stops, because our tools are the whole of what we are and we never leave that.

We also have to motivate ourselves for each performance. Coming back to the issue of warm-ups, a dancer exercises the body, a pianist exercises the fingers, a singer will exercise breath and voice. Actors use hands, legs, the face, the whole body and voice and all the inner apparatus of imagination, senses, emotions, mind and will, so it is ridiculous if we don't prepare that whole instrument. In performance, every entrance needs preparation each time we make it. We have to bring on whatever has happened to the character between scenes through our imaginations.

**Keep fit and ready**. In the wider perspective, we have responsibility for our own fitness, vocal quality and acting technique, so it's advisable to do regular workouts, vocal exercises and work with other actors, whether in paid classes or sessions set up by actors themselves to explore technique, examine new scripts or devise work. We shouldn't stop learning and developing, but we can't rely on constant work to prompt this. For most of us, there are periods of painful unemployment and we need to keep our hand in by doing something connected with our craft. Some actors get a bit sniffy about classes, and it is true there are actors who only seem to do classes as opposed to work. However, to work regularly does not negate the value of continuous training. One actor I spoke to, who has actually monitored training in drama schools for the National Council of Drama Training, was dismissive of this: it isn't necessary if the actor's drama school training was good, and work itself provides the training for professionals. Established actors like Paul Newman and Anne Bancroft didn't turn their noses up at doing exercises at the Actors Studio. The RSC now provides classes for the company's actors. The Maly Drama Theatre keeps training continuous for its ensemble company.

**Prepare**. Auditions are a chance of employment, to get to do what we've trained for and live for. They need preparation. Be on top of a script if you've been sent one. For TV we sometimes get 'the sides' by e-mail, so take advantage of that to become very familiar with the lines, to get a sense of the character and work out the objectives, and to be able to lift your eyes from the page when you read for the director, producer, casting director, and camera and whoever's reading the other lines to you in a completely blank and unhelpful manner! If you're reading for a known play, read the play beforehand. If you're doing a speech, work on it sufficiently so that you are confident and can control nerves, while keeping easy and flexible and able to do it in different ways. It goes without saying you need to know the whole play from which it comes.

**Do it yourself**. If you've left acting school and no agent has taken you on and no casting director or director wants to see you, you are not alone! You can always take the initiative and set up your own work: get some scenes together with friends and organise a showcase or put on a play. Of course these things cost money, mainly the hire cost of the theatre, but you can pool your resources and possibly pay off debts with money from the job you may get as a result. Get good photos, a clear, well laid-out CV and a succinct but interesting letter and promote yourself to casting directors, agents, theatre, TV, radio and film directors, and if you have an agent don't rely on them solely. Don't stint on letter writing and making contacts whenever you can.

**Be positive**. It's best to see other actors as colleagues, all in the same large boat tossing on stormy seas, rather than as stealth bombers trying to blow you out of the water. We need to develop friends who are constructive, resilient and forward-looking rather than negative cynics who only drag us down. Try to be glad when your friends get work. Gore Vidal, the American writer, said 'Whenever a friend succeeds a little something in me dies'. At some time many of us will have had that sinking feeling of envy when we hear a friend has got work rather than us, but we need to get things in perspective: they haven't taken *our* job, they're most likely not in direct competition, and at least it shows there are jobs out there to be had! Envy and self-pity decay our spirits. Also, if we're generous and supportive maybe we'll get the same back.

**Pay the rent**. If things get really bad financially, you might have to take a 'fill-in' job, preferably something which keeps you in food, clothing, shelter and the odd bottle of wine, is not so involving it takes your mind off acting, and which allows you to go to interviews at a moment's notice. It helps to work part-time and to be doing some other form of creative work like teaching, aerobics, or photography, or a job like temping or market research where you can decide what hours you work.

**Create**. Some consolation in periods of unemployment can be gained by taking up another artform or skill: singing in a choir, learning the guitar or how to ride, sculpting or writing, for example. At least you're releasing those creative juices and what you do may become useful in your acting.

**Keep in the flow**. We need to stay in touch with the business and friends who are working so we see what's on and what it's like. Not easy – when we're working we can't get to shows, when we're unemployed we can't afford it. Of course, you can always give up smoking!

**Engage**. Finally, why not engage socially or politically and do something for someone else? Collect for Amnesty, join your Equity Branch, or get involved in that political party you say you agree with.

In short, we need to do whatever is required to get us into shape, keep us sane, and give us confidence so we have the best chance of doing a good job in all circumstances.

## Absorption

As we work, all the information we receive, the discoveries we make, the experiences we have need to be assimilated and absorbed so that all this raw material is actually turned into creative progress. Some actors turn up to work every day like *tabla rasas*, or chicks just out of the egg, as though nothing has penetrated. This wastes energy and time and is very frustrating. We need to be like sponges not granite balls. Every thing that happens to us, however unpleasant, can be used in the creative process. Bad rehearsals, awful auditions, poor performances can be of use providing we are willing to *learn* from them. It's too easy simply to sulk, and it's very easy to be lazy and inattentive.

**Take notes!** We won't remember everything a director says to us, particularly if it's our turn to get a full frontal assault, and the notes include minor technical points as well as deeper points on characterisation. We need to write the notes down. We then need to refer to them at home, go through them one by one, and work them through – possibly on our feet – so they are implemented in the next rehearsals. It's not advisable to make a director have to repeat them. After you've given the same note four times, your temper starts to wear a little thin.

**Diligence**. It's an old theatrical adage, but true: *Acting is 99% perspiration and 1% inspiration.* As should be evident from the rest of the book, we spend a lot of time researching, exploring, trying things out to get to that point where we can take off. The more talented the actor the more concern will there be for developing technique and solving problems. Another famous quote, from the architect Mies van der Rohe: 'God is in the detail'!

**Exploration**. The whole process of creating a theatre production, TV or radio programme, or film involves a search if it is to go beyond the glib and mechanical. Even if we have a strong sense of a character and the meaning of a script we have to find ourselves within them and find them within us. There is a process of objective and subjective exploration. Acting is about immersion in life and how we react to it. It's true that we may never fully understand ourselves or other people or the world we live in, and we shouldn't pretend we do. However, people choose to be artists of whatever nature not to present confusion and spread ambivalence but to try to make sense of things and help others to make a little more sense as well. We should beware fashionable philosophies which abnegate artistic responsibility for finding answers as the world becomes increasingly dangerous and complex. They produce blank and mannered performance. It is not the job of artists to throw up our hands in despair and say we know nothing and can know nothing. What we can know is what issues emerge in a writer's script, and what the characters do. We can examine why they do these actions and what stands in their way. We can explore the action, and through that, our senses, emotions, will and mind will be engaged and things will happen in performance that take on a meaning we may not be aware of and cannot control. That's the nature of art. What's important is that we search for answers, clarity and the truth of human experience. Finding all the answers is impossible, but searching is everything.

**Humour**. Of course, some invoke sense of humour as a secret weapon against seriousness, process, methodology, commitment, etc. Don't let the shallow get a monopoly on fun! It's perfectly possible – and necessary – to work with serious commitment and have a sense of humour and the ability to laugh and play in rehearsal. Working with humourless people can be as much a misery as working with superficial candyfloss. Humour also brings insight into dramatic works. It is a rare script without any humour and we need the sense to bring it out. Humour is an aspect of the childlike quality we need to open up, remove blocks and let our imaginations fly. It's also a great leveller; being able to laugh with someone breaks barriers and establishes bonds. Humour eases tensions in rehearsals and promotes ease in performance. Some directors believe conflict in a company produces edgy, exciting work. Actors know this is rubbish. We need trust in rehearsal, sensitivity and generosity; not a policy of divide and rule through which the director governs by fear and humiliation, or vagueness and indecision. These negative attributes, which many actors will have experienced, may cause us to bind together albeit in a bad production, but more likely will bring out all the actors' insecurities and arouse competition, backbiting and disruption. Directors' egos often become more important than the play, the actors, or the audience.

To conclude, we need to be as fit as an athlete, as sensitive as a child, and as searching as a detective to develop artistically – and as tough as old boots to deal with the industry!

# 16 Working together

*Collective creativeness, on which our art is based, necessarily demands ensemble*

Stanislavski

Actors don't work alone. The painter or sculptor can disappear to create solitarily for days. Pianists can play concert performances on their own. Actors need other actors, unless we're doing the atypical one-person performance, and even then you need stage management, possibly a director, and lighting and sound technicians. Actors have to work with other people, and the whole effort to mount a production is a collaborative one, including not just the creative team but front of house staff, administration, marketing and publicity, finance and all the maintenance staff and ushers. If any part of this collective is not functioning well it could have a damaging effect on the experience of the audience, and on their experience of the actors' work. Although we live within a competitive capitalist society many organisations, including the ones actors work in, need, at least on certain levels, to use co-operation to produce the best results. We know it works. Many heads and creativities all working towards a common goal are bound to produce better results than the many working to do each other down. Even the uncreative and repetitive factory production line relies on a clear, co-ordinated division of labour. However, the very un-Christian prevailing values of western societies encourage us all not to share wealth and love each other, but to make as much profit as possible at whatever expense to the environment and the general standard of living here and in developing countries. Adverts, always a good reflection of current mores, are full of this materialistic edge. Remember the car advert where a woman fearfully moves her car from under a window rather than help a man precariously hanging from it? Of course, there are humanistic values held by many, and I'd say most people in the arts, in opposition to these values, which appear to make more sense for the healthy survival of the human race: co-operation is just one of these. That it's constantly opposed by competition, which seeps into our consciousness and actions, is a contradiction we have to live with.

One of the reasons actors act is to express themselves, to communicate great work and ideas, to explore the range of human personality and contribute to change. All these reasons provide an escape from the more alienating modes of work in which people feel trapped on a treadmill, separated from other people and what is finally produced, and separated from their own feelings, aspirations and potential. Working in a theatre company, or even in television is not like working on an assembly line or in a call centre. People do work more closely. The director may be more approachable than the factory production manager. The theatre executive director may be more friendly than the Chief Executive Officer of Halliburton. We don't produce a piece of work such as a fridge for sale in the marketplace. However, we don't have a control as part of a collective. This *is* the case in Germany where actors in many companies have three or more year contracts and participate in selecting the plays and even the director. Here, we hardly get to discuss the play we're acting in. The director and designer give us the design, the period in which the production will be set and the concept, and then you get down to rehearsing that – pretty amazing when you consider we're dealing in communication and creativity, ideas and experience and the recreation of human life! We don't have a say in how the production will be presented and marketed, and normally that wouldn't be possible because we're short-term workers. That work has been started by other full-time employees before we even get off the train. When our work in TV, film, and commercials is repeated or sold to another company we have to fight to gain some control over the 'exploitation' of our work by gaining a decent 'use' fee. Some media commentators are critical of this practice seeing it as unjustified, as if they would question something equivalent like the hire fee for a taxi or a DVD. This sort of negotiation would be done by our trade union, Equity, but we individually operate as one-person businesses. We train as actors, we perform for an audience, but we're employed by companies to whom we contract out our artistic labour. Our artistic lives are mediated by economic relations. We want to create but have to market ourselves as commodities and we have to deal with 'industrial relations' at work, for example, when a management breaks the terms of our agreed contract by not paying overtime or contributions into the pension scheme. Bad relations with a management can create a bad atmosphere and affect performances. Defending our rights can mean we don't work for a company again. We don't do our creative work in isolation but neither do we have control over it.

While we may want to work as a team with actors in a company, we've had to compete for our job with many other actors who were rejected and are probably now out of work. The competition in all the media is increasingly harsh: there are greater numbers of actors, fewer jobs and a basic lack of civility in the casting process. Interviews are often cold and impersonal affairs recorded on the ubiquitous camera. Nobody even rings you anymore to say you've *been* rejected; there's just silence. David Mamet, in one of his slashes at the 'business' side of what we do, says, 'The audition process selects for the most blatant (and not even the most attractive) of the supplicants. As a hiring tool, it is geared to reject all but the hackneyed, the stock, the predictable – in short, the counterfeit' (*True and False*). This will be a comforting balm for us when we don't get the job, but there is some truth in it.

Television is full of a shallow culture of makeovers, 'reality' shows, a 'cult of celebrity' and talent competitions, and much acting now falls into the mode of 'giving it attitude' and playing a manner, of dishing up some half-baked notion of 'style' rather than real substance. Of course, at the other end of the spectrum is the final *Prime Suspect* or *The State Within*, both with universally fine acting.

Once we do get a job, competition doesn't go away because we are usually only in this job for a short time and may be thinking about getting the next job, and looking better than the other actors, and getting the best reviews, and so on. This may translate into actively undermining other actors in performance by a whole array of devices such as pulling focus from them, cutting into their lines, doing something out of character to throw them, speaking out to the audience instead of to the actor, competing for laughs, etc. Usually, this sort of tactic is counterproductive and an act of desperation, but it certainly won't help the production. Since most companies are 'scratch' companies of actors who have never worked together before, we often find there are different varieties of acting onstage at any one time and the most showy ones will be competing for attention. Having said all that, you get companies who, despite the pressures of the business, gel personally and artistically and do good productions.

## The ensemble

For there to be genuine collaboration between actors, without whom drama would not be brought to life, and the rest of the creative team; for there to be more collective control of material and process; for there to be common aims and a unified process of working, we need ensemble companies. Ensemble means *together*. In practice, though, what is an ensemble company? We used to have a network of repertory companies throughout Britain that employed actors for a season of plays lasting for four months or more, in which the actor would play probably six or more varied parts. The audience got to know the actors and enjoy their creative transformations from one week to the next, the actors developed their skills and versatility, and the theatres gained a particular character. Today, most companies cast each production separately, or two together. The influence of television has taken over. Many directors believe the best cast can only be attained by picking a fresh crop for each play. There is distrust, or lack of consideration, of the idea of actors' ability to act. It's assumed that a new, special cast, possibly with a TV name in it, is the guarantee of artistic excellence and bums on seats. We know from experience this is not the case. We know from the mediocrity and distinct lack of excellence of many of our productions here that this is not the case. We know from observing the quality of European ensembles this is not the case. This is not to say that the old-style rep system produced consistently wonderful work; the pressures of short rehearsal periods denied that possibility. So, the existence of a company working together over a number of months is not in itself an ensemble. Even a company working over years may lack the vital ingredient to make it a true ensemble, and that is the development of a common set of values, goals, and artistic processes that are not just those of the director but are created by collaboration with a whole team of actors and other creative, technical, and administrative staff.

At the Ensemble Theatre Conference, organised by Equity and the Directors' Guild of Great Britain in November 2004, most of the contributions from British directors focused on the amount of time people are together, how long rehearsals are, organisational aspects, the position of actors in a company, funding, and relationship to the audience: all important issues, but hardly anybody mentioned the nature of the work, the process which largely creates it, and the philosophy behind it. Those who did were from the European companies, the Maly Drama Theatre and the Stary Teatr from Krakow in Poland, who were universally admired but clearly not emulated in their chief concerns. Although contributors acknowledged the actor-centred nature of ensemble there is no record in the conference transcript of anybody who is essentially an actor speaking or being requested to speak.

Mikhail Stronin, former Literary Advisor and International Relations Manager of the Maly, said, 'Ensemble means working together and working together means, in the first place, ideology. Ideology – not in the vulgar understanding of Soviet times but ideology: what the actors think about art; what they think about style of acting; what they want to say ... I remember very well what Lev Dodin (the Artistic Director) used to say when he went to very good theatres, like the Moscow Art Theatre, to many other theatres: seventy percent of the time was spent on working out a common language ... the formal presence of the permanent company and the presence of a repertoire doesn't ensure the ensemble in the true sense of the word. It is one body with many heads – but many heads who work in the same direction. But now Russia is in great danger of disintegrating as far as ensemble theatres are concerned. Still the majority are repertoire theatres but the ideology is rather attacked from the side of the commercial theatre due to different reasons (mainly economic reasons). Well, it's paradox. Britain is speaking about the ensemble theatre and there are voices in Russia who say: "Let's follow the British or the Western system. Why should the state finance the theatre? Let theatres provide for themselves." This is because the government and maybe some artists do not understand what, practically, theatre is and what language theatre should speak.'

In an interview for Theatre Scotland in 1994, Lev Dodin emphasised: 'I don't think artists should consent to the situation when they find themselves in a small recess on the side of life in which society has put them ... artists should fight for the right to speak about eternal human problems.'

Agata Siwiak from the Stary Teatr disagreed with Stronin about many heads looking in the same direction: 'We want to have arguments in the theatre. We want to have a lot of various thinkings. We want to have the place where people meet and discuss and argue. And we have sometimes very hard discussion ...

But I believe that – from this kind of very hard atmosphere, very hard discussions – can come something really fresh which is the mixture of tradition (of that which we have from our big theatre directors, big older actors) and of something that can bring on the young artists'.

Nevertheless, talking of Krystian Lupa, the renowned director who works with the company, she said, 'Sometimes I am at rehearsals and I know that the process of working is very important for actors. They told me that they change as people after a few years of working with Krystian. From being very closed people, they started to discover incredible things as humans in themselves. I think that something like that wouldn't be possible in the system when the actors are chosen by casting. It's something deeper and everything that is really deep needs time'.

She also made the point, though, that the Stary's actors have freedom to work in other theatres and in film while keeping the company as their base.

In Britain, 'ensemble' has often been a dirty word, interpreted as meaning ossified companies and productions, complacent mediocre performers and no stars, too much deafening ideology and restrictive methodology, too much emphasis on the dull group and not the charismatic individual, and most actors won't want to commit for long periods anyway, and so on. What we actually see, when companies continue to explore and do not rest on their laurels, are companies of actors who are all stars, all important, all interesting to watch, performing specific characters and circumstances while drawing out universal human dilemmas, and working as an organic, seamless whole, full of layers, spontaneity, power and passion. Many actors *will* want the opportunity to do that sort of work. Here, we've had some companies which are notable exceptions to the norm and organised as ensembles: touring companies like Theatre de Complicité and Shared Experience, political companies like Belt and Braces and Women's Theatre Group, and a few building-based companies like the Royal Shakespeare Company in its early days, the Stoke Victoria Theatre (now the New Vic in Newcastle-under-Lyme), Northern Stage and Dundee Rep, and before them all, Shakespeare's own company.

The current RSC has two-year contracts and continuing training. The Artistic Director, Michael Boyd, has this to say, 'How can you build future generations of leading players with range, depth and stamina if you don't create a situation where they can be happy to stay put and learn for a significant amount of time? How do you escape the shallows of a career dominated by money, status and celebrity? Where do you nurture the art and craft of our trade, the rigour, the self-respect and the sense of pride in our profession? A shelter from "short-termism", opportunism and the fear of unemployment ... Is it impossible to reconcile our egos in consensus or can an ensemble company act in some sense as ... a better version of the real world on an achievable scale which celebrates the virtues of collaboration, the collaborative skills of theatre as something valuable beyond the pragmatic promiscuity of "loveydom" which is so reviled by our culture?'

Alan Lyddiard set up the Northern Stage ensemble in Newcastle in 1992 as a result of meeting Lev Dodin in St. Petersburg and seeing the Maly perform. On becoming director, the first thing he did was to invite the Maly Theatre with *Brothers and Sisters*, and Peter Brook's company with *The Man Who*. His own company of local actors performed Max Frisch's *Andorra*, and did workshops, warm-ups and training with the other companies. The same company is still working and doing a wide range of projects from an opera for children in Darlington to a project with Calixto Bieito's company in Barcelona. Lyddiard aimed for a house style and bringing in directors who are close to that.

Hamish Glen ran the ensemble at Dundee rep between 1999 and 2003, and that is now continued by James Brining and Dominic Hill. Glen was also inspired by European companies, having worked at Eimuntas Nekrosius' company in Lithuania, and observed Maly rehearsals. The Dundee company consisted of eleven actors and three apprentices, graduates from Scottish drama courses on one-year contracts. He organised weekly skills classes, run by outside specialists, including singing, dance, musical instrument tuition, mask, and dialect work. Shows stayed in the repertoire and toured; for example, they took *The Winter's Tale* to Iran. Glen favoured an eclectic approach to rehearsal: one director might use units and objectives, while he favoured external exercises to explore their psychological effect. He saw the advantage of ensemble as being 'to make work of a different quality possible', to achieve 'truthful and beautiful' productions. Because actors were not insecure about work and the next job, he maintains there was an uncompetitiveness, ease, and joy in performance. Rehearsals lasted six weeks to three months, so skills could be absorbed and acting given greater depth and richness. Casting could be unexpected and exciting, and he makes the point that bringing in names to play lead parts at the RSC breaks the spirit of ensemble. The company strengthened through playing varied roles, and the audiences were delighted and grew through seeing transformation which Glen regards as crucial for actors. The actors came to see the theatre and audiences as *theirs*, and they were able to influence the choice of directors and plays. They stopped worrying about the size of part offered, and sometimes also directed. Glen could leave the actors to try scenes out on their own initiative, seeing himself as a co-ordinator, encourager and platform provider rather than a controller. Actors were also allowed out of the company so they could perform other theatre shows or do TV provided enough notice was given, so flexibility was part of the mix, too. It took about a year before the actors really gelled and could start to simply 'be' rather than 'act'.

The point was made at the Conference that here were theatre people trying to make the case for ensemble work, when it would be unthinkable to make the obvious point that established orchestras play better than ones thrown together from scratch. The Berlin Philharmonic or London Symphony Orchestra are great because they are on contracts that have allowed them to work together for a long time, they exercise collective control, they choose the conductors. Why should it be different for actors? Nobody is talking of imposing ensemble on unwilling victims, but where the value is recognised and there is a desire to set up such companies there should be encouragement in terms of practical support and finance from funding bodies and other arts organisations. A wide variety of directors and other theatre practitioners at the Conference agreed that the future health of British theatre depended in part on reviving ensemble practice. Back in 1963, Olivier wrote to Tyrone Guthrie that, 'study and observation of the last thirty years has led both Peter Hall and myself to the same conclusion, that a permanent ensemble is the only way to keep the standard consistently on the rise.' Of course, what each ensemble creates, through what processes, for what reasons; how they are organised and funded, and what role actors play in the running of them; what the relationship is to the audience and community – all these points give rise to a wide range of artistic, social and political questions and answers. No one ensemble need be the same as another, and that appears in practice to be the case.

Clearly, ensembles which keep flexible and explorative offer many advantages to actors, directors, company reputation, audiences and the community as a whole, who benefit economically, socially and spiritually from prestigious and successful companies. The Stanislavski approach, which requires an ensemble rehearsal process, also benefits most from organising a company and building in the ensemble manner.

I believe central and local funding bodies should encourage the establishment of ensembles throughout the country, learning from what works and doesn't work in the European models, and the government should provide adequate and sustainable funding at the highest European levels to enable the success of this project. To maintain a permanent ensemble for fifty weeks of the year may prove more expensive than casting by the show and they will say they can't afford it. Instead they are already (in July 2007) squaring up to deliver another round of cutbacks to the arts; but budgeting involves making priorities and I think most people in this country would prefer more money to go into creativity than into weapons of mass destruction and their deployment and use overseas.

## School links

Another issue arising is the relationship between theatre companies and acting training. We do not have a tradition of strong links between the two and of students from a school moving into an associated company. In St. Petersburg, the Academy of Theatre Arts is linked to the Maly Drama Theatre. Lev Dodin runs a rigorous five year course, for around twenty to twenty-five students a year and from this selected students will join the Maly company. In the production of *King Lear* which came to the Bite Festival at London's Barbican in 2006 there were four students in their fourth year playing the major parts of Goneril, Regan, Cordelia and Edmund. Training for them and all the other actors continues during the work of the company.

In Moscow, the Moscow Art Theatre School is linked to the Moscow Art Theatre. Mikhail Mokeiev, a renowned Russian actor, teacher and director whom I talked with while we were both working at a leading acting school, trained as an actor and director at the Art Theatre School and then became an actor and director in the MAT for ten years. He then became a teacher at the school. He now runs a four year course at the Russian Academy of Theatre Arts (RATI), formerly known as GITIS, the Government Institute of Theatre Art, and the biggest and oldest acting school in Russia. The Opera and Dramatic Studio, where Stanislavski worked on recording his approach in the last three years of his life, was connected to GITIS; he and other MAT actors taught there. Mokeiev also finds time to do freelance theatre work and has directed a massive historical television series in Russia.

The Ensemble Theatre Conference recommended that links between schools and companies should be developed here, to create continuity in theoretical and practical understanding of acting and a common language to save time in rehearsal and deepen the work, and to connect students to the professional world, revitalise the professional company, and enhance the identity of each. Some actors are also provided with quality work early on in their careers, an important consideration given that many of our young actors start off with bits of TV or a commercial. Glen's incorporation of three acting student 'apprentices' into his company is a fine example of what is possible here.

## Training

It's possible that some British drama schools can cover varied acting and theatre 'styles' without necessarily delivering enough on basic acting process in a way that makes students feel confident, easy and equipped to deal with full and truthful character creation in any period and form. There may be a sometimes overwhelming pot pourri of subjects and projects to cover in very short periods of time, and not enough time to absorb technique in an unpressured way. Training cannot be done properly in a panic, or in a climate of fear and anxiety, or in an undisciplined or passive state. Staff know this as much as students, and the situation becomes ever more difficult and pressured as some of the universities overseeing acting schools press for greater student numbers but don't provide enough cash for enough teaching staff. Of course, some schools are better funded than others. Creative work has organic gestation periods. Some European directors insist that this principle be honoured. Krystian Lupa from the Stary Teatr, because of the ensemble method of working, has been able to postpone the opening of plays – if not ready after three months, he works for another few months, and opens when he is ready. In RATI, Mikhail Mokeiev only presents a project when he considers it ready, and not according to a deadline. We could not do this under the pressures of commercial theatre and limited public funding or in crammed acting school courses. The St. Petersburg Academy runs a five year course. A Bosnian student on a course I used to run told me that her first course in Sarajevo lasted four years. Mokeiev's course is four years. Michel Saint-Denis, in *Training for the Theatre*, recommended a four-year training consisting of a Discovery Year, in which students discover their talents and what is needed to develop them; a Transformation Year, which focuses on imaginative expression and transformation into someone else; an Interpretation Year, exploring different styles of play and communication with an audience; and a Performing Year, concentrating on the presentation of a variety of plays on different stages to varied audiences, and a final repertory season. This obviously relieves some time pressure and allows for learning to sink in more and for projects to be done in more depth.

In Britain, full-length acting courses are three years. If a four-year training were adopted here a problem would be whether students could afford an extra year now that the government has replaced free education with £3000 a year tuition fees and student loans. However, students on art and music courses manage on their four year courses, acting schools do offer some scholarships and the government gives small grants to students in difficulty at, for example, RADA and LAMDA (London Academy of Music and Dramatic Art). Also, before the universities entered the field of acting training in the 1990s students usually had to rely totally on their own or their families' resources, or scholarships; discretionary local authority grants were rare. Some students do accomplish four years' training by doing a foundation course first or an MA later but the only four year course here is Queen Margaret University College's acting course.

There are other differences between our schools and the Stanislavski-based schools abroad. Some of our courses – at Guildhall and Bristol Old Vic schools, for example – may take in less than twenty-five students a year, around the same number as abroad, but many courses admit forty or more.

There is more consistency and continuity in the Stanislavski training. Mikhail Mokeiev works with his group of students throughout their course, instead of handing over leadership to several different tutors with different processes and terminology, as is often the case here. To emulate the variety actors may find in the business while they are in training may not be a virtue. Understanding, absorption and consolidation may be more valuable virtues.

The working day is also much longer. Students start at 9a.m. and finish at midnight, from Monday to Saturday. Here the day starts between 9 and 10a.m. and ends around 6.30p.m., from Monday to Friday, with performances taking place on some evenings. There, they will do skills classes in the morning; theoretical studies on drama, literature, art, economics, etc. in the afternoon (which Mokeiev believes is too much like university academic study); and acting classes and rehearsal in the evening. The MAT school does acting in the morning and evening and skills in the afternoon.

A fifth difference is that the whole of the first year of the RATI course is devoted to acting process, exercises and improvisation: they cover different elements of the Stanislavski approach such as ease, attention, release, responsiveness, adaptation, objectives, imagination, atmosphere, and Michael Chekhov's psycho-physical exercises. The aim is to allow actors to understand who they are and explore how to be themselves truthfully in different circumstances. In the second year, various types of text are used, e.g. Bulgakov, Brecht, Beckett, Chekhov, Aristophanes, to discover different types of truthful connection. In year three, work is begun on scenes from writers like Racine, Moliere and Lope de Vega and then finished in year four. There are also full productions. All the work addresses how to start with you and then reach a fully physicalised transformation. Year four operates as a rep theatre with rehearsals in the morning, classes in the afternoon and performance in the evening. The working day may be excessively long, but clearly the creative baby is not being forced out and, therefore, is less likely to be damaged at birth. Mokeiev believes two months is an absolute minimum for any rehearsal period: '*You have to give them time to go through the truth*'.

In conclusion, I think our acting training would benefit from some East European influence: not necessarily a much longer working day, but a four year training; more concentration on basic acting process, exercises, and improvisation; consistency and continuity of theory and practice; a more rigorous awareness of what is truthful organic acting and what isn't; and closer links between training schools and companies. An encouragement to this would be a more enlightened and affirmative policy towards theatre and training from the government, removal of tuition fees and huge student debt, provision of higher funding for schools and a commitment to a sustainable future. This is about investing in our youth and their creativity for the benefit of all.

We will only *be* the best in the world if we do what is needed to make us the best, otherwise we are simply being delusional, chauvinist and arrogant. It is not a helpful concept, however, to talk of being 'the best': artists form an international community and we should aim to be as good as we can become. For that to happen we need the conditions outlined above for companies and training, and a much greater awareness of the highest acting standards elsewhere and of both our own limitations and huge potential.

# 17 An open conclusion

> *But the actor is not his own master. It is his nature which creates through him, he is only the instrument*
>
> Stanislavski

We act to recreate humanity in our simplicity and in our complexities and contradictions, at our most loving and at our most barbaric, at our funniest and most tragic, and we do it through different theatrical forms and in different media. By doing this audiences can be inspired, moved, enlightened, and through that, and usually only through that, entertained. The view of this book is that we present humanity most perceptively and truthfully if we observe natural processes and experience each person as unique, rather than diminishing them by representing and describing them from the outside. Stanislavski observed and learned from the great actors of his time who put the reality of nature at the core of their performance, and based his approach on this experience not abstract theory. Nevertheless, he has been misunderstood, misrepresented, and misapplied so that what we are told about his process and how we see it used can be the opposite of what he intended and miss the crucial point: that it is aimed at organic involvement in a role, the creation of 'the life of the human spirit' with a fully physicalised form, as opposed to personal indulgence or cerebral intellectualising.

We need to see this approach as a whole and not simply take bits of emotion memory or study of actions and pump them up in isolation so they become independent systems of working. Seeing the interconnection of all the different elements is vital. 'Separate elements of art can fulfil the purposes of creativeness no more than separate elements of the air can serve man for breathing' (*My Life in Art*). Having said that, the process cannot be tackled like a manual for understanding a car engine. We have to *become* the process and learn through doing and exploring elements that engage our natures and trigger responses. This is why I've avoided using the terms *method* and *system*, which give the impression of a fixed formula. I've preferred *approach*, which feels more like fluid and creative guidelines. It's been suggested recently that acting is *first nature* not an acquired *second nature* (*The Actor and the Target*, Declan Donnellan, Nick Hern Books, 2002); but the playing of particular roles in life is not the same as playing another person in performance. One is reality, the other is an imaginary reality. Although in acting in performance we use ourselves and recreate human life we are engaged in an artform. To achieve imaginative, truthful creations within this artifice we have to remove blocks to our receptivity, sensitivity and free expression so that we can absorb information and experience and act action with clarity and subtext. We also have to learn techniques to help us bring a character to full life, just as a painter and musician learn techniques; for example, how to really affect and change someone through playing an objective, how to recreate heat or physical pain, how to develop an atmosphere, and what the components are for unblocking what *is* first nature like listening and responding. These need to be developed to the extent that they become *second nature*, automatic and possessed, and we make audiences believe that what they are seeing and hearing is *first nature*, that we are real human beings for the duration of the performance. Good technique, as Michael Chekhov insists, is the key to unlocking an actor's talent and inspiration regardless of physical or psychological obstacles. It is also a means for freeing us from dependence on a director. Again, the approach is not like a car manual where you open at a page and find out how to turn the lights on. It is much more a way of life. Stanislavski liked to say: 'The difficult should become habitual, the habitual, easy, the easy, beautiful.' By the time we get to the stage of performance, the scaffolding of technique should have been pushed away and made invisible so what we do appears completely natural and easy. A fine dancer or pianist are not thinking about their feet or fingers while they perform. Their technique has been learned, and will continue to be developed, but is forgotten, or more accurately put out of conscious mind, when performing. We go from the conscious to the subconscious.

Acting is as much a skill and artform as any other, and the most directly human, and we owe it respect. If we respect it we can respect ourselves, and we can start to reassess what sort of training and companies produce the highest quality and be willing to learn with humility and confidence, rather than dismiss with arrogance and insecurity.

Stanislavski believed that the greatest wisdom is to recognise one's lack of it. What we can actually *do* as actors is to commit to our art, rely on our natures as human beings and never stop exploring with compassion and understanding.

# Glossary

**Action/s** The basis of drama. Everything that is done in the inner and outer life of the character as psychological, verbal and physical action. The means to fulfil the objectives in a justified and consecutive manner.

**Method of Physical Action** Stanislavski's later process by which the actor moves to the inner life of the character by exploring the objectives and actions in the text through improvisation.

**Analysis through action/Active Analysis** The whole process of reading, discussing and improvising the action of the text to uncover everything that gives rise to the actual words.

**Activity** What you're doing while playing objectives and actions, e.g. washing the dishes, smoking, knitting.

**Atmosphere** The objective feeling suggested by the text and created by all the actors through imagination and action. **Individual feelings** may be in empathy or opposition to this.

**Circles of attention** Small, medium and large areas radiating out from oneself within which attention is focused.

**Object of attention** The thing or person on which you focus your attention and which stimulates action.

**Communion** Awareness of everything present in performance: objects, people and sensory elements surrounding you. Connecting with different parts of oneself, e.g. head to feelings. Communicating with others through alertness, receiving and radiating thoughts, feelings and actions: a process of **adaptation**, spontaneous responsiveness in the moment.

**Emotion memory** Also known as 'affective memory' it is our bank of emotional experience, which can release emotions under the influence of the action of a script.

**Emotion recall** The conscious recall of one's own experiences to produce an emotion analogous to that of the character's, most associated with the Method.

**Episode** A large section of the script defining a significant stage in the development of the characters and the events.

**Given circumstances** All the circumstances given by the play and production for each scene.

**Previous circumstances** What has happened before the action and which imaginatively informs it.

**The 5 Ws** The imaginative embodiment of the circumstances by the actor.

**'I am'** The state of believing in yourself in imaginary circumstances or as a character; the sense of 'being' through doing and experiencing, living through the role in each moment.

**'If'** *If* I am in these circumstances what do I do? The imaginative question that launches us into inner and outer action.

**Imaginary body** The character's body existing in the space of your own.

**Imaginary centre** The place where you imagine your character experiences themselves to be.

**Inner motive forces** The main elements driving our psycho-physical makeup: *mind*, centred in the head; *feeling*, centred in the chest or solar plexus area; *will*, centred in the lower body.

**In the moment** Responding freshly to each stimulus as it arises, without premeditation and conscious calculation; being 'here, today, now'.

**Life of the human spirit of a role** The whole inner life of the part, including the mental, psychological, spiritual, imaginative and emotional elements: its creation is the core aim of Stanislavski's approach and is to be communicated through 'artistic form' and full physical expression.

**Moment of orientation** The moment of entering a new situation and becoming aware of it and acclimatising yourself as if for the first time.

**Objective** What I want to achieve and change in a unit or scene, expressed actively in a way that stirs and drives me.

**Superobjective** My overall objective in life, and in an episode of the script or the script as a whole. Or, the **Ruling Idea** of the play as a whole.

**Obstacle** What is in my way and I need to overcome to fulfil my objective.

**The stakes** How important it is to achieve my objective.

**Organic moment** The point where an emotion may be triggered or begin to fade.

**Perspective** The shaping and balancing of a performance with a sense of the whole.

**Physical score** Everything that is seen, heard, smelled, tasted and touched in a scene.

**Psychological gesture** An expressive full-body physicalisation of the psychological essence of the character, with its Superobjective and will at its core.

**Psycho-physical** The dynamic relationship between inner impulse and physical expression, and physical action and inner response.

**Second plan** The life of characters off script in the period before it actually starts or between scenes.

**Sensation of feeling** The creation of a sensation of a quality or feeling to arouse a genuine feeling.

**Sense memory** Recreating the physical sensation of an action without using objects. Recreating a physical sensation from one's own experience analogous to that in the script – heat, cold, sickness, etc.

**Subtext** Every inner thought, feeling, image or motivation that lies beneath the words and actions in a text.

**Tempo-rhythm** The speed and rhythmic quality of a character's inner workings and outer action, which can stimulate the feelings.

**Through line of action** The coherent sequence of objectives and actions which leads to the fulfilment of the Superobjective of the character and the play.

**Counteraction** The action of a character in opposition to the main line of action in the play; for example, the protagonist's through line will face a counteraction from the antagonist.

**Emotion through line** The sequence of emotions in response to the through line of action.

**Unit** A unit of action, within which characters have objectives that create a specific dynamic between them.

# Selected bibliography

Adler, Stella, *The Art of Acting*, compiled and edited by Howard Kissel, Applause Books, New York, 2000.

Arts Council England, 'Economic impact study of UK theatre', April 2004.

Benedetti, Jean, *Stanislavski and the Actor*, Methuen Drama, London, 1998.

Boal, Augusto, *Games for Actors and Non-Actors*, translated by Adrian Jackson, Routledge, London, 1992.

Boyer, Paul and Nissenbaum, Stephen, *Salem Possessed: Social Origins of Witchcraft*, Harvard University Press, 1974.

Brook, Peter, *The Empty Space*, Penguin Books, Harmondsworth, 1972.

Calderone, Maria and Lloyd-Williams, Maggie, *Actions, The Actors' Thesaurus*, Nick Hern Books, London, 2004.

Carnicke, Sharon M., *Stanislavski in Focus*, Routledge, London, 1998.

Chamberlain, Franc, *Michael Chekhov*, Routledge, London, 2004.

Chekhov, Michael, *Lessons for the Professional Actor*, edited by Deirdre Hurst Du Prey, Performing Arts Journal Publications, New York, 1985.

Chekhov, Michael, *On the Technique of Acting*, edited by Mel Gordon, preface and afterword by Mala Powers, Harper Perennial, New York, 1991.

Chekhov, Michael, *The Path of the Actor*, edited by Andrei Kirillov and Bella Merlin, Routledge, London and New York, 2005.

Chekhov, Michael, *To the Actor*, Harper & Row, New York, Evanston, and London, 1953.

Chekhov, Michael, *To the Actor*, Routledge, London, 2002.

Dodin, Lev, *Journey Without End*, translated by Oksana Mamyrin and Anna Karabinska, Tantalus Books, London, 2005.

Donnellan, Declan, *The Actor and the Target*, Nick Hern Books, London, 2005.

Engels, Frederick, *The Origin of the Family, Private Property and the State*, Lawrence & Wishart, London, 1972.

Equity and Directors' Guild of Great Britain, Transcript of *Ensemble Theatre Conference* held at The Pit, The Barbican, London, 2004.

Hall, Peter, *Shakespeare's Advice to the Players*, Oberon Books, London, 2003.

Hagen, Uta, *A Challenge for the Actor*, Scribner, New York, 1991.

Hagen, Uta, *Respect for Acting*, Macmillan Publishing Company, New York, 1973.

Hartnoll, Phyllis, *A Concise History of the Theatre*, Thames & Hudson, 1985.

Hirsch, Foster, *A Method to Their Madness, The History of the Actors Studio*, Da Capo Press, New York, 1984.

Lagarde, André and Michard, Laurent, *XIXe Siècle, Les Grands Auteurs Français du Programme*, Les Editions Bordas, Paris, 1967.

Lewis, Robert, *Advice to the Players, Robert Lewis on Acting*, Theatre Communications Group, New York, 1980.

Mamet, David, *True and False, Heresy and Common Sense for the Actor*, Vintage Books, Random House, New York, 1997.

Meisner, Sanford and Longwell, Dennis, *Sanford Meisner on Acting*, Vintage Books, Random House, New York, 1987.

Merlin, Bella, *Konstantin Stanislavsky*, Routledge, London, 2003.

Miller, Arthur, *The Crucible*, Penguin Books, Harmondsworth, 1968.

Miller, Arthur, *Timebends*, Methuen, London, 1987.

Moore, Sonia, *The Stanislavski System, the Professional Training of an Actor*, The Viking Press, New York, 1974.

Newlove, Jean and Dalby, John, *Laban for All*, Nick Hern Books, London, 2004.

Redgrave, Michael, *In My Mind's Eye, An Autobiography*, Weidenfeld & Nicolson, London, 1983.

Richards, Thomas, *At Work with Grotowski on Physical Actions*, Routledge, Oxford, 1995.

Saint-Denis, Michel, *Training for the Theatre*, Heinmann, 1982.

Sartre, Jean-Paul, *Sketch for a Theory of the Emotions*, Methuen University Paperback, London, 1971.

Shakespeare, William, *Measure for Measure*, Penguin Books, Harmondsworth, 1969.

Shaw, Bernard, *Plays and Players, Theatre Essays by Bernard Shaw*, Oxford University Press, London, 1952.

Shevtsova, Maria, *Dodin and the Maly Drama Theatre, Process to Performance*, Routledge, London, 2004.

Stanislavski, Constantin, *An Actor Prepares*, translated by Elizabeth Reynolds Hapgood, Penguin Books, Harmondsworth, 1967.

Stanislavski, Constantin, *Building a Character*, translated by Elizabeth Reynolds Hapgood, Methuen University Paperback, London, 1968.

Stanislavski, Constantin, *Creating a Role*, translated by Elizabeth Reynolds Hapgood, Eyre Methuen, London, 1981.

Stanislavski, Constantin, *My Life in Art*, Methuen Drama, London, 2001.

Stanislavsky, Konstantin, *Stanislavsky on the Art of the Stage*, translated and introduced by David Magarshak, Faber & Faber, London, 1960.

Strasberg, Lee, *A Dream of Passion*, Methuen Drama, London, 1989.

Toporkov, Vasili, *Stanislavski in Rehearsal*, translated by Jean Benedetti, Methuen, London, 2001.

Willett, John, *Brecht on Theatre*, Methuen Drama, London, 1964.

Worrall, Nick, *The Moscow Art Theatre*, Routledge, London, 1996.

# Index